# Localiz

## A Global N

D0283300

*Colin Hines*

Earthscan Publications Ltd, London and Sterling, VA

*Dedicated to my much missed father Tom Hines.*
*Also for my mother Lillian, my wife Ann and children*
*Clare and Pip*

First published in the UK in 2000 by
Earthscan Publications Ltd
Reprinted 2001
Copyright © Colin Hines, 2000

A catalogue record for this book is available from the British Library

ISBN: 1 85383 612 5

Typesetting by PCS Mapping & DTP, Newcastle upon Tyne
Printed and bound by Creative Print and Design, Ebbw Vale
Cover design by Andrew Corbett

For a full list of publications please contact:

Earthscan Publications Ltd
120 Pentonville Road
London, N1 9JN, UK
Tel: +44 (0)20 7278 0433
Fax: +44 (0)20 7278 1142
Email: earthinfo@earthscan.co.uk
http://www.earthscan.co.uk

22883 Quicksilver Drive, Sterling, VA 20166–2012, USA

Earthscan is an editorially independent subsidiary of Kogan Page Ltd and
publishes in association with WWF-UK and the International Institute for
Environment and Development

This book is printed on elemental chlorine-free paper

# Contents

# PART THREE HOW LOCALIZATION MIGHT COME ABOUT

# Preface and Acknowledgements

This book is the result of endless conversations, discussions and arguments with many friends and colleagues. The biggest debt of constant gratitude is to my fellow 'new protectionist' heretic Tim Lang, who kept the faith despite having a four letter word (Prof) placed in front of his name. Also lured into day-long discussions about the potential shape of this localization alternative were Nick Hildyard and Alan Simpson MP. This book would not have happened without the invaluable ideas and encouragement of the three of them.

The second great debt is to Jerry Mander and Doug Tompkins for setting up the International Forum on Globalization (plus Debi Barker, Shawnee Hoover and Victor Menotti). This network has allowed me access to many of the key people in the world working against globalization. I would particularly like to mention those members who I have spent most time with discussing my ideas and in the process ruthlessly stealing theirs (suitably referenced of course): Maude Barlow, Harriet Barlow, Walden Bello, Agnés Bertrand, Brent Blackwelder, John Cavanagh, Tony Clarke, Herman Daly, Ramón Durán, Susan George, Teddy Goldsmith, Richard Grossman, Randy Hayes, Martin Khor, Andy Kimbrell, David Korten, Sara Larrain, Anuradha Mittal, David Morris, Helena Norberg-Hodge, Jean-Pierre Page, Carl Pope, Jeremy Rifkin, Mark Ritchie, Wolfgang Sachs, Vandana Shiva, Steven Shrybman, Lori Wallach and Tracy Worcester.

Others who played an important part in providing inputs for the book included: Charlie Arden-Clarke, David Baldock, Catherine Barr, Kevin Bundell, Tord Bjork, Stewart Boyle, Gabriel Chanan, Barry Coates, Pat Conarty, Chris Fisher, Shaun Geoghegans, Arthur Fountain, Ronnie Hall, Olivier Hoedeman, Paul Hohnen, Charlie Kronick, Jeremy Leggett, John Lovering, Caroline Lucas, Duncan McLaren, Ed Mayo, Brian Padgett, Andy Rowell, Michael Shuman, Andrew Simms, Richard Tapper, Thomas Wallgren, Erik Wesselius, David Wheeler, Alex Wilks, Angela Wood, Jessica Woodroffe.

Doug and Steve Hellinger and Fred O'Reagan, co-founders of the Development Group for Alternative Policies were amongst the first people I shared 'new protectionist' ideas with nearly 20 years ago.

Thanks also to the indulgence shown by Jonathan Sinclair Wilson and the rest of the Earthscan team as deadline after deadline slipped.

True patience was also exhibited by Kath and Geoff Tansey, the stalwalt and punctilious editors.

Finally, I would like to thank my friend and uncompromising mentor of decades Teddy Goldsmith, for encouraging the Goldsmith Foundation to financially support me during the writing of this book. (with the help of Jon Cracknell and Zac Goldsmith). Thanks also to the Polden Puckham Foundation and Network Foundation for funding the unfashionable.

These funders have allowed me to have to commute only as far as my art deco loft/eyrie in order to write this book. My family has thus had the dubious pleasure of me being around most days. However my working from home has allowed me to partake of my only practical contribution to localization – chairing my children's school PTA.

As ever the book is my responsibility entirely.

# An Intemperate Introduction

*'Globalization is not a policy choice, it is a fact.'*

Bill Clinton[1]

*'Globalization is "irreversible and irresistible".'*

Tony Blair[2]

This book is an attempt to provide an optimistic alternative to the statements of Mr Clinton and Mr Blair above. They represent a fatalism that grips not just politicians. Far too many concerned citizens and organizations working for a fairer world also seem to have been bamboozled into accepting globalization and international competitiveness as inevitable. Yet these are not God given. Indeed the briefest perusal of the Bible's Ten Commandments reveals that there is not a single Commandment saying, 'Thou shalt be internationally competitive'. It's a modern construct, elevated to a theology.

*Localization: A Global Manifesto* has been written to contribute to a 'mindwrench'. This involves a move away from acquiescence to the new theology of globalization towards considering the possibility of its replacement with a localism that protects and rebuilds local economies worldwide. This mindwrench requires courage, almost of the order of an economic 'coming out', in order to reject the orthodoxy's ceaseless mantra chant of the need for international competitiveness. It needs to challenge head on this constant reiteration by a self-serving priesthood of mainstream economists, commentators and the new 'masters of the universe' – big business leaders and international financiers.

The clarion call to be internationally competitive has become so powerful that it has infected the thinking of those who should know better. These include trades unionists, small businesspeople, farmers, and those concerned about making commerce more ethical and environmental. All seem duty bound to pepper their public utterances with fervent assurances that were their aims to be achieved, then it will hurry society further down the path to competitiveness.

The global commandment that every nation must contort its economy to outcompete every other country's is an economic, social and environmental nonsense. It is a beggar-your-neighbour act of economic warfare. There have to be losers, because no matter how much a specific market may be growing, if its needs can be supplied by a competing range of outside sources, then large numbers, often the domestic producers, have to lose.

The alternative is that everything that could be produced within a nation or region should be. Long-distance trade is then reduced to supplying what could not come from within one country or geographical grouping of countries. This would allow an increase in local control of the economy and the potential for it being shared out more fairly, locally. Technology and information would be encouraged to flow, when and where they could strengthen local economies. Under these circumstamces, beggar-your-neighbour globalization gives way to the potentially more cooperative better-your-neighbour localization.

Part One of this book defines globalization and localization and briefly catalogues the adverse effects of globalization on society, equity and the environment. It then debunks the myth that concentrating on the cheapest supply source is nationally and globally efficient (comparative advantage) and the idea, already in tatters thanks to the Asian economic crisis, that money should flow unfettered in order to make the world run more effectively (capital advantage).

Part Two details a *Protect the Local, Globally* set of policies that can bring about localization. These involve:

- safeguarding national and regional economies against imports of goods and services that can be produced locally;
- site-here-to-sell-here rules for industry;
- localizing money flows to rebuild the economies of communities;
- local competition policies to ensure high-quality goods and services;
- the introduction of resource and other taxes to help pay for such a fundamental and expensive transition, and to guide it in such a way that adequately protects the environment;
- fostering democratic involvement in both the local economic and political systems;
- a redirection of trade and aid, such that it is geared to help the rebuilding of local economies, rather than international competitiveness.

Such a fundamental challenge to the power of transnational companies (TNCs) and global finance can not take place in one country alone, but will probably need to begin in the two blocs powerful enough to face down such forces – Europe and North America. Once such a debate even begins, however, it is likely to ricochet around this unstable world.

Part Three deals with why and how such a fundamental change should come about. It explains how globalization and international competitiveness are leading to rising unemployment and a concomitant decline in effective demand. The book also makes the case for why the politically active are far more likely to achieve their aims if they get out of their issue-specific ghettos, and put their campaigns within a localization framework.

Public questioning and opposition to globalization have never been higher. In December 1999, in Seattle, against a background of massive street protests, the World Trade Organization's (WTO) attempt to foist a new Millennium Round of trade expansion on developing world delegates collapsed in a shambles. The highly publicized trade wars between Europe and the US over bananas and hormone-pumped beef have raised more widespread concerns amongst the general public. The Europeans lost twice at the court of unrepresentative trade bureaucrats – the WTO – and faced massive trade sanctions. Yet all this stands to pail into insignificance when the next trade war looms over genetically modified foods.

These instances should have presented an enormous opportunity for pressure groups to challenge trade rules fundamentally and call for a completely different end goal for trade. Few have done this, although as will be seen in the Conclusion, issue-specific resistance is growing. Alas, such is the mental sway that globalization has over even the politically active, that they seem to accept that their best shot is 'a dare to be cautious approach'. This involves calling for a labour standard here, an environmental add-on there, in the hope that the system can be adjusted into being a little kinder and gentler to their own specific interests. Some haven't even gone this far. Those concerned about domestic issues such as health, education and transport still put their focus and energies into impotent calls for their governments to spend much more on this or that issue. They fail to grasp that the dictates of international competitiveness cause continuous curbs on public expenditure. This is what is demanded of governments by business which otherwise threatens them with relocation or withholding of investment.

These largely futile efforts by political activists to tame globalization fundamentally mistake the nature of the trade liberalization beast. These attempts are like trying to lasso a tiger with cotton. It is now time to return this tiger to its original habitat. Trade was initially a search for the novel; Europeans went to India for spices and other exotics, not coal. That is precisely the *Protect the Local, Globally* approach. Long-distance trade is only for acquiring what can not be provided within the region where people live. The rules for this diminished international sector are those of the 'fair trade' movement, where preference is given to goods supplied in a way that benefits workers, the local community and the environment.

The politically active need to demand a new direction and end goal for trade rules. The latter must contribute to the rebuilding and protection of local sustainable economies. In the process the myriad goals of movements for social and animal welfare, development, human and labour rights and environmental protection have much more potential to be met.

In short, it is time that those wanting a fairer, more environmentally sustainable world, where everyone's basic needs are met, had a radical rethink. They must stop pinning their hopes of campaign success on tweaking the direction of globalization. They must stop acting as if trade rules were governed by some kind of Olympian logic that comes down from on high, with the intention of eventual global benefit. They must set their campaigning ambitions higher than deferential adjustments to the onward march of globalization. Instead, trade rules should be seen for what they are: a grubby set of global guidelines drawn up at the behest of the powerful for the benefit of the powerful. It is time for a radical change.

Finally, this book is not against rules for trade. It wants them to have the different end goal of protecting and rediversifying local economies, rather than the present one of forcing all nations to bow the knee to the false god of international competitiveness. It proposes leaving trade liberalizers a GAST – the General Agreement on Sustainable Trade.

This book is not trying to put the clock back. Globalization is doing that as it reduces the security, basic needs provision and employment prospects for billions for whom things had been improving since the Second World War. *Protect the Local, Globally* could return us to a path that advances the majority and doesn't mire them in cruel insecurity. It is not against trade, it just wants trade where possible to be local. The shorter the gap between producer and consumer, the better the chance for the latter to control the former. Adverse environmental effects are more likely to be experienced through long-distance trade and lack of consumer control over distant producers. Local trade should significantly lessen these problems and make possible the tighter regulation required.

This book is an attempt to help move the debate about globalization away from issue-specific horror stories such as GM food, banana wars, leg-hold traps and so on. It focuses instead on what should be the goal of world trade and how radical change might be achieved. It is a blatant and heretical call for the rejection of the worldwide theology of globalization. Unless this occurs, campaigners will win the odd skirmish, but continue to lose the war. As will be seen in the Conclusion there was never a better time to drop any pretence of humility. Instead, it is crucial to play the globalizers at their own game. They have a clear end goal: maximum trade and money flows for maximum profit. Tough luck for the growing number of losers. From this end goal comes a clear set of policies and trade rules supporting this approach. Those seeking a more just, environmentally sustainable future need to have their own clear end goal and policies for achieving it. This is the debate this book was written to help kick-start. It will hopefully result in the mindwrench away from impotent fulminating against globalization towards considering the policy route to its alternative – the localism of *Protect the Local, Globally.*

# Acronyms and Abbreviations

| | |
|---|---|
| ACP | Africa, Caribbean and Pacific |
| AIC | Alternative Investment Code |
| AIDS | acquired immune deficiency syndrome |
| AMF | Asian Monetary Fund |
| AOA | Agreement on Agriculture |
| APEC | Asia-Pacific Economic Cooperation |
| ART | Aston Reinvestment Trust |
| BECC | Border Environmental Cooperation Commission |
| BSE | bovine spongiform encephalopathy |
| BST | bovine somatotrofin |
| CBD | Convention on Biological Diversity |
| CDLF | Community Development Loan Fund |
| CEC | Commission for Environmental Cooperation |
| CED | Community Economic Development |
| CITES | Convention on International Trade in Endangered Species of Wild Flora and Fauna |
| CTE | Committee on Trade and Environment (WTO) |
| EC | European Commission |
| EMU | European Monetary Union |
| EPA | Environmental Protection Agency |
| EPZ | export processing zone |
| EU | European Union |
| FAO | Food and Agriculture Organization of the United Nations |
| FoE | Friends of the Earth |
| FTAA | Free Trade Area of the Americas |
| G7 | group of seven industrialized nations: Canada, France, Germany, Italy, Japan, United Kingdom, United States |
| GATT | General Agreement on Tariffs and Trade (WTO) |
| GAST | General Agreement on Sustainable Trade |
| GATS | General Agreement on Trade in Services (WTO) |
| GM | genetically modified |
| GDP | gross domestic product |
| GNP | gross national product |
| IATP | Institute for Agriculture and Trade Policy |
| ICC | International Chamber of Commerce |
| ICFTU | International Confederation of Free Trade Unions |

| ICI | Imperial Chemical Industry |
|-----|----------------------------|
| ILO | International Labour Office |
| IMF | International Monetary Fund |
| IPR | Institute of Policy Research |
| ISA | individual savings account |
| IT | information technology |
| ITO | International Trade Organization |
| LETS | local exchange trading schemes or systems |
| MAI | Multilateral Agreement on Investment |
| M&As | mergers and acquisitions |
| MEA | Multilateral Environmental Agreement |
| MEP | Member of European Parliament |
| MFN | Most-Favoured Nation (WTO) |
| MMC | Monopolies and Mergers Commission |
| MMPA | Marine Mammal Protection Act (US) |
| MP | Member of Parliament (UK) |
| MTA | Metropolitan Transportation Authority (New York) |
| NEF | New Economics Foundation |
| NGO | non-governmental organization |
| NIC | newly industrialized country |
| NAAEC | North American Agreement on Environmental Cooperation |
| NAALC | North American Agreement on Labor Cooperation |
| NAFTA | North America Free Trade Agreement |
| OECD | Organisation for Economic Co-operation and Development |
| OFT | Office of Fair Trading |
| OPEC | Organization of Petroleum Exporting Countries |
| PFI | private finance initiative |
| PPM | non-product related process and production |
| PSBR | Public Sector Borrowing Requirement |
| rBGH | recombinant bovine growth hormone |
| R&D | research and development |
| RMALC | Red Mexicana de Acci-n frente al Libre Comercio |
| RPM | retail price maintenance |
| SIA | social investment account |
| SMEs | small- and medium-sized enterprises |
| SPS | Agreement on Sanitary and Phytosanitary Measures (WTO) |
| TABD | transatlantic business dialogue |
| TBI | transitional basic income |
| TBT | Agreement on Technical Barriers to Trade (WTO) |
| TED | turtle excluder device |

| | |
|---|---|
| TEP | Transatlantic Economic Partnership |
| TINA | there is no alternative |
| TNCs | transnational companies |
| TRIMs | Agreement on Trade-Related Investment Measures (WTO) |
| TRIPS | Agreement on Trade-Related Aspects of Intellectual Property Rights (WTO) |
| TUAC | Trade Union Advisory Council (to the OECD) |
| UNCTAD | United Nations Conference on Trade and Development |
| UNICEF | United Nations Children's Fund |
| US | United States of America |
| VAT | value-added tax |
| VER | voluntary export restraint |
| WDM | World Development Movement |
| WEA | Workers Education Association |
| WHO | World Health Organization |
| WIPO | World Intellectual Property Organization |
| WLO | World Localization Organization |
| WTO | World Trade Organization |

*Part One*

# The Problem – Globalization

*Chapter 1*

# Globalization – What it is and the Damage it Does

## THE OFFICIAL VIEW

*'The government remains firmly behind a comprehensive new round of negotiations in the WTO as the best way forward for the UK, for developing countries in particular, and for the world economy as a whole. We are working for a more transparent WTO which promotes sustainable development and fosters the rule of law in international trade.'*
Richard Caborn MP, UK Minister for Trade[1]

**Trade liberalization is not the cause of the problems of the world's economies, but the answer to them.**

*'By securing better access to overseas markets for producers, by reducing trade barriers, and maintaining and improving the supply of competitively priced goods and services to consumers, trade liberalization brings widespread welfare benefits and helps to improve the efficiency with which the world's resources are used. That is why the Government supports the EU's call for a comprehensive new Round of trade liberalization, which has already met with support from a number of developed and developing countries.'*

**Trade and environment:**

*'Our overall aim is to work towards sustainable development in accordance with the principles set out in the Rio Declaration adopted in 1992. The Government will work to ensure that trade liberalization contributes to this aim, including action to safeguard the environment and the interests of developing countries. By enabling developing countries to derive more benefits from increased access to overseas markets and to*

*inward investment, we can help them to increased prosperity which in turn has the potential to enable them to raise their standards of environmental and social protection.*

*The Government believes that the evidence shows strongly that trade liberalization is in the best interests of developing countries as well as developed countries. The OECD has found that in the last decade countries which have been more open to trade and investment have achieved twice the average annual growth of more closed economies. This is of particular importance to those countries which need to grow faster to deal with their greater infrastructure and capacity weaknesses.'*

Brian Wilson MP, former Minister for Trade[2]

## The Critics' View

*Globalization* – the ever-increasing integration of national economies into the global economy through trade and investment rules and privatization, aided by technological advances. These reduce barriers to trade and investment and in the process reduce democratic controls by nation states and their communities over their economic affairs. The process is driven by the theory of comparative advantage, the goal of international competitiveness and the growth model. It is occurring increasingly at the expense of social, environmental and labour improvements and rising inequality for most of the world.

Or more bluntly:

> *Globalization n.1. the process by which governments sign away the rights of their citizens in favour of speculative investors and transnational corporations. 2. The erosion of wages, social welfare standards and environmental regulations for the sake of international trade. 3. the imposition world-wide of a consumer monoculture. Widely but falsely believed to be irreversible. – See also financial meltdown, casino economy, Third World debt and race to the bottom (16th century: from colonialism, via development).[3]*

## An Alternative

*Localization* – a process which reverses the trend of globalization by discriminating in favour of the local. Depending on the context, the 'local' is predominantly defined as part of the nation state, although it can on occasions be the nation state itself or even occasionally a

regional grouping of nation states. The policies bringing about localization are ones which increase control of the economy by communities
and nation states. The result should be an increase in community
cohesion, a reduction in poverty and inequality and an improvement
in livelihoods, social infrastructure and environmental protection, and
hence an increase in the all-important sense of security.

Localization is not about restricting the flow of information,
technology, trade and investment, management and legal structures
which *further* localization, indeed these are encouraged by the new
localist emphasis in global aid and trade rules. Such transfers also play
a crucial role in the successful transition from globalization to localization. It is *not* a return to overpowering state control, merely
governments' provision of a policy and economic framework which
allows people, community groups and businesses to rediversify their
own local economies.

## GLOBALIZATION VERSUS INTERNATIONALISM

It is crucial to make a clear distinction between, for example, a global
flow of technology, ideas and information to rebuild sustainable local
communities, ie a supportive 'internationalism', and the process of
globalization. In essence, the latter is the systematic reduction of protective barriers to the flow of goods and money by international trade rules
shaped by and for big business. It pits country against country, community against community and workers against workers. That is the point
of it, because such a structure and process is the route to maximizing
profits. Internationalism can be thought of as the flow of ideas, technologies, information, culture, money and goods with the end goal of
protecting and rebuilding local economies worldwide. Its emphasis is
not on competition for the cheapest, but on cooperation for the best.

Linguistic clarity is vital since the advocates and beneficiaries of
globalization misuse the indisputable benefits that can accrue from
such constructive international flows to justify the destructive process
of globalization. In tandem with this misleading approach is invariably a promise that someday the growth resulting from globalization
will somehow trickle down to benefit the majority.

## DOWNSIDES OF GLOBALIZATION

There are a vast number of books and other publications which
authoritatively detail the adverse effects of globalization, and how it is
directly guided by the priorities of transnational companies (TNCs)

(see Suggested Reading). It is not the intention of this book to go over that ground again other than in the briefest of summaries. The main purpose of this chapter is to summarize the faulty theoretical under-pinnings of what has now become an international theology. This then clears the way to consider its diametric opposite localization – along with the policies that can bring it about.

Up until the Asian crisis that began in July 1997, supporters of a global economy built on trade liberalization, usually described it as a win–win game. The theory is that the economies of all participants grow as countries specialize in what they are good at providing. They then import what they are less proficient in, what economists term 'comparative advantage'.

Although it is conceded that this process has increased income disparities in most countries, the theory is that the resulting growth will eventually result in benefits for the majority. All countries are supposed to benefit by providing the cheapest exports, and for the resulting growth to trickle down to the general populace. This rarely happens in practice. What does occur is that hand in hand with rising gross national product (GNP) statistics and – until recently – booming world-wide stockmarkets has come a global rise in inequality, declining social and environmental conditions and a loss of power by sovereign states, local governments and citizens. The major beneficiaries have been the TNCs and international capital, the major losers have been the poor and the rising numbers who have lost their jobs, or are underemployed and underpaid.

In its reports in the latter half of the 1990s, the International Labour Office (ILO) catalogued that one third of the world's willing-to-work population was either unemployed or underemployed, the worst situation since the 1930s.[4] The income inequalities that have come in globalization's wake are illustrated by the fact that in 1960 the combined incomes of the richest fifth of the world's population were 30 times greater than the poorest fifth. By 1991 it was over 60 times and in 1998 the UN's latest figures put this as 78 times as high.[5] The stock of wealth of the 447 (mainly American) dollar billionaires listed by *Forbes* magazine in 1996 has been estimated by the Institute of Policy Research (IPR) in Washington DC to exceed the annual income of the poorest half of the world's people.[6] The richest three have assets that exceed the combined GDP of the least developed countries with a total population of more than 600 million.[7]

To sustain this 'success', ever less trade barriers, minimal constraints on capital flows, privatization, deregulation, flexible working and strict curbs on public expenditure goals are demanded. Virtually all the world's economies are geared to maximum inward investment and cheaper exports. It is constantly asserted that these measures are really succeeding in delivering prosperity. Until the Asian crisis this tended to be defined in terms of rising GNPs, stockmarket valuations and trade statistics. Globalization's supporters also claimed that one day the process will provide the surplus necessary to tackle environmental and social problems. In any case there is, most establishment commentators still agree, no alternative.

Until the Asian crisis it was of course possible to list from a conventional economic perspective a number of gains from trade liberalization. Between 1975 and 1995, the proportion of East Asians living in absolute poverty declined from 60 per cent to 20 per cent. In Latin America in particular, inflation was sharply reduced from a regional mean of 196 per cent in 1991 to 19 per cent in 1996.[8] Unfortunately the July 1997 Asian economic crash and the cuts in Latin America's public expenditure have resulted in an increase in the number in absolute poverty.

## GLOBALIZATION IS DE-LOCALIZATION

*'Behind all these "meanings" of Globalization is a single underlying idea which can be called "de-localization": the uprooting of activities and relationships from local origins and cultures. It means the displacement of activities that until recently were local into networks of relationships whose reach is distant or world-wide. Domestic prices of consumer goods, financial assets such as stocks and bonds, even labour – are less and less governed by local and national conditions; they all fluctuate along with the global market prices. Globalization means lifting social activities out of local knowledge and placing them in networks in which they are conditioned by, and condition, world-wide events.'[9]*

Of course however far globalization proceeds it is not omnipotent. It will always be true that some dimensions of a society's economic life are not affected by world markets, though these may change over time. Modern information and communication technologies have meant though that people's traditional cultures are far more deeply influenced than ever before.

Globalization also doesn't bring total homogeneity. Business when it invests abroad adapts to some extent to local conditions in order to maximize local demand for their products or services and to minimize the chance of their being discriminated against by trade or investment barriers. This process is known as glocalization, and has been defined as: '.... a company's attempt to become accepted as a "local citizen" in a different trade bloc, while transferring as little control as possible over its areas of strategic concern.'[10]

Despite these minor caveats, the gap between rich and poor in this overall process of de-localization is widening, in large part, according to the United Nations Committee on Trade and Development (UNCTAD), due to the uneven impacts of globalization, inequalities which UNCTAD believes could cause major social upheavals.[11] Taken as a whole the pressure for trade liberalization, pushed by TNCs, economists, commentators and more recently by politicians has been to the detriment of the majority globally, to social cohesion and to the environment (see Part Three).

*Chapter 2*

# History and WTO Enforcing of Comparative Advantage

## A Very Brief History of Trade

There have been four major phases of development in trade.[1] The first was associated with a mercantile division of labour, where a surplus of commodities was generated through the accidents of geography, climate, and the spread of plants and animals. While merchants were swapping these goods, they began to organize labour, in particular as plantation workers and slaves. Plants such as potatoes, cotton, tea, sugar, rice and rubber were moved round the world to make better use of supplies of labour.

The second phase came with the *industrial* division of labour as machines began to replace the production and processing of tropical commodities. Europe drew in labour from its farms to factories in the towns. Workers were increasingly dependent on wages. Some countries with a shortage of labour pulled in workers form elsewhere – the US pulled in over 35 million peasants from farms in Europe. Infrastructures such as international canals, roads and rails were built. These developments gave rise to the first strikes and workers' protests.

These conflicts lessened as money from the home countries moved to other colonies where sufficient profits were produced to fund modest improvements for workers at home. This is often called the *imperial* division of labour. Workers in European colonies grew food and dug up materials which were exported to Europe, and Europe's new working classes made the manufactured goods that were exported throughout the world. Peasant proprietors in the colonies became cash crop producers tied to the world markets, and European trade unions slowly became partners rather than protectors in the process.

The world is now entering a fourth phase, the *transnational* phase, characterized by a transnational division of labour, where power has centred on the US and until recently Japan. This leaves in place many previous trading relationships, but has restructured industrial production in the developed countries, imported migrant labour to those countries, and internationalized key sectors such as the oil giants, car companies, and electrical goods. Most recently there has been a shift of manufacturing to South East Asia, although this process has stalled somewhat since the Asian economic crisis.

## THE MENTAL FRAMEWORK SUPPORTING THE UNSUPPORTABLE

*'In nineteenth-century England, the free market ran aground on enduring human needs for economic security. In the twentieth century the liberal international economic order perished violently in the wars and dictatorships of the 1930s. That cataclysm was the precondition of post-war prosperity and political stability. In the 1930s the free market proved to be an inherently unstable institution. Built by design and artifice it fell apart in confusion and chaos. The history of the free market in our time is unlikely to be much different.'[2]*

*'Economists like to talk about externalities. The costs of job dislocation, rising family violence, community breakdown, environmental damage, and cultural collapse are all considered "external". External to what, one might ask?'[3]*

Trade liberalization has been built on the theory of comparative advantage, the diktat of being internationally competitive and the promise of growth today, generating wealth for all tomorrow. The free trade theory underpinning all this rests largely on the concept of comparative advantage. This theory was first developed by the British economist Adam Smith in 1776 and refined by David Ricardo in 1817.[4]

### The Theory of Comparative Advantage

Economists claim that all nations benefit by trade because of this principle of 'comparative advantage'. According to Smith and Ricardo nations do best from international trade when their industries specialize. By mass producing those goods where they can make maximum use of the factors of production (whether land, climate, natural resources or labour) which are in abundance locally, countries are able to gain a price advantage over their competitors. Thus a nation should narrow its focus of activity, abandoning certain industries while developing those in which it has the largest 'comparative advantage'.

If a country has a significant amount of low-cost labour, for instance, it should export labour-intensive products: if it has a rich endowment of natural resources, it should export resource-intensive products. By exporting what they can produce most cheaply and importing what others can produce more cheaply, international trade, according to the theory, would grow as nations export their surplus and import the products that they no longer manufacture. As a result, efficiency and productivity would increase in line with economies of scale and prosperity would be enhanced.

As producers vie with each other to improve production and sell their goods, they become more efficient. Efficiency and competition thrive off each other. The trader ensures that goods get to where there is the most appropriate market. The nature of comparative advantage for a country may alter completely through long-term planning, education and investment. Japan has made its wealth on manufactured goods, despite being poor in natural resources and energy. But for poor countries, as their economies now stand, free trade would mean continuing in their role as low-cost producers of primary goods for Western consumption.

For Adam Smith, prosperity was dependent on specialization, which made workers more productive. Since one worker produced one thing more efficiently, there were more total goods to go around. This requires a market for the goods. But the more specialized the production, the larger the market needed to assimilate it. This division of labour is thus limited by the extent of the market, as is the prosperity which can be generated. Smith argued that the case for specialization and large markets does not stop with national boundaries. The same advantages gained by trade among free citizens within the nation would apply unchanged to exchanges between citizens and firms in different nations. The ideal, according to the theory, is a completely open global market in which goods and services pass freely over all national boundaries.

Thus, the basic thesis of free trade is that, instead of a country being self-sufficient, each one should produce what it can produce most cheaply, that is the things in which it has a 'comparative advantage'. It would then exchange its goods for what could be produced more cheaply elsewhere. As everything would be produced more cheaply, everyone would be better off. The 'invisible hand' of market forces would direct every member of society and every nation, using the dynamo of self-interest, to the most advantageous situation for the global economy as a whole. This theory runs into difficulty where one country can produce a number of products more cheaply than others, and has no incentive to trade, or where a country has little or no comparative advantage in anything.

Ricardo attempted to address the former by using a semi-fictitious example to illustrate how the theory of comparative advantage works to everyone's advantage. Say, Portugal is capable of producing both wine and cloth with less labour (hence less cost) than England. However, Portugal can make the most money by transferring all efforts to the production of its most profitable commodity, in his example wine, and importing cloth from England. This comparative advantage would be big enough to overcome the fact that Portugal can produce cloth cheaper than England can. From England's perspective, although it has to give up producing wine in order to produce enough cloth for its exports, the cost differences between the two products internally, when compared with the cost advantage of ceasing wine production and just trading cloth, mean that England also enjoys a 'comparative advantage' by engaging in this trade. Both countries appear to gain.

## Capital Flows Spoil the Theory

Today, Ricardo's example would be upset by the capacity of capital to move, since the UK like many economies has de-regulated controls on capital, especially internationally. Today Portuguese capital would at first flow to wine, increasing its productivity and output and the price would drop. Capital would therefore flow to cloth where Portugal also has a comparative advantage. The result would probably be such a drop in the price of Portuguese cloth that the English cloth producers would eventually be forced out of the market, due to cheaper Portuguese imports. English capital would also flow to Portugal to supplement Portuguese capital, making even more inevitable the situation where both wine and cloth are produced in Portugal. Under the European Union (EU), English labour might also move to Portugal, thus reducing labour costs even more because of the competition for jobs involved.

The free flow of capital and goods, and not just of goods as was basically the case in Smith's and Ricardo's time, means that investment is now governed by absolute profitability and not by comparative advantage between countries. Neither Ricardo nor Smith thought that capital would be so mobile. They assumed that it would remain in the country of its owners. Smith, in the famous 'invisible hand' passage, took it for granted that it is in the personal interest of capitalists to invest at home:

> 'By preferring the support of domestic to that of foreign industry, he intends only to his own security; and by directing that industry in such a manner as its produce may be of the great-

*est value, he intends only his own gain, and he is in this, as in many other cases, led by an invisible hand to promote an end which was no part of his intention.'[5]*

Ricardo also felt it would be perceived as desirable to keep capital at home:

*'...the fancied or real insecurity of capital, when not under the immediate control of its owner, together with the natural disinclination which every man has to quit the country of his birth and connections, and intrust himself with all his habits fixed, to a strange government and new laws, checks the emigration of capital. These feelings, which I should be sorry to see weakened, induce most men of property to be satisfied with a low rate of profits in their own country, rather than seek a more advantageous employment for their wealth in foreign nations.'[6]*

## The 'Overlooked Advantage' of Power

What is entirely absent from Smith and Ricardo's original theory is any notion of power and the bargaining advantage that it gives. Traders, for example, are assumed to be equal partners, making rational decisions based on objective evaluations of the productive factors available to them and others. Within a market economy, however, there are no transactions amongst equals. Some traders enjoy the backing of huge military machines, others access to subsidies not enjoyed by their competitors.

Moreover, their bargaining power is largely determined by their past histories. The demise of Portugal's cloth industry in the 19th century, for example had less to do with comparative advantage than with Britain's use of its political power to stifle the growth of the textile industries of Portugal in the 18th century, thus leaving the market open to British manufacturers. Likewise, Britain's dominant position in world trade during the 19th century rested to a large extent on its victorious wars against the Spanish in the 16th century, the Dutch in the 17th century and the French in the 18th century. These wars 'helped to ensure that British ships would be free to trade where and when they pleased'.[7]

Competitiveness is thus less a reflection of the 'natural advantages' enjoyed by traders as of the historical, geopolitical and organizational advantages they enjoy: in particular their ability to exploit those social and political forces that distort markets – state power, subsidies, cartels, externalized costs and political favours. Success in the market-place, nationally and internationally, rests primarily on a firm's ability to organize an external and internal political infrastructure that enables it to control labour, ensure access to raw materials, markets and subsidies, manage resistance, and mould a regulatory environment favourable to its expansion.

During the 19th century, such organizational advantage rested with the small, specialized, regionally concentrated firms that grew and prospered during Britain's industrial revolution. Their competi-tiveness derived from their ability to control labour through the factory system, plus the military and financial backing they received from the British government. Abroad they could rely on British military power to prise open new markets and then to deny those markets to others by bringing them under direct colonial rule. State power ensured the enclosure of common land and thus the creation of a labour force for the factories. It also opened up internal markets via the construction of canals, waterways and railways, all subsidized by the government. With this State help and with protected access to the resources and markets of Britain's colonies, British firms enjoyed a 'comparative advantage' that to many contemporaries abroad seemed virtually unassailable.

Today power has passed to the US and TNCs. They too use the same devices but this time with the additional armoury of the WTO's international trade rules, to ensure the global economy is skewed to their advantage. The result is that 47 of the top 100 economies of the world are TNCs, 70 per cent of global trade is controlled by just 500 corporations and a mere 1 per cent of TNCs are responsible for half the total foreign direct investment in the world.[8] While the global economy increases by between 2 and 3 per cent each year, large corpo-rations typically grow by 8 to 10 per cent annually. Constant mergers and acquisitions (M&As), which make up 80 per cent of all foreign investments, further fuel TNC growth. In 1997, transborder M&As reached US$342 billion and the trend has accelerated. These have mostly occurred in financial services, insurance, life sciences, the media and telecommunications.[9]

This globalization process, and the trade rules that guide it, has been fuelled over the past three decades by the world's leading business and governmental elites regularly meeting in forums such as the Council On Foreign Relations and the Trilateral Commission. They have secretly agreed on common approaches such as global economic integration, deregulation, and an economic philosophy of free trade and international competitiveness. They have pushed for free trade agreements such as the General Agreement on Tariffs and Trade's

(GATT) Uruguay Round (spearheaded by the International Chamber of Commerce), the North America Free Trade Agreement (NAFTA) (pushed by the US Business Roundtable of TNCs and big banking and insurance interests, and Canada's equivalent, the Business Council on National Issues) and in Europe for the Single Market and Currency (via the European Roundtable of Industrialists).[10]

## WTO – THE GLOBAL ENFORCER OF COMPARATIVE ADVANTAGE

The GATT rules of the WTO, a Geneva-based agency set up in 1995 has as its aim the reducing of trade barriers, preventing increases in tariffs, and promoting multilateral negotiations to lower tariffs. It provides a set of rules and processes for such trade liberalization, as well as providing a mechanism for implementing them. Although it seeks a world free trade order as its ultimate goal, it is primarily concerned to create what it sees as a fair, open, non-discriminatory, multilateral, rules-based trading system, much of its work focusing on the detail of trade relations.

The WTO is the successor to the GATT: which set out rules for world trade aimed at eliminating tariffs and other barriers to trade. The WTO provides a global executive branch to judge a country's compliance with its rules, enforce the rule, with sanctions and provide the legislative capacity to expand the rules in the future. The WTO has no mechanism for non-governmental organizations (NGO) involvement and requires that all members agree to be bound by its rules and that the laws of every nation must 'conform' to the WTO and each other.

The central principles of GATT rules are:

1   Liberalization or 'market access' – this is the goal of gradually reducing most forms of protection and fixing or 'binding' these reduced levels. This involves an undertaking initially to fix maximum tariffs or other measures at the agreed level; actual tariffs can be below this level, but if set at higher levels, compensation may be claimed or retaliatory actions taken by countries adversely affected.

2   Reciprocity – the negotiating process whereby each country makes successive tariff reduction offers until a schedule of mutually agreed reductions is reached.

3   Non-discrimination – this concept, implying equality between WTO members, takes three forms: first, WTO rules apply equally

to imports and exports; second, trade concessions granted to any country must be extended equally to all other WTO members – the 'Most Favoured Nation' (MFN) principle; third, no tariff, tax or other measure should discriminate between domestic and foreign suppliers – the 'National Treatment' (NT) principle.

4   Transparency – any form of protection a signatory chooses to use within the framework of WTO rules should be clearly and firmly stated, should be consistent and ideally should take the form of visible tariffs.

The WTO's greatest power lies in its dispute settlement body and its cross-retaliation provisions, both of which enable it to force nations to comply with WTO rules. The increasing number of controversial rulings in which the WTO dispute settlement body has upheld corporate interests over those of people and the environment has increased public opposition to the WTO.

Within the WTO system, any member state can complain to the dispute settlement body about any other member's policies or laws that are perceived to restrict the free flow of trade. If the panel, composed of unelected bureaucrats, finds a government guilty of non-compliance with WTO agreements, the offending country must change its legislation or face retaliatory trade sanctions by the complaining party, even in sectors unrelated to the dispute. The offending country may also face heavy financial penalties.

During the first four years of the WTO's existence, the Dispute Settlement Mechanism has been invoked predominantly for disputes between the EU and the US. These include the banana and beef hormone disputes (see Chapter 19) which provide evidence of an anti-environmental and anti-poor approach and the central, although often behind the scenes, role played by TNCs.

Globalization is reducing the power of governments to provide what their populations require all over the world. TNCs and international capital have become the de facto, new world government. Their increasing control over the global economy is underpinned by the free trade orthodoxy.

Yet the theories behind this bear no comparison to today's reality. The original theorists, Adam Smith and David Ricardo, expected most capital to stay in the country where it was generated. Today, there are very few constraints on the flow of capital. The increased size and the global spread of TNCs has been paralleled by a massive increase in the amount of capital flowing round the world. Developments in computing and information technology, plus a deregulation of controls on capital by nation states now mean that around US$1.5 trillion (US$1,500 billion) is transferred every day around the world.[11]

# Chapter 3

# Theory and Attempted Enforcement of Capital Advantage

## THE THEORY OF CAPITAL ADVANTAGE[1]

*'Practical men, who believe themselves to be quite exempt from any intellectual influences, are usually the slaves of some defunct economist. Madmen in authority, who hear voices in the air, are distilling their frenzy from some academic scribbler of a few years back.'*

John Maynard Keynes[2]

Capital advantage is the theory that the global economy will work more effectively if constraints on the flow of money are continuously reduced. The three main benefits claimed for liberalizing capital markets are:

1   to provide more efficient allocation of global savings to their most productive uses;
2   to provide valuable services to financial investors, especially by allowing them to diversify risks across countries;
3   to provide healthy 'disciplines' for national governments by rewarding those that adopt 'sound' policies.

The case against depends on four major criticisms:

1   Capital markets are plagued by severe and endemic information problems, which prevent international capital flows from achieving their intended efficiency gains.
2   Capital mobility severely constrains national monetary autonomy.
3   The threat of capital flight leads to a contractionary or 'deflationary' bias in macroeconomic policy making.
4   The volatility of international capital flows worsens real economic instability by fostering exaggerated boom–bust cycles.

In addition, the international financial crisis of the 1990s has led to further questioning about the effects of liberalized capital markets. It has become more and more clear that liberalized capital flows can become extremely volatile and have contributed to the spread of financial crises around the world.

## 1 Information Problems

International investments, in essence, involve placing bets about an inherently uncertain future. Purchasing goods on the other hand involves information that is generally known (eg quality and price). An investor however cannot know for sure whether an asset (eg shares) will hold its value, whether borrowers will be able to service their debts, or whether a currency will depreciate. There is a degree of certainty about government bonds, guaranteeing to repay at a certain date and paying fixed interest at regular intervals by the state. But even these are usually compared with more risky investments, in case the latter bring higher yields. Decisions about international investment are therefore based on purely subjective evaluations of the probabilities of future events, or even on mere feelings of optimism or pessimism about a country's future prospects.

Investors are also driven by a herd instinct, typified by their 'trend is my friend' approach. Thus, investors pile in or out of shares or currencies for fear of missing out on expected gains, or fears of losses. This can result in a rise or fall, even if conditions didn't merit such a fluctuation. Thus financial markets can be characterized by 'self-fulfilling expectations' resulting in assets' prices skyrocketing in a 'bubble' and subsequently collapsing in a 'panic', without regard to the underlying fundamentals that should theoretically determine the true value of the asset (eg expected future profits for a company). Given these weaknesses in the process, the efforts by the like of the G7 group of rich nations to improve information to the market are unlikely to contribute greatly to achieving significantly more certainty of stability.

The inherent uncertainty and incomplete information involved in investment will always occur, even by those investing in their own country. However, the situation is far worse in the global economy. Here the simultaneous liberalization of capital markets in a large number of countries makes it even more difficult to evaluate the widespread information available. Thus decisions about any individual country's true prospects are weakened even more. There can therefore be no presumption that capital is flowing towards those countries where it will be most productively used.

## 2 Constraining National Economic Autonomy

Global financial liberalization undermines national central banks' autonomy to set national monetary policy: that is money supply, bank interest rates, government expenditure and borrowing. These are the main levers of economic power and control for a nation. International banks and offshore currency markets created pressures that encourage the deregulation of domestic banking and financial services such as insurance, thus reducing governments' influence. Offshore currency markets originally arose out of efforts by large banks and depositors to avoid national regulations which curbed their potential profits. These included interest rate ceilings and reserve requirements (ie the minimum percentage of their total assets which banks and other financial institutions are required to hold in cash or short-term Treasury bills of exchange, which can be easily changed into cash with minimum delay and risk of loss). The offshore currency markets were also set up to evade national capital control in the 1960s and 1970s.

Once external and unregulated, or less regulated, markets existed, domestic financial institutions lost deposit and loan business to offshore competitors. This competition in turn placed pressure on domestic governments to relax and abolish domestic regulations as well as external restrictions. In short, a race to the bottom. This undermines the ability of governments to control the allocation of resources within their countries for socially desirable purposes. For example, restrictions on interstate banking in the US and on international capital flows in all countries can force banks to relocate savings within depressed regions domestically, instead of pumping the funds into booming areas elsewhere in the country or in the world.

Another crucial lever of national control over the economy is interest rates (the internal price of credit) and this is constrained by international capital mobility. The tightness of such constraints depends on whether the exchange rate (the external price of a country's currency in terms of another) is fixed or managed within certain fluctuations. The latter tends to have to be accepted by smaller and less developed countries, the larger and richer ones having more autonomy to set their own interest rates.

Inward speculative capital flows can also constrain policy makers' room to manoeuvre to maintain policies they consider pertinent and 'sound', eg constraining economic activity if inflation is thought to be increasing unacceptably. These flows can temporarily suspend ordinary constraints on growth for a country, only to cause a subsequent crisis when investors revise their expectations of a country's situation and quickly withdraw. Openness to volatile capital flows is a common feature to all recent crises in Latin America, East Asia and other regions.

Thus, the operation of unfettered financial markets interferes with national efforts to maintain economic policies in the public interest.

## 3 Deflationary Bias

Capital mobility allows those controlling such finance to threaten to leave a country introducing a policy they do not like (eg increasing corporate or other taxation). Since they are intent on preserving and enhancing the value of their financial assets, investors are very fearful of inflation (a persistent tendency for prices and money wages to increase, creating a potential spiral where prices rise to keep up with increased production costs). Inflation redistributes income from creditors to debtors, since the real value of the money originally lent is reduced over time. Hence the repayment of the original loan at a later date means that the repayment's real cost is considerably less, as is its value to the creditor when it is repaid.

This is why financial investors prefer to invest in countries that prioritize low inflation through price stability. For this to be maintained demand levels have to be constrained such that they don't exceed supply and hence don't result in significant price rises. This tends to mean a favouring of higher interest rates and lower public expenditure resulting in low budget deficits (the excess of a government's expenditure over its income) or positive budget surpluses. The more that financial markets and capital flows are liberalized the easier it is to pull out, or threaten to do so, should a country desire to adopt a more 'tax and spend' approach to, for example, create jobs or improve social or physical infrastructure.

Of course, some foreign direct investment is geared partially to ensuring eventual access to what is seen as a significant future market; this is particularly true of China and parts of Eastern Europe. However once these foreign investors are entrenched they urge the same set of policies on such countries.

International financial flows thus tend to reward those countries that constrain public expenditure and taxation, particularly on investment income, and that deregulate financial markets, privatize state enterprises and liberalize trade. The result is countries with open capital markets tend to be pushed in the direction of slower growth, higher unemployment and part-time and less-secure employment, and more unequal distributions of income than was the case when capital was more constrained.[3] The recent long-term US boom that seemed to buck this trend is in fact based on what is widely considered to be an overvalued stockmarket and historically low savings levels. These have resulted in a consumer boom, which is not expected to be sustainable.[4]

## 4 Boom–Bust Instability

The theory is that more sustainable, long-term economic growth, is supposed to be delivered by channeling savings from all countries to the most efficient investment outlets around the world. The reality is that capital market liberalization has worsened economic instability in countries where unsustainable booms were initially fuelled by rapid capital inflows, and subsequently cut short by panic-stricken outflows. Rather than investing where the long-term prospects are greatest, investors move their funds in and out of countries in a herd-like fashion. This is based on poorly informed expectations that can change overnight from overtly optimistic to unduly pessimistic. Moreover, while open capital markets were supposed to allow investors to diversify their risks internationally, their herd-instinct has ended up increasing the level of risk in the entire global economy by causing synchronized waves of currency crises, financial panics and contagion effects. The end result is a global economy that is more unstable rather than being more efficient.

# THE MAI WAY TO CAPITAL ADVANTAGE

Just as those TNCs trading in goods had secured a beneficial set of rules overseen by the WTO, so those concerned with international investments wanted these rules to be expanded dramatically to cover their interests. Accordingly they pressed for what became known as the Multilateral Agreement on Investment (MAI), that was initially negotiated in secret at the Paris Headquarters of the Organisation for Economic Co-operation and Development (OECD). However, an alliance of NGOs and some governments starting in the developing world, then spreading to America and eventually to the rest of the OECD, has succeeded in stopping this initiative. This treaty for corporate rights and privileges would have granted transnational investors an almost unrestricted ability to buy, sell and move business assets wherever and whenever they wanted.

It would have forced countries to treat foreign investors as favourably as domestic companies, severely inhibiting protective laws such as those mandating the purchase of material from local vendors or the employment of local managers. Subsidies for domestic business and limits on foreign ownership would be forbidden. This would severely threaten the work of community revitalization, since much of it depends on initial or sustained subsidizing of enterprises run for and by the community.

Increasingly known as the International Bill of Corporate Rights, it had been dubbed in the US a 'virtual constitutional amendment' because of its potential to transfer power away from state and local government in favour of multinationals. It would have enabled the latter to bypass national courts. Challenges to national laws such as protection for local jobs or the environment would have instead gone before an international panel of industry experts that would interpret the MAI and issue binding rulings.

Furthermore the MAI would have given transnational companies the right to binding dispute resolution legislation enabling them to initiate lawsuits against national and local governments to protect their interests, and against those of local communities. Thus, these corporations would be able to challenge legislation such as recycling content laws, local hiring requirements and other community-based legislation. Their grounds would be that since it is harder for them to comply with such regulations, the laws are discriminatory and would therefore be illegal under MAI. This would severely curb the rights of governments and their citizens to control the entry and behaviour of transnational companies and restrict the ability of nations, both North and South, to control and improve their domestic economies.

Encouragingly, however, in the face of worldwide opposition – both NGO and governmental – in April 1998 the OECD had to call a halt to the negotiation of the MAI. The international opposition came from NGOs, unions, the European Parliament, as well as from non-trade or finance ministries in negotiating countries. Also attempts to change the International Monetary Fund's (IMF) charter to extend its jurisdiction to the liberalization of capital movements is also meeting stiff opposition in the US Congress.[5]

However, attempts to revamp the MAI are occurring through the Transatlantic Economic Partnership (TEP), which seeks to reduce barriers to trade between the US and the EU, and were attempted at the Millennium Round of the World Trade Organization. (Similar approaches are also to be found in the negotiations for the NAFTA expansion Free Trade Area of the Americas (FTAA), the International Monetary Fund (IMF) and the Asia-Pacific Economic Cooperation (APEC) forum.)[6]

The European Commission's recommendations for the TEP uses the pretext of removing 'technical barriers to trade' to reconsider health, social and environmental protection regulations. Its ultimate goal is to 'reach a general commitment to unconditional access to the market in all sectors and for all methods of supply' of products and services, including health, education and public contracts. The aim is gradually to draw up common minimum regulations 'based on the recommendations of enterprises' in order to 'create new outlets' for them. This agreement has been influenced by TNCs via the powerful lobby of the Transatlantic Business Dialogue (TABD). Indeed the TABD has been labeled the 'new paradigm for trade liberalization' by its proponents. This is because it eliminates the 'middle man' from trade policy making. That middle man is the EU and US governments, and by extension EU and US citizens, community activists, consumers, trades unionists and environmentalists.[7]

The result of such an agreement would be to strip 'the EU, member governments and local authorities of their ability to pursue their own policies, be they economic, social, cultural or environmental'.[8] This strikes at the heart of any attempts to rebuild local communities by using local business and local money, sudsidized or pump primed by the state, since this would be an impediment to trade for foreign companies.

*Part Two*

# The Solution – Localization

# Chapter 4

# From Globalization to Localization – A Potential Rallying Call

## THE CASE FOR A LOCAL APPROACH

As already introduced in Chapter 1, localization is a process which reverses the trend of globalization by discriminating in favour of the local. Depending on the context, the 'local' is predominantly defined as part of the nation state, but can be the nation state itself or even, occasionally, a regional grouping of nation states.

The adverse effects of globalization have been assiduously documented over the last few years (see Suggested Reading). This includes the way is reduces the power of governments to provide what their populations require and how TNCs and international capital have become the, de facto, new world government, aided by the WTO, IMF and the World Bank. Their increasing control over the global economy is underpinned by the orthodoxy of trade liberalization. While outside businesses could be advantageous if they strengthened the local economy (see Chapters 7 and 8) in most instances they harm the local economies in countries both rich and poor.

### The Re-think Begins

The international economic crisis that began in Asia in July 1997 has led to more and more attempts to re-think the future direction of the global economy. This has ranged from disagreements between sections of the World Bank and the IMF, to Malaysia and Russia introducing curbs on financial flows, through to grass roots reaction to specific adverse events. When considering what direction global economics should take, it is crucial to be aware that at the core of most of the issue-specific demands of the huge range of politically active groupings are certain basic rights.

The Council of the Canadians in a report highlighted this fact:

> 'As citizens in a democratic society, we all have rights. The
> Universal Declaration of Human Rights and other interna-
> tional covenants and charters enshrine a number of these,
> including the right to adequate food, clothing and shelter; the
> right to employment, education and health care; the right to a
> clean environment, our own culture and quality public
> services; the right to physical security and justice before the
> law. Central to all of these is the right to participate in
> decisions that affect our lives.'[1]

The key question for advocates of localization is whether the present
global economic upheavals will provide an opportunity for them to
articulate a rights-based 'localist' alternative. More than that they must
convince active citizens that this approach provides a roadway towards
achieving these rights. This second part of the book therefore explains
what the local is, why localization can overcome the adverse effects of
globalization and then details the *Protect the Local, Globally* set of
self-reinforcing policies which might bring this about.

## LOCALIZATION – THE 'RIGHTS' ROUTE

Many are now proposing discriminating positively in favour of the
local, as the way to potentially achieve the basic rights agenda
mentioned above.[2] Terms differ and include localization/local
economies first/protect the local globally/from global to local/going
local. For the purposes of this book, 'localization' will be used as the
catch-all term.

Michael Shuman of the Washington-based Institute for Policy
Studies in his groundbreaking book *Going Local* described the aims of
the localization process as one that:

> '...does not mean walling off the outside world. It means
> nurturing locally owned businesses which use local resources
> sustainably, employ local workers at decent wages and serve
> primarily local consumers. It means becoming more self suffi-
> cient, and less dependent on imports. Control moves from the
> boardrooms of distant corporations and back to the commu-
> nity where it belongs.'[3]

The prerequisite for achieving such a relocalization of the world
economy is to replace the accepted wisdom that globalization is all
that is on offer with a cogent alternative. The policies involved must

be seen as a plausible way to reverse the instability and insecurity that trade liberalization has wrought upon the world. The essence of these policies is to allow nations, local governments and communities to reclaim control over their local economies; to make them as diverse as possible; and to rebuild stability into community life.

This does not mean a return to overpowering state control, merely that governments provide the policy framework which allows people and businesses to rediversify their own local economies. It would ensure a transition from the present situation, to one where whatever goods and services that can be provided locally are done so. The reduction of product or service miles (distance from provider to consumer) is also an environmental goal. In short, there is a positive discrimination in favour of the local.

## LOCALIZATION FOR WHAT AND FOR WHOM?

Former US House Speaker Tip O'Neill made famous the phrase 'All politics is local'. At one level this is a statement of the obvious, at another it glosses over three key issues. Firstly, what is meant by the local. Secondly, how much is the local constrained by decisions and priorities made at a more national or international level. These include national spending plans for domestic regions, and international or regional bloc trade rules. Thirdly, who actually has the power at the local level and whose interests do such local agendas serve.

### What Constitutes the Local?

Richard Douthwaite suggests that for developed countries the local should be taken as the circulation areas of local papers.[4] These have established the spatial limits within which the readers are interested in each others' doings. Of course newspaper areas of circulation overlap, and so will the boundaries of what constitutes a local economy for different products and services.

In terms of personal interaction, sociologists refer to 'social fields' which have been characterized as local towns of 1500–10,000 and via commuting their hinterland can be extended to a 10–15-mile radius. For urban dwellers, the area, excluding commuting to work, is more likely to be bounded by the distance from the nearest supermarket, shopping centre, school and other parts of the social infrastructure. For developing countries, the local is more likely to be the village or township, again sometimes excluding longer distances travelled to work.

## Economic Boundaries

What constitutes the boundary for localization will depend on what goods or services are being considered. This should reflect the views and the needs of the communities affected, but will ultimately, in terms of allocation of the necessary supportive resources, be a political decision by those countries and any regional blocs concerned.

The parameters of the area within which each industry would site would be predominately the nation state, although for some goods (eg agricultural products), the area might be sub-national. For very large industries, such as aeroplane production, the delineation might be the actual grouping of countries which make up the geographical bloc.

Each bloc can put limitations on imports to the group of countries concerned in order to encourage domestic production. To further this goal inside these regional blocs, larger countries may have their own national barriers. Smaller ones may choose to join together until they have attained a grouping that they feel is an optimal size to maximize production of their needs. This new grouping may then have its own protective controls to allow for as much internal production as possible. The guiding light for such decisions will be to ensure that production is as local as possible for every country. For most sectors a gradual increase of energy costs will lead to production being sited as close as is feasible to the markets.

In terms of capital controls, the costs of rebuilding local economies could, in the short term, be partly funded from a Tobin/Speculation Tax (a small tax of around 0.5 per cent on each international capital transaction) to curb currency speculators. This is vital since such predatory activity has resulted in enormous job losses for the Asian Tigers and elsewhere. Broader reregulation of finance capital is also required. To ensure that money was more grounded and redirected to the local would require controls on capital flows, taxes on short-term speculative transactions, and tightening of easy credit that allow speculators to multiply the size of their 'bets' way beyond the cash required to cover them. A coordinated attack on corporate tax evasion, including offshore banking centres, is also crucial. Equally important is the regulation of corporate investments in a manner involving the wishes and wellbeing of the affected communities.

## How Much Local Control Exists?

It is crucial to make clear the distinction between different levels of political control and geography. Some local political powers clearly control the day to day running of a defined local area (eg a local authority), and should in theory be more accountable to local residents. Many local economies are dominated by the agenda of national governments, which need not be in their interests. Examples include tax incentives for foreign investment rather than support for local firms, or making a locality an export zone. Finally, more and more national priorities are subsumed to the demands of regional and international free trade agreements, eg competitive tax cutting, low environmental and labour standards, wages and security (see Part Three).

### Priorities of the Local

A key end-goal is to ensure that the transition to a more localized economy has at its core the aims of providing basic needs sustainably, improving human rights, reducing the power gaps between different groupings and genders, and increasing equity and democratic control over decision making. Should these guidelines gain general acceptance, then the policies for localization suggested in the sections below, or any others proposed, have to be constantly evaluated in these terms. This holds whether these measures are being discussed or being put into practice. The politics of localization must also be inclusive and supportive of localist measures elsewhere that are aimed at improving the lives of the vast majority. This is what used to be termed internationalism.

Internationalism covers any interaction that benefits the majority in local economies, and involves communities in the decision-making process. Such flows of information, technology, management and legal structures, trade, aid and investment between continents, would strengthen local economies.

## LOCALIZATION – SOMETHING DONE BY PEOPLE, NOT SOMETHING DONE TO THEM

*'Individuals are the engine that makes a healthy local economy grow. It is individuals, working independently and collectively, that form the fabric of community life. It is the skills, abilities, and experience of these individuals that can be mobilized to develop a vibrant local economy.'*[5]

Historically, significant community development tends mostly to take place when people in a local community are committed to investing their time, skills and resources in the effort. In the US, John Kretzman and John McKnight summarized successful community-building initiatives in hundreds of neighbourhoods across America.[6] They found that a key was to 'map' their local human, institutional and resource assets and to combine and mobilize these strengths to build stronger, more self-reliant communities and hence local economies. This consists of utilizing individuals' skills, the local associations where people assemble to solve problems or share common interests, and the more formal institutions which are located in the community. These include private businesses, public institutions such as schools, libraries, hospitals and social service agencies.[7]

This has led to the beginning of processes which reinvigorate the local economic and physical assets. Local government officials have been most useful where they have supported local problem solvers and strengthened and connected more effectively the other local assets. The most helpful approach has been one where local government representatives have asked how they can assist local citizens in their development efforts. (The more usual approach has been to ask how local citizens can participate in the government's efforts.) At a national government level the priority is the need to ensure that a substantial part of government expenditure provides direct economic benefits in terms of local jobs, contracts and purchases.[8]

The way that the policies necessary for localization can further community regeneration is considered in more detail in the next chapter.

## A NEW OVERARCHING ECONOMIC ARCHITECTURE

Michael Shuman makes the point that 'every locality must find its own way'.[9] While this is true, it is also crucial at a national and international level to galvanize those supportive of localization to replace the present dominant paradigm of globalization. The 'architecture' to achieve localization would bolster local initiatives by providing the macro-policies which would allow then to flourish. It would also discriminate in favour of local production, rather than the cheapest global source. Adverse effects of any increase in prices would be compensated by increased employment opportunities and benefit increases for the poor via local taxation.

The major task is clearly to develop a credible set of overarching policies which will secure the end-goal of relocalizing economies worldwide. These will need to be discussed, refined and used as organizational and lobbying tools by a wide range of active citizens and movements in order to bring about such a dramatic political turnaround. The result should be worth the enormous effort involved. It would put governments at a local, national and regional level back in control of their economies in order to benefit the majority. This would enable economic activity to be relocalized and rediversified.

Central to this process must be the involvement in the final development of such policies of the wide range of grass-roots activists, who are already developing such initiatives at a local level. They must be convinced that they, and their concerns and communities, would benefit from such a policy framework, and that it could ensure that their efforts can be replicated more easily and on as wide a scale as possible.

Such a reorganization of the global market is needed to allow both rich and poor countries to have any real chance of moving towards relocalized economies. For this to be successful it must be underpinned by a commitment by the OECD countries to the two way, free flow of sustainable technologies and relevant information with the developing world and Eastern Europe. A spur to such a change in direction by the rich countries could well be the fact that a worsening global economic situation for the world's majority will adversely affect them. It will not merely be the usual economic concern about lost markets, there will also be the domestic implications for OECD countries of the increased movements of people displaced by globalization's economic failures and its concomitant adverse environmental effects. The Red Cross now estimates that there are more 'environmental refugees' than those displaced by armed conflict.

## POTENTIAL ADVANTAGES OF THE LOCAL

The term potential is used, since local control need not guarantee increased democracy, equality, environmental protection and so on, it just makes it more likely. In times of rising insecurity, as is now being generated by globalization, this can often bring out non-progressive forces in support of a more local emphasis. Such groupings often also use the language of racism, xenophobia and religious fundamentalism as part of their platform. Examples include the Freedom Party in Austria, the National Front in France, and the Bhartiya Janata Party (BJP) in India.

However, this is sometimes used as an excuse by more progressive forces not to emphasize the need to protect and rebuild local communities less there be guilt by association. This can leave the right with a clear run to capitalize on the growth of insecurity and leave the progressives concentrating on more limited issue-specific battles. This defensive approach can be at the expense of concentrating on the fundamental shifts required to deal with the very insecurity which is the springboard for the rise of extremists.

The main potential advantages of localization are summarized under the following headings.

## 1 Maximum Devolution of Political Power and Democratic Accountability

A diverse local economy is likely to be inherently democratic, since it involves a wide range of people's active involvement to make it work. This wider economic involvement needs to go hand in hand with wider political and democratic control and accountability at the local level. Every effort needs to be made to ensure such participation is genuine, rather than token. To use an environmental metaphor, it invokes the stability of diversity as compared with globalization's move to ever fewer providers. The recent rash of mergers and acquisitions involving banks, oil companies, information technology (IT) companies, car producers and the like is the latest testimony to this trend towards economic monoculture.

## 2 Taking Control of the Economy

The sub-national, national and regional prioritizing of the goal of localization should, if the countries concerned acted in concert, return control of the local economy to the locality. This is because it is here that in most cases the good or service would have to be produced. This approach would stop TNCs and others relocating or threatening to do so, since they would thus lose access to the market concerned.

Such localization could make more feasible the breaking up of such large companies and makes them subject to greater transparency and stakeholder power. They would not just be geared to the needs of shareholders, but also to the desires of workers and the local community. Company and accounting law could control transfer pricing and the siphoning off of company profits and individual earnings off shore. These policies would allow for the level of company taxation deemed necessary by local and national governments. Democratic control over capital is also a key to providing the money for governments and communities to improve social and environmental conditions and job opportunities.

## 3 Protecting the Environment

Ecological taxes on energy, other resource use and pollution would help pay for the radical economic transition to localization. They would be environmentally advantageous and could allow for the removal of taxes on labour. Competition from regions without such taxes could be held at bay by positive discrimination in favour of local production. For the environment in general, relocalization would mean less long-distance transportation and energy use and resulting pollution.

Also, any adverse environmental effects would be experienced locally, thus increasing the pressure, impetus and potential for control and improved standards. The transition to more environmentally sustainable local economies would of course have huge job-creating potential. Examples include improving energy efficiency of most of the building stock, developing renewable energy sources on a substantial scale, increasing public transport and making agriculture organic and hence more labour intensive.

## 4 Improving Social and Environmental Conditions, Plus Positive Technological Developments

These measures may of course lead to a greater price rise than would be the case if every country could obtain its needs from the cheapest global source. However, as more and more regional blocs adopt the localization approach, the features that often made their exports cheap (ie low wages, inadequate environmental standards and cheap transport costs) will no longer apply, thus improving the economics of local production.

Also this approach, because of the increased sense of security it should bring, could improve the overall social cohesion and reduce the high social costs inherent in the present beggar-your-neighbour emphasis of international competitiveness. This includes high unemployment, increasing inequality and inadequate resource allocation to deal with poverty. This is the inadequately recognized flip side of the cheap goods argument favoured by trade liberalizers.

The economics of smaller amounts of production for more local markets can be improved increasingly by new computer-controlled technological developments. These are allowing ever smaller numbers of products to become more and more economic to produce, and with less throughput of resources.

## 5 A Positive Role for Competition

A limit should be set for the market share of products by any one company. New firms should be encouraged by grants and loans to enter the marketplace. This guarantees the local competition needed to maintain the impetus for improved products, more efficient resource use as well as the provision of choice. The transfer of information and technology globally would be encouraged where it improved the efficiency of local competitiveness.

## 6 Trade and Aid Rules for Self-reliance

The GATT rules at present administered by the WTO would need to be revised to become a General Agreement for Sustainable Trade (GAST) policed by a World Localization Organization (WLO). Their remit would be to ensure aid policies and flows, information and technological transfer, and residual international trade should incorporate the rules of 'fair trading' and be geared to the building up of sustainable local economies. The goal should be to foster maximum employment through sustainable regional self-reliance.

# TIMELINES

The world economy will remain unstable in 2000 and beyond. The US stockmarket is expected to falter and the pressures on the OECD economies at a time of burgeoning exports from Asia is likely to see a rise in protectionism against long-distance trade. This could follow the 1998 rise in protectionism from long-distance capital flight that occurred in the wake of the Asian crisis that began the year before. The latter led to currency controls moving from being heresy to a short-term salvation for a country like Malaysia. The continual economic instability worldwide and the global slow down likely in the wake of the much-predicted fall in the US stockmarket could well create a similarly fundamental rethink in the way global trade is organized and more calls for it being curbed.

Indeed the WTO Ministerial meeting in Seattle in December 1999 attracted opponents of globalization from around the world. Huge, internationally reported demonstrations, the 'fiasco' of the collapsed meeting itself, plus open revolt from disillusioned developing countries' delegates seriously dented public perceptions of the WTO. At a grassroots level Seattle also saw the emergence of an alternative future. A 'Citizen's Millennium Round' included the demand from over 1600 organizations worldwide that further trade liberalization be halted and trade rules reviewed and revised. This trend, and the growing public unease about WTO rulings from bananas to hormone beef, could be the other half of a pincer movement with the macro-economic concerns mentioned above, which could result in a radical shift away from globalization and towards localization (see Part Three and the Conclusion).

*Chapter 5*

# Localization – Increasing Community Renewal

*'A sustainable community could be described as one in which
there exists, from a mixture of internal and external sources, a
self-renewing basis of economic viability, quality of services
and social capital sufficient to support a good quality of life
for all inhabitants, improve conditions and opportunities
where they are inadequate, face new problems creatively as
they arise, and pass on to future inhabitants the tangible and
intangible assets to achieve the same or higher standards.'*[1]

This chapter considers in detail what is required to build sustainable
communities. The policies of localization must help to foster such
entities, since it is these which in essence make up the 'local'. Achieving
this will be the litmus test of whether localization really helps to rebuild
the local economy on a permanent and inclusive basis.

Later chapters will look at how localization can further the aims
of a wider range of movements concerned with improving social
infrastructure (such as schools, housing, hospitals, transport, etc),
environmental protection and the economic position of the majority
in the developing world and Eastern Europe. The actual policies for
bringing about localization are looked at in detail in the next seven
chapters.

To achieve the shift from acceptance of globalization to its replacement by localization will first require a fundamental 'mindwrench'.
This needs the growing opposition to globalization to develop into
proposals for alternatives. This process will need the links to be made
between successful active campaigning for local on-the-ground
improvements and the need for a drastic change in macroeconomic
policies. Community activists will have to consider and be convinced
that the localization agenda is likely to benefit their interests.

When eventually governments have been convinced (see Part
Three) of the pivotal need to set an overarching framework which
reallocates national budgets, investments, taxes, interest rates, public

jobs and trade rules to this 'localist' end, one key step remains. The way these measures are actually utilized must be shaped and informed by the practical experience and opinions of those on the ground, where most of the control should reside.

# ACHIEVING SOCIAL COHESION PLUS ECONOMIC RENEWAL

## Defining 'Community' and its Needs

*'A community in which people know and care about each other is the basic building block for all other civilised activities, whether commercial, political, social or spiritual. If we cannot care about our neighbours, we will never develop the capacity to care about our nation or world. And there is no better expression of caring than to create a local economy which meets the basic needs of every one of our neighbours, and to help other local economies throughout the world to do likewise.'*[2]

The sustainability of a community could be judged by the following ten points.[3] The first seven of these are concerned with material issues which are dependent on a mixture of internal and external sources. The last three are concerned with the life of the community itself – its internal relationships, activities and its capacity to take a major role from within in the decision-making areas which govern development. The ten criteria are:

1   good housing, shops and other facilities, accessible to all with the help of high-quality, reliable public transport;
2   good education, training and work opportunities and a flourishing local economy that stimulates local enterprise and meets local needs;
3   diverse wildlife and good air, water and soil quality;
4   low energy use and waste, coupled with warm homes and resource-efficient businesses;
5   sustainable lifestyles, requiring less unhealthy and unnecessary consumption and resource use, encouraged and facilitated by education, information and opportunities supporting lifestyle change;
6   a safe and healthy environment, contributing to people's physical, mental and social well-being;

7   quality information enabling the monitoring of social, economic and environmental progress;
8   a vibrant and creative culture, characterized by thriving community groups and pride in the local economy;
9   high levels of public participation in decision making, including often-excluded groups;
10  the means to facilitate on-going improvements in the area.

## Action in the Community

Community activity is found in an incredibly wide range of activities. These include:

- owner and tenants groups involved in housing development, management and maintenance;
- groupings supporting local authority and state provision in: education, health, care for the elderly, youth programmes, physical activity and recreation, community centres, improving the environment and open space, rehabilitation of run-down buildings and the redevelopment of empty and derelict land, transport, energy saving and recycling projects, cultural activities and the development of the local informal and formal economy;
- informational support and training to bolster community activities in the areas of benefit, financial, welfare and legal advice, banking and financial services;
- capacity building for local communities and community groups;
- business formation, development and support, training; advice and specialist service delivery for local businesses;
- use and spread of information technology; provision of work and office space, shops, community centres etc.

The New Economics Foundation (NEF) has identified an enormous range of entities which facilitate what it calls 'community economic action'.[4] They estimate that in the UK one-and-a-half million people now take regular part in such action. These entities have been categorized with some overlap and include:

- *Community Enterprises* have social aims, are financially viable and owned and run by local people. They tackle local social and environmental issues and provide work, training opportunities and local services. They include: community businesses such as childcare schemes, community cafes, managed workspaces; community cooperatives such as housing and food; credit unions and commu-

nity-based housing associations. There are 275 community enterprises in England and Wales and 170 in Scotland, the latter
supporting some 3300 jobs and training places with a collective
turnover of approximately £18 million.

- *Development Trusts* are community-led enterprises with social
objectives actively involved in economic, environmental and social
regeneration of an area. Their core values are mutuality (sharing
of benefits within the community); empowerment (creating opportunities for local people's involvement and control) and acquiring
an asset base (leading to financial self-sufficiency). They help to
rebuild communities and tackle unemployment by providing
workspace, training facilities, child care, recreational and social
facilities, environmental improvements, open spaces, promoting
tourism and heritage etc. There are now around 150 development
trusts, mostly urban based but with a growing number in rural
areas.

- *Credit Unions* are owned and run by their members who save
regularly into a common fund. Members must share some common
bond (eg community or workplace) and those needing small to
medium personal loans can make repayments, according to their
ability, at affordable rates. Altogether 400,000 people now benefit
from the services of more than 700 credit unions in the UK[5] and
assets of £30 million.

- *Community Recycling Schemes* range from large-scale kerbside
collections operating on contract to the local authority, employing
a number of full-time workers to small-scale voluntary groups
concentrating on one or two materials for fundraising purposes.
There are over 500 schemes operating throughout the country.
Wyecycle is a community enterprise employing three full-time and
three part-time workers and recycles about 1000 tonnes of waste
from a dozen villages in Kent and also runs a successful compost-
ing scheme, It is partly self-financing and also receives 'recycling
credits' from the local authority.

- *Community Self-builders* are groups of people in need of housing
who work together to build their homes. They account for £30
million of building and have built over 500 self-build homes.

- *Community Transport* covers a wide range of transport initiatives,
roughly 2500 schemes in the UK, which put local people at the
heart of planning and delivering new transport options. Many are
based on collective transport in minibuses, and are often key parts
of community development initiatives offering dial-a-ride to the
elderly, disabled, vulnerable women or rural communities.

The above are the largest categories of examples, but a myriad of other initiatives are to be found including: Local Exchange Trading Schemes or Systems (LETS); Box Schemes linking local organic farmers and about 35,000 consumers; Managed Workspace providing local small-scale businesses affordable, small-scale offices, studios, workshops and light industrial space; Community Shops and Pubs and Ethical Shops (with community product sourcing); and independent charities known as Community Trust or Foundations.

## MANAGING WITHIN THE PRESENT ECONOMIC CONTEXT

*'Regeneration works best when local residents are actively involved. Community involvement in local development means that a large proportion of local residents:*

- *are involved in their own local organizations, networks and initiatives, each of which enhance local life directly in some way;*
- *know what is being planned for their locality by authorities, and feel that they have effective channels for influencing it;*
- *co-operate actively with official schemes, adding value through their voluntary effort;*
- *are stimulated and given hope by the climate and opportunities of regeneration, and so develop themselves personally through their contribution to the joint effort;*
- *feel ownership of what is achieved by development schemes, are confident that the local population will benefit, and therefore preserve and enhance the achievements.'*[6]

### *Organization and Funding Sources*

Regeneration tends to start in the local neighbourhood, since this is where immediate incremental improvements can be made, in the process building trust and experience. Specific improvements can be provided by a single group, or their competence or capacity can be enhanced by a network of local groups or from the outside. Some initiatives start at the street level and expand to the district, city or region. Others will start as a regional initiative and subsequently split into neighbourhood projects. LETS and food co-ops can be set up without outside support. Advice and seedcorn grants are likely to be needed by nurseries and schoolclubs. Continuous funding is required for handicapped and elderly care, business start ups and training and capital funding for the likes of transport, arts centres and environmental schemes. Poorer areas can receive in the case of Europe various regional funds from the EU.

Investing in people active in their community must not be viewed as an excuse for future institutional abandonment by local or national governments. Instead a national commitment to create policies and a supportive financial, legal and administrative framework is required. The role of the local authority is to facilitate in terms of resources and expertise, such that a process occurs whereby the local community can have control over sufficient resources to ensure the long-term economic and social wellbeing of the neighbourhood.

One example of a group which is both impressively effective on the ground and which has been very successful in obtaining continual financial assistance for local, national and even European resources is the Wise Group based in Glasgow. The Wise Group was set up in 1984 and more than 12,000 people have benefited from participating in its programmes with 6000 going on to a job. For 15 years, through a local partnership between local communities, Glasgow City Council and, the Scottish Office and Europe, the Wise Group has been finding solutions to the problem of unemployment. It now employs over 800 people and will have a turnover of £19 million in 1999.

The Wise Group provides training and work experience to long-term unemployed people in some of the most deprived areas of Britain, while at the same time, delivering energy conservation, home security, community care environmental improvements and call-centre training. By the mid 1990s the group had insulated over 115,000 houses (resulting energy savings of over £5 million per annum), planted 800,000 trees, improved the environment around 3000 houses in the worst parts of Glasgow and made 35,000 houses more secure. It also used this model to improve industrial sites and derelict land.

In carrying out its business, the Wise Group has pioneered what has become known as the 'Intermediate Labour Market'. This market 'adds value and provides people with self worth and a stepping stone into regular work'. In order to help spread its techniques, the company now also operates in East London, Motherwell, Falkirk, Clackmannan and Ayrshire and is transferring good practice to other parts of Britain. This involves helping to create local capacity in regions which would be locally controlled, without having to reinvent the wheel and which develops a clear long-term strategy and funding structure.[7]

## Limitations

The acceptance of the need to design national policies to meet the needs of globalization, and its imperative of international competitiveness, results in an undermining of community cohesion. Firms threaten to relocate or to go out of business unless provided with ever cheaper production facilities and lower taxes. This has contributed to the formation of regional development policies which meet these demands. They have helped fund and encourage companies to congregate where communications and infrastructure are the best for the transportation of their goods to the rest of the country or the world. This has led to the by-passing of marginal and peripheral communities. In Wales, for example, the focus has been on south-east Wales with little benefit to other areas.

### Fickle Big Business Disappoints

Also, decisions by major participants in foreign direct investment (FDI) programmes have been reversed. One of the most spectacular examples was the Korean electronics company LG. This took a government grant reportedly worth around £400 million and promised to open a factory in Wales that the then Prime Minister John Major termed the largest job-creating project ever brought to Europe. Once the Asian crisis hit, such plans were mothballed.[8]

The negative effect of past investments both in terms of employment and the environment are illustrated by the case of the oil industry in Pembrokeshire. Here each expansion phase of the oil industry has left higher unemployment in the region as the promises of new jobs have proved to be over-estimates. The construction phase has drawn in more non-locals to fill temporary contracts, many of whom have remained once the job has finished.[9] That a more local small enterprise emphasis is required was illustrated by the Scottish Federation of Small Businesses calling for Scottish Enterprise to be wound up early for 'totally failing the small business sector'.[10]

## Wales Looks to the Local

The Welsh Party, Plaid Cymru, has taken a lead in looking for a different and more locally self-reliant approach. It recognizes that too much emphasis has been placed on trying to attract jobs by beggar-your-neighbour competition with places outside Wales. The same approach sets the regions of Wales against each other in an unproductive race to attract competitors. With a rare prescience they also recognize that growing competition for mobile investment from other regions in

Europe with high unemployment, and the entry of new nations to the EU have and will expose the futility of this pattern of development.

In its place they call for a rejection of economic development strategies which continue to place an ill-defined competitiveness above employment. This approach must be replaced by one which redefines the purpose of public economic intervention as the creation of sustainable employment. To achieve this will require maximizing the impact of public policy on the number and quality of Welsh jobs as well as the more usual widening of access to training and job opportunities.

Plaid Cymru asserts there should be no further subsidy to foreign investment at a very high cost per job, when other sectors promise to provide employment far more cheaply. Industrial support should be judged on cost per job as the main criteria for the use of public funds. This is expected to result in more support for sectors and areas bypassed by recent economic development policies, including small and medium-sized businesses and community enterprise.

In the medium term, Plaid Cymru intends to persuade the new Welsh Assembly to take a more ambitious approach to the EU. It calls for cooperation with other countries and regions to press for an improvement in the macroeconomic context, and European employment policy. At present this still emphasizes the failed and self-defeating policies of equipping areas to compete for jobs both with neighbouring areas, Eastern Europe and the developing world.

## LOCAL DIRECT INVESTMENT – THE LARGE-SCALE JOB GENERATOR?

As will be enlarged on in Chapter 14, globalization presents a huge threat to future employment via its acceleration of automation, relocation to cheaper labour countries and tax curbs which cut the labour-intensive public sector. This is resulting in global deflation in large parts of the world and inadequate demand. Boosting demand to generate the new jobs required must not take the form of the traditional encouraging of more sales of cars and other consumer goods, with built-in obsolescence and produced and utilized in a way that threatens the environment. Instead, the answer must lie in encouraging economic activity which deals with the basic needs of people in their communities in a way that is labour intensive.

The key is for jobs to be rooted in communities where people live. Of course settlements from villages to cities have tended to evolve around employment opportunities. For many cities technological and trade changes have robbed them of many former sources of work. If enough resources could be allocated to cities, then their new job generators would not just be factories, small businesses, shops or offices, vital as these are. The new employment dynamo could be urban infrastructural regenereration.

The growth point would be the rebuilding and refurbishment of energy efficient housing and public buildings, as well as renewing sewers, improving public spaces, leisure facilities, the public transport system and all the other public and private requirements of the city. In rural areas, the job potential comes from producing safe food through a large-scale switch to more organic farming, local food processing and marketing. Whether urban or rural the other great source of local jobs is more face-to-face caring. This ranges from areas such as health, education, care for the elderly through to the more esoteric shores of aromatherapy and the like.

If people were employed locally, and a whole range of new businesses and services sprung up to meet such a programme, much of the huge costs involved could be offset by reduced unemployment benefits, and lower health and policing costs. The former is related to factors such as substandard housing and the stress of unemployment and the latter to the fact that more jobs are likely to ensure that crime no longer increases. In addition, there will be an increased tax take from the employed and businesses.

The money would also be more likely to stay and be recycled in the community, once it had been invested there or found from local public and private resources. To some extent, aspects of such programme financing were presaged in the government's Urban Taskforce report.[11] This called for the formation of 'regeneration companies', a partnership between businesses and local councils. The latter, in turn, will be allowed greater freedom to raise money locally, and recycle cash for further development in priority areas. It also calls for some of the additional cash generated by business rates in the 'urban priority areas' to be retained by the local authority.

English Heritage has had some experience with a similar approach. Between 1994 and 1999 it invested £36 million pounds in renovation grants in a conservation area partnership programme. This involved working with local authorities and private investors in 357 projects to help businesses in run-down but unlisted historical buildings in conservation areas. These ranged from restoring a decaying old Customs House in Hastings to become a bucket-and-spade shop, through to a fish shop, hairdressers and the more predictable designer shops and wine bars.

Its first audit showed that for every £10,000 spent by English Heritage, £58,000 was obtained in matching funds from the public and private sectors. This resulted in one new job, one safeguarded job, one improved home and 177 sq metres of improved commercial space. It also argued that recycling existing buildings is both more environmentally efficient and more socially useful, boosting community spirit and preserving a sense of history.[12]

A further advantage to the country as a whole from such a localist revitalization of cities is that it reduces pressure on green field sites, and the concomitant increase in commuting, congestion and health problems. Such a change would also protect pension income. Millions of people have their pensions either directly or indirectly through investment tied up in the rental income received from town-centre shop properties. Many of these have halved in recent years. Depressed rentals in many town centres as a result of out-of-town developments, have already affected the pension income of many people.[13]

Historically, such calls for adequate money for local direct investment have received inadequate funding because of the entrenched perception of the need to prioritize resourcing and encouraging a competitive export sector. This has been the national priority to generate the wealth to fund public expenditure and pay for the imports required. Under localization, however, imports of goods and services would be substantially reduced, as would the need for such a national export emphasis over time.

## ROLE OF BUSINESS IN MORE SELF-RELIANT COMMUNITIES

Activities in communities worldwide include business entities anchored in the community, for example:

- locally owned and operated for-profits, non profits, cooperatives, and public enterprises;
- community corporations meeting local needs for energy, food, water and materials;
- local finance through special banks, currency unions and microloan funds;
- local currency systems allowing purchase of local goods and services;
- local governments targeting of municipal grants, tax relief, investments, contracts, and hiring.

All the above need to be seen as part of a package in which sectors reinforce each other. The cornerstones are investing in locally owned business, focusing on import-replacing rather than export-led development: ie reducing dependence on distant sources of energy, water, food and basic materials and demanding governments change their subsidies, tax and trade laws to rebuild local communities.

Much of this chapter concentrates on community groups and NGO activities, but business will need to be centrally involved in local regeneration. Based on US experience, nine basic steps for business involvement in a community committed to self-reliance have been identified.[14] These are listed in Box 5.1.

## To the Community's 'Mutual' Advantage

A report by the London-based think-tank Demos[15] surveyed the scale of mutuals in Britain. It concluded that when they are well run, when they serve the appropriate market and when they are organized on the right scale, then they have significant advantages over the private and public sector organizations with which they compete. The report expects that mutuals could flourish because at their best they can harness two ingredients critical to success for modern enterprise – trust and know how. These two factors are also a crucial 'glue' for effective community activity and involvement in the regeneration of sustainable local economies.

They also potentially excel at bringing forth ideas and know how that more hierarchical and bureaucratic organizations such as local authorities find hard to reach. This must not however be seen as a recipe for pulling back state provision, but rather as a vehicle for community involvement in service provision decisions, rather than being passive recipients. Indeed well-run and properly funded services for everyone are vital to a society in which the state and individuals are deemed to have mutual and reciprocal obligations. Whether they are provided publicly or privately requires using the yardstick of the quality of service on a case-by-case basis. The crucial thing is that there should be no decline in the public experience of service provision.

The biggest gains in public-sector productivity, crucial to a successful and widespread infrastructural renewal programme could come from a new alliance between professional services and mutual self-help. The Demos report claimed that public health will be improved by health professionals and communities working more closely together. Social housing is invariably run more effectively and imaginatively when tenants are involved in management and budget setting. Similarly, community safety will depend on the police working with neighbourhood-watch patrols and the like. Schools need to build on

# Box 5.1 US Business – Community Cooperation for Rebuilding the Local Economy

## 1 Community Bill of Rights

The community and local businesses should participate in a series of meetings resulting in a statement of economic principles and practices. This Community Bill of Rights states what constitutes community-friendly business and consumer behaviour, and is distributed to every household. Businesses would be monitored and good practice publicly noted via an awards system.

## 2 State of the City Report

- economic security through community-monitored pensions, savings accounts, loans, inflation rates, wages, taxes and income distribution;
- ecological integrity through an inventory of consumption to see if local renewable resources (energy, trees, fish, wildlife, agricultural land and water) are being used sustainably, are they replacing non-renewables like fossil fuels, copper;
- quality of life through rates of longevity, divorce, hunger, homelessness, illness and crime;
- political empowerment such as participation rates in all elections, progress towards gender and racial equity.

The most dramatic example of this type of approach is Chattanooga, Tennessee, once labelled the 'dirtiest city' in the US. Following a launch by the city in 1984 of 'Vision 2000' public participation resulted in 40 goals being agreed for 2000. By 1993 substantial progress had been made on most of them, 223 projects had been launched, creating 1380 jobs and triggering investments of US$750 million. Another example is Sustainable Seattle which has kept track of more than 100 indicators in surrounding King County since 1980. In Jacksonville, Florida, residents decided on 74 key indicators and have set a series of community goals to be reached by 2000.[16]

Input–output models of community economies have also been found useful. They have prompted efforts to curb the outflow of money to absentee landlords, interest payments to outside banks and money spent in stores outside city limits and help small, rural towns revive themselves.

## 3 Anchor 'Community Corporations'

A thorough State of the City Report will highlight business opportunities in fulfilling unmet needs, utilizing unused or underused resources, or replacing goods and services at present produced outside the community. A community willing to put its money where its goal of self-reliance is will attract such businesses, ranging from locally grown food in farmers' markets through to recycling. In the US the recycling business grosses more than US$30 billion. More than 4000 companies are in the National Recycling Coalition and 200 US cities are now making money by recycling more than half of their solid wastes.

Community self-reliance does not mean isolation but expanding the economic base to produce necessities for residents and to focus existing resources on more value-added industries.

## 4 Community-friendly Business Schools

Community-friendly business schools to provide the required skills and confidence to set up a business. These can range form adult education establishments through to pressure groups like the Washington-based Institute for Policy Studies. This set up the Social Action and Leadership School for Activists (SALSA), which has provided night classes on running NGOs for more than 1500 adults a year.

Transforming business schools and economics departments also needs the shifting of emphasis from personal profit to community service. The extent of the shift needed was seen when Cornell University found that economics graduates donated less than half to charity than their counterparts in other disciplines. Their charitable giving declined further with more years of training and reached its nadir when they became professors.[17]

## 5 Community Finance

No business can survive without adequate capital, in the US nearly 70 per cent of small businesses fail within eight years primarily because of under-capitalization. Localizing banks through demands that commercial banks, building societies or credit unions set up a division that invests locally to attract the localist's savings and provide loans for local businesses. To make things even easier for smaller enterprises, the bank could set up a special community-development fund in which no-interest loans are exchanged for equity shares and some management responsibility. This is the approach taken by the huge Mondragon enterprise in Spain, a network of 160 affiliated cooperatives, 90 of which are industrial users. It is Spain's biggest refrigerator and machine-tool manufacturer, and its only producer of computer chips.[18]

Such a community bank could also set up an internal trading system among all loan recipients, as the Swiss Economic Circle does. This is an association of 60,000 business and individual members who once they qualify for a loan must use it exclusively to purchase goods and services from businesses within the circle, and repaid exclusively with the proceeds from sales to member businesses.[19]

## 6 Community Currency

Local money such as LETS schemes, eg Ithaca Hours. Such approaches raise awareness about who lives in the community, which citizens are committed to self-reliance, and what and where goods and services are locally available. Any business that doesn't take local currencies isn't supporting the community, so the chances are that the community will no longer support the business. Local government could also ensure that more of its contracts and purchases were with local businesses and pay some salary and pay-rises in local money.

## 7 Community-friendly Local Authority

Local government could ensure that the only beneficiaries of local invest-ment, contracts, purchases and, in the US, local bonds are 'community corporations'. It could also change regulations and allocate resources to this end and even provide scholarships to ensure that selected graduates set up local businesses.

## 8 Political Reform to Allow a Lobby for Localism

Of course politicians may well be sympathetic to much of the above but the policies proposed often clash directly with the trade and investment agree-ments that national governments are increasingly signing. Thus, the EU's Single Market legislation prohibits too much positive discrimination in favour of the local in areas such as government tendering. The proposed MAI, had it been agreed, would render many of the above ideas very difficult to put into practice. So too do the rules of the WTO should any measures to protect local markets from 'imports' be required.

Local politicians have to take a lead in any 'devolution revolution'. However, the centralizing trend of national governments taking ever more power to the centre whilst doling out ever-more responsibilities to the local tiers of government must be reversed to give the latter real powers over the local economy. At present, they receive inadequate financial help, often have inadequate labour resources or are without the revenue-raising capacity to pay for them.

## 9 Translocalism

A key to a globally minded community moving towards self-reliance is to cooperate with and to help other communities worldwide to do likewise. This requires the transfer of information and technology which leads to such an end. More than 2000 communities in the North have some kind of relationship with an equal number of communities in the South that could be built upon along these lines. In Europe, they are called 'twinnings' or 'linkings' and in North America 'sister cities'.

At present, those in the US celebrate new contracts for export-orien-tated businesses, rather than the necessity for municipal partners to work together to reduce their dependence on long-distance trade. In Europe, more positive approaches can be found. The city-state of Bremen in Germany has spread biogas technology to help communities become more self-reliant in energy. It has funded technology transfer for biogas digesters in communi-ties in Mali, Ethiopia and Tanzania.

Over 150 European municipalities are fighting global warming through the Climate Alliance. Most of their activities concentrate on energy conser-vation, public transport and selective purchasing. They are also providing financial and legal support to South American communities, primarily those of indigenous peoples to survey, demarcate and protect Amazon rain forests.

many innovative state schools where mainstream education has been combined with social and environmental services, a healthy living centre and a housing project. West Walker in Newcastle delivers a better education in a very deprived area, because it has been the focus for mutual self-help and community renewal.

Demos estimated that in the UK about 30 million people are already members of mutuals which have a combined turnover of close to £25 billion. Much of the country's food comes from 550 agricultural cooperatives with a turnover of £7.4 billion and nearly a quarter of a million members. The member-run branches of the Workers Education Association (WEA) are one of the largest adult education providers, serving 116,000 students a year. The largest 80 Friendly societies providing insurance still have 4.76 million members and manage £11.4 billion. About 215,000 people are members of credit unions and 120,000 in Neighbourhood Watch schemes.

In the UK as well as mutual organizations being found in education, childcare, housing and agriculture, new sectors such as software retailing and internet services are being developed. New mutuals are also proliferating in areas of acute social and economic distress, in the form of credit unions and micro-credits. In addition to areas of social and financial exclusion mutuality is spreading to employee credit unions, LETS schemes and social and ethical investment. However, at present such initiatives rarely strengthen wider social networks.

One new initiative that has the potential to do this in an initially modest way is the Sheffield Employment Bond. This involves local people making five-year zero-interest loans for the city's regeneration. The revenue generated will create job opportunities and deliver local grants and loans. The bond plans to raise more than a million pounds by selling up to 5000 bonds. Research by the project's organizer Citylife has shown that 57 per cent of the relatively affluent people in Sheffield said that they would consider buying such a bond.[20] The local newspaper, *The Star*, has bought £10,000 worth of bonds and urged its readers to invest the minimum of £200. Celebrities with connections with Sheffield, such as actors Michael Palin and Sean Bean, as well as the UK's Education Minister David Blunkett, have already purchased bonds.

Seventy-five per cent of the money raised is lent to North British Housing Association to secure a contract with Sheffield Rebuild. This is a community enterprise company committed to recruiting and training local unemployed people for the construction of social housing. This money attracts a government Social Housing Grant of 40 per cent of the total project value. The remaining 25 per cent of the bond, after administration costs, goes to the South Yorkshire Community

Foundation, the Sheffield Enterprise Agency and the Sheffield Community Enterprise Development Unit.

The first of these can, on average, leverage out twice what it receives from the bond from European and government Single Regeneration Budget or other resources. It makes grants to local voluntary and community-based support groups, which in turn can offer unemployed people on-the-job office training. The Sheffield Enterprise Agency can get up to eight times as much in matching funds from Midland Bank. This is used to lend to new and growing small businesses that find it hard to get money from traditional capital providers. The Sheffield Community Enterprise Development Unit is able to get matching funds up to six times that received from the bond from a wide range of sources.[21]

The Projects Manager, Dr Martin Clark, summed up its philosophy and hopes as attracting 'charitable loans' rather than donations. 'Sheffield has a strong local identity and is fairly self-contained. We want the whole city to get involved in tackling its own problems and take ownership rather than waiting for government or private sector to solve everything.'[22]

Another encouraging example of mutuality in action is to be found in Aston, Birmingham's second-poorest ward. It is an inner-city development bank, Aston Reinvestment Trust (ART), launched in 1997. It is Birmingham's first mutually owned community reinvestment fund for job creation, financing businesses, voluntary organizations, housing, energy saving and regeneration ventures. It was inspired by US initiatives and legislation which set up around 50 non-bank community development loan funds (CDLF). These jointly invested US$350 million between 1986 and 1996, financing 60,000 units of affordable housing and creating 10,000 jobs. Their investment in urban and rural areas, where banks' branches have declined, has attracted another US$3 billion from mainstream financial institutions, government bodies and other investors.

Investors receive little, if any, dividend income in the first few years of a CDLF's development, but thereafter small annual dividends are either distributed or waived by members to promote further community reinvestment work. The Birmingham equivalent ART may, over time, offer investors a modest dividend of up to 3 per cent. But, as its brochure puts it, the 'real returns in ART are social... with the knowledge that you are helping to create and develop economic activity with a wider social purpose, in neighbourhoods that badly need it'.

ART is owned on a 'one member, one vote' basis by its investor members. All borrowers must also financially contribute to the ART Share Funds and become members. It is thus similar to the original building societies, but since it targets local investments more broadly than housing development alone (eg small business expansion and social enterprise seed financing), it describes itself as a 'rebuilding society'. The organization has already set up an energy-saving loan facility for small firms and voluntary organizations and plans to scale up the pilot fund into a £1 million Birmingham energy-saver's fund. It has made a £60,000 loan, in partnership with the Industrial Common Ownership Finance, to Ashiana Community Project, which provides employment services and training, to buy and renovate its building.

A Rebuilding Society Network has been set up involving many of the other community reinvestment funds similar to ART, eg Glasgow Regeneration Fund, ICOF Community Capital, the Totnes Investment and Loan Trust, CAF Investors in Society, Radical Routes, the Local Investment Fund and Hackney Enterprise Fund. To be really effective and widespread, some form of government encouragement will be key. The Dutch Government, for example, gives incentives for green investment through tax relief.

Pat Conarty, the founder and director of the Rebuilding Society Network, has called for similar measures by British politicians to galvanize local social and environmental investment. He has suggested that the Treasury and the Social Exclusion Unit set up an SIA (Social Investment Account) to accompany the ISA (Individual Savings Accounts) which have been designed for fully commercial investments. If the prospects and opportunities for those in run-down urban areas and neglected rural areas are to be revived, Pat Conarty asserts that regular local investment will be essential. One potentially huge source of such funding could be 'regional economic development bonds', known in the US as 'civic bonds'.

## REGIONAL ECONOMIC DEVELOPMENT BONDS – USING PRIVATE MONEY WITHOUT PRIVATIZATION

*'New York shows that you can get private capital into a system without privatising it. And it works.'*
Senior Banker involved in New York's Metropolitan
Transportation Authority's first round of bond financing[23]

A bond is a contract document promising to repay money borrowed by local or national government, a company or a financial institution at a certain date. The money is normally paid at a fixed interest rate at regular intervals. Government or local authority bonds (called Treasury and Municipal bonds in the US) are seen as key funding mechanisms in several European countries and throughout the US. Regional Development Agencies (in Europe) and Economic Development Corporations (in the US) are frequently empowered to assemble or encourage bond programmes for private investment in response to clearly demonstrated need.

The national or local government is the borrower and the bond issue constitutes public debt. Government uses its own levers and powers to enable the bonds to come about, and it does so according to public policy priorities, such as regional economic development. Such levers include a subsidy of the overheads involved in establishing the feasibility of investment projects, grant aid to prime the initiatives themselves, technical assistance and facilitation of the bond issue, and in many cases, tax relief to make the bonds more attractive.

In the UK the system is rarely used because the Treasury under both Labour and Conservative Governments opposes any public entity raising its own financing.[24] It is also concerned to limit any increases in the Public Sector Borrowing Requirement (PSBR), particularly given the government's hope to eventually enter the Single Currency, which insists on strict curbs on the PSBR. This has led the government to favour Public Private Finance Initiatives where private money takes a stake in the enterprise and so the money drained off by the private owners is much greater than the repayment on bonds, where ownership is retained in the public sector.

Yet, methods for calculating the PSBR vary from one country to another, and, in the case of the US for example, bond-based borrowing by government at the sub-state level does not feature in PSBR calculations. The experience of the New York Metropolitan Transportation Authority (MTA) shows how bonds can turn around a seriously underfunded public enterprise.

There was widespread criticism of declining service and crumbling infrastructure, since hardly any money had been spent on the New York public transport system since the city's effective default in 1975. In 1981 the MTA was reorganized and it was allowed to issue bonds. The MTA's remit was extended to cover the subway and buses as well as the profitable Triborough bridge and tunnel. This meant that investors had a sense that the MTA would not go bust and default on future payments. The private sector bond investors paid for nearly two-thirds of the authority's transport infrastructure. Tax incentives mean that significant numbers of very small investors are attracted to such municipal bonds.

Since 1982 almost US$13 billion has been raised from bonds to improve the city's public transport infrastructure. This has included the renovation of 100 stations, purchase of 1080 new trains, rebuilding of hundreds of miles of track and installation of automatic fare collection on all buses and subways. The fare anywhere in Manhattan is still just US$1.50 (around £1), 1.7 billion trips are made each year, including four out of five rush-hour commuters. The MTA has proposed to issue another US$8 billion in bonds for the five years to 2004, subject to State approval.[25]

## Bonds for Broader Regeneration Schemes

Across the US and Europe, bonds are used for a range of economic development projects, and it is increasingly common to package a number of smaller projects into a portfolio for a bond issue. In New York, bonds have been used for Urban Regeneration initiatives such as the Time Square redevelopment, as well as for the wider regional economic development programme.

In the UK, the Millan Commission Report, 'Renewing the Regions', which recommended measures to improve the targeting and effectiveness of government investment, particularly in terms of regional disparities, suggested that:

*'One option that an incoming Labour Government could consider is to provide for the establishment of regional bonds, financed by pension funds, savings institutions, and others, which would generate additional finance for investment in the regions, particularly among SME's. There are many regionally based financial institutions, including local authority pension funds, which would be likely to welcome the opportunity to add their own region's bonds to their portfolio of investments. Provided that there was an adequate rate of return, regional bonds would be an attractive addition to existing fixed income investment opportunities. Initially, a strictly limited bond issue could be allowed as an experiment, and a wider issue could follow later.'[26]*

## An Existing UK Model in Social Housing

Housing Associations are private charitable bodies who build, own and manage social housing and other developments. The government agency, the Housing Finance Corporation identifies national priorities for social housing, manages government investment in the social housing stock and allocates its grant aid on a regional basis.

After scrutinizing the Housing Association's plans, the Housing Finance Corporation allocates a proportion of the cost of the proposed programme as grant aid (up to 40 per cent) and the Housing

Association has to raise the rest. Housing Associations use bond issues, currently in the region of £3 billion, as one method of raising the money required. They have found willing investors locally and regionally for their programmes. This they have been able to achieve based on a record of a clear programme of investment, the tacit support of government and their own track record, assets and guarantees. Crucial to any bond issue is a clear stream of future income to repay the bonds.[27]

### Bountiful Bonds

The advantage of bonds are that they hold the potential for uniting huge sources of funds, especially local authority, trades union and individual pension schemes, and insurance money with potentially secure, government-underpinned, returns. At the same time, they help rebuild sustainable communities where the majority of the contributors to such funds live, generating potentially huge amounts of local employment and opportunities for small- and medium-sized enterprises (SMEs).

Of course, the key is some kind of secure income stream against the activity that the bond is being raised to pay for. Obviously profitable areas like road tolls, public transport fares, rents and so on could be bundled in with work that requires upfront funds for considerable, but later returns (eg energy conservation and renewables, comprehensive recycling, a move to cleaner production and building up local markets for the shift towards organic food production and processing).

Should the expected downturn in the US bubble economy and stock market lead to a global retreat from less secure investments, then the bonds for local regeneration should provide a welcome home to such a 'wall of money'.[28]

## GLOBALIZATION'S TRIPLE THREAT TO SUSTAINABLE COMMUNITIES

*'The rise of community economic action shows that the struggle for community and sustainability is happening everywhere, often against increasing odds. What it offers is a practical, local response to the insecurity and powerlessness felt by the majority in a whirlwind, global economy.'*[29] [emphasis added]

*'We have a choice of mindsets, as a country:*

*the first is a continuation of the current paradigm of laissez-faire. This is the mindset of those who promise growth and a better tomorrow but connive at cutting communities adrift through the rationing of welfare and resources.*

*the second is a commitment to a new paradigm in which communities can become agents rather than victims, with programmes that enable them to attack the structures of dependency and retake control of their destiny.'[30]*

Although the existing positive instances mentioned above are often inspiring, it is crucial to see what factors prevent them becoming replicated everywhere. There are three ways in which the globalization process, its trade and investment rules and trends in production, agriculture and marketing are acting as roadblocks to widespread community renewal. Once these roadblocks are identified it is then vital to consider what policies for localization can turn these roadblocks into roadways (see Chapters 6–12).

## More International Competitiveness, Less Public Expenditure, Less Community Activity

Most of the community initiatives featured in this chapter require a degree of government or local authority or even EU financial and other support. There are of course exceptions, such as food co-ops and LETS, but predominantly there is always official assistance at some stage or other.

It is frequently overlooked when measures to rebuild communities are called for just how much public expenditure is likely to be required to get from the cheap option of pilot studies to national replication. Enormous amounts of up-front resources in terms of grants, loans, tax breaks etc, will be required to pay for the transition to vastly increased community renewal. This is true regardless of whether the service is eventually provided publicly or privately. (Of course there is a substantial amount of money in existing government budgets spent on projects geared to longer distance trade such as motorways and airports that could also be transferred to local regeneration.)

Similarly, if countries are to shift their food and agricultural system towards organic farming, local food production and marketing, and more healthy, fresh and less highly processed food, this too will require enormous funds to pay for such a dramatic shift. Money will also be required to enable the poorer sections of society to be able to afford more expensive, but sustainable, farming and food products.

Another feature is, that taken as a whole, this broad variety of community-run activities tends to require the money invested in it to remain available locally. This is both because the activities might need continual assistance themselves, or linked entities may require financial support, or the money might simply be required to provide some of the demand locally.

Yet, the reigning in of public expenditure is an explicit part of trade liberalization policies. It is at the heart of the single currency process in Europe, and the IMF and World Bank structural adjustment programmes for the developing world, Eastern Europe and Russia. Thus globalization promises severe limitations on the government funding of community initiatives.

This push to minimize government expenditure succeeds because of the general unquestioning acceptance by politicians of the need to be internationally competitive. Yet virtually all significant community improvements require a tightening of regulations that constrains and reorientates business behaviour. This can take the form of insisting that they remain in a locality, that they buy local inputs, have adequate pay and conditions, obey environmental laws and so on. It also requires, as has been seen, substantial amounts of money to pay for the upfront costs of the transition, a great deal of which will have to come from the public purse, funded either by personal taxation or green taxes.

But to be internationally competitive all governments are deregulating and bowing to the demands of business, currency speculators, bankers and the IMF to cut or curb taxation, to deregulate, to privatize their public sector and to minimize controls on trade or money flows. In short, to give up many of the levers of power that need to be marshalled to regenerate communities.

In the face of this, any meaningful effort to protect and rebuild communities through tighter regulation or more funding through increased green or other taxes is halted by the politician's mental roadblock of not impeding competitiveness.

## Opening of Government Procurement to International Competition

'...the US pointed out: "*Procurement markets worldwide account for trillions of dollars in commercial transactions. Large, commercially attractive procurement occurs at all levels of government.*" It cited as examples: municipal government procurement for police, fire departments and local public works; provincial government procurement for health and social security programs: central government procurement for national telecommunications networks, electrical power grid *and transportation systems. The problem, said the US is that although governments are the largest purchasers of goods and services in the world, procurement activities are not subject to basic WTO rules..." "Future steps towards full integration will generate increased opportunities for suppliers to compete on an equal basis in government procurement markets worldwide."...there should be no exemption or lower standards for developing countries...'[31]*

The Ministerial meeting of the 134 WTO members in Seattle in November 1999 was supposed to revise the 1994 Marrakesh accords agreed when the WTO was formed. These covered agriculture, services and intellectual property. In 1999, government procurement, competition, and investment were added for consideration. In the case of government procurement, it was proposed that foreign firms would eventually have the same rights as national ones for all local, regional and national public contracts.

This is a vast market running into many trillions.[32] Of course a huge range of community activities revolve around control of public provision of services. To discriminate in favour of local production is therefore a vital piece of government policy that could be the next victim of the globalization process. In the EU, the Single Market legislation already demands that any large-scale, public procurement programme has to put to tender throughout the community.

When the WTO considers competition, it too implies that countries would no longer have any control over public purchase, offers and mergers. All would have to be open to foreign involvement. What the Northern countries tend to mean by 'competition policy' within the WTO is new rights for big international companies to obtain unlimited access to markets which now have restrictions on them. Examples include rules on the percentage of foreign ownership of transportation, communication and utility service providers; tax and procurement preferences given to local small enterprises, and government or government-controlled monopolies found especially in infrastructure, health and educational services.

Some community activism in developed countries will be adversely affected by this WTO attack on local control. However, it is the governments of developing countries and those organizing at a community level to improve or maintain basic needs and rights that will be most seriously affected. Their loss of control over who provides their local services – domestic or foreign firms – further weakens their government's sway over the national economies and strengthens that of TNCs.

Such threats to developing world livelihoods have not only concerned the disadvantaged. In India, the BJP Government had originally stood on an anti-globalization and pro-Swadeshi (increased self-reliance) programme.[33] A survey of urban graduates, aged between 18 and 40, showed that this approach wasn't just supported by the rural masses. It found a 'stunning groundswell' of support for Swadeshi policies. Around two-thirds were in favour of buying Indian, protecting Indian companies from foreign takeovers, opposing foreign companies producing consumer products and only allowing multinational companies into high-technology areas. Three-quarters said the new government should work towards protecting Indian companies.[34]

## Agriculture is for Competition, not Feeding People Locally

Given that the largest percentage of the population in most developing countries are rural, defending and improving local food systems is a big priority for developing world community groups. In the North many community groups are linking with their nearest farm sources and working for increased local food production and marketing, particularly if grown organically.

Globalization takes the world's food system in completely the opposite direction. The thrust of agricultural policies regionally and globally is to produce the cheapest product to sell in as wide a market as possible. Despite growing consumer preference for organic agriculture and local food consumption in the OECD, the trend is still towards ever more intensive agriculture and more long-distance transportation of food. In the developing world and Eastern Europe, where traditional farming and local markets are more common, they too are coming under increasing pressure to reduce the barriers to cheap imports. Indeed, this was one of the priorities for the WTO Ministerial Meeting in Seattle, with potentially disastrous effects for small farmers. In addition, the export emphasis on aid and investment packages to poorer countries means that they have no choice but to reorientate their agriculture further in this direction. As a result, smaller farmers, producing more for local needs, are frequently being squeezed out in favour of larger, usually more export-orientated agriculture.

To adequately protect and rebuild local small farming communities in poor, predominantly rural countries and to revitalize rural communities in the process will require a shift in emphasis. This must favour maximum sustainable local production and bring about a reduction in long-distance trade in food. The exception would be traditional cash crops that can only be grown in certain areas, eg coffee, tea and bananas traded under 'fair trade' rules.

## CONCLUSION

This chapter has looked at what community activity is, and how it is being fostered, and what is required further. It also identified how globalization, with its emphasis on international competitiveness and its concomitant desire to reduce public expenditure, deregulate and open up local markets to large corporations and investors, is taking the world in the opposite direction.

The *Protect the Local, Globally* set of policies detailed in Chapters 6–12 will allow the emergence of adequately funded, more self-reliant communities. They could result in the individual, positive community examples seen in this chapter being turned from the noble exception to the replicable norm.

## Chapter 6

# 'Protect the Local, Globally' – A Route to Localization

The prerequisite for achieving the relocalization of the world economy is to challenge the accepted wisdom that the process of globalization is inevitable and can be made beneficial. At the same time it is crucial to propose a cogent alternative. Its policies must be judged by whether they are seen as a plausible way to reverse the instability and insecurity that trade liberalization has wrought upon the world. This chapter, and the next six, detail a set of self-reinforcing policies that are encapsulated by the term *Protect the Local, Globally*.

The essence of these policies is to allow nations, local governments and communities to reclaim control over their local economies; to make them as diverse as possible; and to rebuild stability into community life. This does not mean a return to overpowering state control, instead governments merely provide the policy framework which allows people and businesses to rediversify their own local economies. It would ensure a transition from the present situation of ever-increasing criss-crossing of the world's seas and skies with the same products, to one where whatever goods and services that can be provided locally are done so. The reduction of 'product or service miles' (distance from provider to consumer) is also an environmental goal. In short, there develops a positive discrimination in favour of the local.

The policies have a goal of maximum self-reliance nationally and regionally in a way that ensures increased sustainable development. The policy mix of *Protect the Local, Globally* will obviously vary to some degree from country to country. Its essence consists of seven, main, interrelated approaches aimed at increasing local control over economies. The end goal of the economy becomes maximum self-reliance, rather than open markets and international competitiveness. The seven basic steps to be introduced, over a suitable transition period are:

- reintroduction of protective safeguards for domestic economies (tariffs, quotas etc);

- a site-here-to-sell-here policy for manufacturing and services domestically or regionally;
- localising money such that the majority stays within its place of origin;
- enforcing a local competition policy to eliminate monopolies from the more protected economies;
- introduction of resource taxes to increase environmental improvements and help fund the transition to *Protect the Local, Globally*;
- increased democratic involvement both politically and economically to ensure the effectiveness and equity of the movement to more diverse local economies;
- reorientation of the end goals of aid and trade rules such that they contribute to the rebuilding of local economies and local control, particularly through the global transfer of relevant information and technology.

A *Protect the Local, Globally* policy is neither anti-trade nor autarkic (ie totally self-sufficient). Its goal is maximum local trade, within diversified sustainable local economies, and minimum long-distance trade. Local is used here to mean a part of a country, and 'regional' a geographic grouping of countries.

Such a dramatic turnaround in the direction of the international economy could not just occur in one country. To take on the powerful international forces of international capital and TNCs would require these policies to be introduced, for example, EU-wide or in the whole of North America. Even the debate about considering such an approach would reverberate internationally at this time of global economic insecurity. Once it was introduced even in just Europe or North America, it would set an example and would almost certainly engender similar approaches in other regions of the world.

A radical alternative to the global economic status quo, such as *Protect the Local, Globally* obviously raises a number of fundamental questions, criticisms and concerns. These are dealt with in Appendix I. The first of the necessary policies, which is a key initial step in the move to localization, is now considered in this chapter and in the following six chapters.

## REINTRODUCING PROTECTIVE SAFEGUARDS TO REBUILD LOCAL ECONOMIES

Controls on imports should be gradually introduced on a national and regional bloc level, with the aim of allowing localities and countries to produce as much of their food, goods and services as they can. Anything that can't be provided nationally should be obtained regionally, with long-distance trade the very last resort. The number of jobs generated using this more diverse, local emphasis on providing for national needs should far outweigh those lost as export markets begin to decline. A transition period of perhaps five to ten years will also provide an opportunity for those threatened to reorientate production towards national and regional bloc markets. Some long-distance trade will still occur for those sectors providing goods and services to other regions of the world that can't provide such items from within their own borders, eg certain minerals or cash crops. Such trade would need to be governed by 'fair trade' rules and with stable export prices adequate enough to allow local economies to flourish.

What constitutes the boundary for such controls will be a political decision by those countries in the regional blocs concerned. (More and more countries are already in or joining regional trading blocs. With the changed end-goal of localism replacing international competitiveness, these blocs can then serve to improve the conditions of the majority in them rather than as at present hindering this process.) Each bloc will have protective safeguards limiting imports to the group of countries concerned in order to encourage domestic production. To further this goal inside these regional blocs, larger countries may have their own national barriers. Smaller ones may choose to join together until they have attained a grouping that they feel is an optimal size to maximize production of their needs. This new grouping may then have its own protective barriers to allow for as much internal production as possible. The guiding light for such decision will be to ensure that production is as local as possible for every country.

## Potential Protective Safeguards

*Tariffs:* a tariff is an import duty, which makes imported goods more expensive. An *ad valoreum* tariff is set as a percentage of the price of the goods imported. A specific tariff is set in money terms per physical unit of the good imported, and does not depend on its price. A non-discriminatory tariff taxes imports from all countries equally; tariff preferences mean that similar imports from different countries are taxed at different rates. Non-tariff barriers are other limitations to trade such as quotas or voluntary export restraints (VER) agreements.[1]

*Import Quotas:* a fixed quantity of a particular type of good which the government allows to be imported This may be set in terms of value or physical units.[2] Mainstream economists argue that any objective achieved by a quota system could be achieved at lower cost by use of the price mechanism, through an appropriate tax or subsidy.[3] However, the price mechanism rarely reflects the hidden costs of wasteful energy and resource use, or the level of payment required to provide adequate wages as well as a taxation source that will allow the building of more equitable and sustainable societies.

Tariffs are likely to be of most use in the transition from globalization to localization. If gradually phased in over an agreed timetable they send a clear message to all exporters that they need to reorientate their production towards more local markets. Quotas will be more useful to regulate trade in goods which cannot be produced locally and that will therefore continue to be imported once localization is established. This is because they can be used to show clear and specified favour to exporters producing goods in a more socially and ecologically responsible way. Tariffs, on the other hand, even tariff preferences, merely add to the cost of all imports covered. Thus, a country could still compensate for this by having dramatically lower export costs by inadequate social and/or environmental protection, and so would still win market share.

Two countries with very similar social and environmental standards would have the potential to charge similar prices. Therefore, increasing import costs through the tariff system might act as a competitive spur to increased socially and environmentally beneficial efficiency, provided such trade was limited to such suppliers.

> *Subsidies:* payments by the government to consumers (eg food subsidies) or producers (eg crop subsidies) which make the prices received by producers greater than that which would be received if the market forces of supply and demand establish the price. Other examples include direct payments, credits, interest rate concessions and tax rebates for both export and domestic industries;[4]

> *Export Subsidies:* subsidy to the exporter such that the price per unit received by the producers of exports is higher than the price charged to foreign customers. Direct export subsidies are prohibited by present international agreements, but other government measures include refunds on tariffs on their inputs, subsidized credit, preferential access to ordinary credit in an economy, or assistance with their capital costs or training

costs. In economies with either currency controls or direct controls on imports, exporters can be allowed priority in the allocation to them of scarce materials or foreign currency. Firms competing with imports which they claim have received export subsidies may be able to obtain countervailing import duties to offset the effects of these subsidies.[5]

Under localization, subsidies would be used domestically to favour methods of production which are socially and environmentally more beneficial, particularly during the transition period towards more protected, diverse local economies. Export subsidies could be used by those producers with a continued export market, by dint of their being able to provide goods that cannot be produced in some other regions. Such export subsidies would again be used in the furtherance of better production methods. Surveillance of such export subsidies would need to be vigorous to ensure that they don't disadvantage small countries with the same high standards of production and national priorities, but with less economies of scale. (This is covered in Chapter 12 when considering trade and aid rules internationally) In the event of this happening then any imbalance can be compensated for by changes in the quota system. These would themselves eventually be required by the importer under the 'fair trade' aims and rules of the *Protect the Local, Globally* route to localization.

## Less Necessary Protective Safeguards

*Other 'Non-tariff Barriers':* in addition to quotas and subsidies, the number of other possible non-tariff barriers is almost infinite. Several major categories include regulations for health and safety purposes; requirement for prior deposit of the costs of imports in blocked bank accounts; the requirements of licences or specific foreign currency allocation.[6] National environmental, social and labour standards could also be used as a reason to discriminate against products produced in unacceptable ways.

Most abhorred by trade liberalizers are the voluntary export restraints (VERS). These occur when the protecting country inveigles an exporting country to 'voluntarily' limit its exports of a particular item, usually backed by implied threats of formal protection such as tariffs or other trade barriers. The limit set may be in terms of quantity, value and market share.[7]

Byzantine measures will become far less necessary once such constraints on trade are put within a clear *Protect the Local, Globally* context.

## LOCALIZATION SIMPLIFIES

The bewildering array and complexity of trade measures stems from countries trying to do two mutually inconsistent things: to gain export market share whilst protecting their domestic businesses. Under localization, such inconsistencies will be considerably lessened. Tariffs, quotas and subsidies will be used to reorientate national economies towards more protected, diverse local economies. The limited long-distance trade involving goods that can't be produced locally will be similarly governed by such tariffs, quotas and subsidies to ensure that such exports contribute to this *Protect the Local, Globally* aim.

*Chapter 7*

# Localizing Production and Dismantling Transnational Companies

## A SITE-HERE-TO-SELL-HERE POLICY

In conjunction with the phased introduction of tariffs, quotas and subsidies designed to ensure the maximum diversity and protection of the local economy, site-here-to-sell-here legislation could, over time, considerably reduce levels of imports. Market access would be dependent on compliance with this policy, ensuring that whatever a country or a geographical grouping of countries could produce themselves they did. Practicalities of this might involve:

- an inventory of what is at present imported;
- an analysis of what can be feasibly produced within the one country or geographical grouping of countries;
- a clear posting that, over the transition period, imports of such goods will be made increasingly expensive through tariffs and quotas;
- encouragement for producers to fill the gap provided by these growing local markets.

Whether filling this increased market is to be facilitated by government assistance (eg set-up grants or training provision) or left to market opportunities, or most likely a mixture of the two, will depend upon the citizens and governments concerned.

The boundaries within which each industry would site would be predominately the nation state. Small nation states might choose to join with others regionally to form a more viable entity. For very large industries such as aeroplane production, the delineation might be the actual grouping of countries that make up a geographically bounded economic bloc such as the EU or North America. For most sectors the gradual increase of energy costs through resource tax rises (see Chapter 10) would act as another inducement for production being sited as close as feasible to markets.

## Maintaining Choice and Standards

After a transition period of perhaps five to ten years such local goods would be the only ones readily available. (Of course if people wanted to import foreign products by preference, feeling perhaps they're of a higher standard, more fashionable etc, they would be able to do so, but would be required to pay import taxes.) During the transition existing or new domestic industries would have inducements not only to fill the market, but also to improve their existing standards by domestic competition policy (see Chapter 9). Also taking the best ideas from around the world and incorporating them in domestic production would be possible via joint ventures with former foreign exporters or other outside entities. This would often be the most cost-effective way for them to have access to the national market concerned.

The site-here-to-sell-here approach would stop TNCs and others relocating, or threatening to do so, since they would lose access to the national market concerned. Their activities could then be brought back more under the control of citizens and their governments. Improvements in labour laws, consumer rights and environmental legislation would be easier to put in place and enforce.

Reasonable levels of company taxation would become feasible, since the excuse of unfair competition from low tax/low wage foreign competitors would no longer be valid. The same would be true of resource taxes such as those on energy which at present are easily constrained by businesses arguing that they would render domestic producers uncompetitive.

In order to ensure that large firms didn't crowd out domestic competitors, they might need to be broken up (see Chapter 9). Business would also be made far more transparent and responsive to stakeholder power, ie not just geared to the needs of shareholders, but also the desires of workers and the local community.

Company and accounting law could be used more easily to control transfer pricing. Under globalization, one third of world trade consists of transactions between various units of the same corporation based in different countries. This enables companies to minimize tax by registering their profits as made mostly in the countries which charge low corporation tax. Under localization, domestic consumption would be satisfied largely by national or geographically close sources. Thus, the potential for this downward competitive pressure would be substantially lessened. The siphoning of company profits and individual earnings offshore would be ruled out under the localizing money policy (see Chapter 8).

E-commerce, which is often claimed to be the big threat to government's ability to tax companies would be taxed at the point of provision. If the good or service were from a foreign country its taxation would be reflected in the final price, which would then shift the advantage to domestic e-commerce. Should a country choose not to tax e-commerce, that would be regarded as unfair competition and the tax would need to be paid by the customer. This could be enforced by making it illegal for computers to be sold without a program to register such e-commerce.[1]

## Coping With Potential Price Rises

These measures may lead to a greater price rise than would be the case if every country could obtain its needs from the cheapest source. Increasingly, however, new computer-controlled technology is making ever smaller numbers of products more and more economic to produce, with less throughput of resources.[2] Most significantly, as more and more regional blocs adopt the *Protect the Local, Globally* approach, the features that often made their exports cheap (low wages, inadequate environmental taxation and standards and cheap transport costs) will no longer apply, thus improving the relative economics of local production. Also, this approach will improve the overall social cohesion and reduce the high social costs inherent in the present emphasis on international competitiveness. This includes high global unemployment and underemployment, increasing inequality, inadequate resource allocation to deal with poverty and the growth of crime internationally. This is the all too rarely recognized flip side of the cheap goods argument, favoured by trade liberalizers.

In the interim, any hardship experienced by the poor, should goods such as food and clothing increase in price, will need to be compensated for by increased benefits, paid out of higher resource, company and personal taxation.

# BIG PROBLEMS FOR TNCS

Given an adequate transition period, such an economic realignment should pose little problem for most small- and medium-sized firms, whose markets are predominantly local. Those dependent on export markets would be encouraged during the transition period to reorientate towards the domestic market. They would be helped by rising tariffs, quotas and subsidies which would mean the market would be served less and less by imports of goods and services that could instead be provided nationally.

In terms of employment, small- and medium-sized companies are the greatest generators of employment within a country. In the UK in 1997, small businesses (fewer than 50 employees) made up 97 per cent of the 1.2 million businesses with employees; medium-sized businesses (50–249) around 2 per cent; and large businesses (250 or more) 0.6 per cent. In terms of numbers of jobs, small- and medium-sized businesses account for 57 per cent of total non-government employment, while the 7000 largest businesses accounted for 43 per cent of non-government employment. Large employers, however, are concentrated in a few specific areas: electricity, gas and water supply and mining/quarrying sectors. In all other sectors 99 per cent of businesses were small- and medium-sized companies.

In terms of generating jobs and ensuring that local economies are regenerated, the major growth sectors are likely to be areas such as the construction industry, most services, computing, recycling and agriculture. These are all areas where small businesses predominate.[3]

The biggest losers in this site-here-to-sell-here approach will be the TNCs. Between 1980 and the mid-1990s the number of TNCs has soared from 7000 to more than 40,000. Of the top 100 economies in the world, 50 are TNCs, 70 per cent of global trade is controlled by just 500 corporations and a mere 1 per cent of the TNCs own half of the total stock of foreign direct investment. Described by the UN as 'the productive core of the globalizing world economy'[4] these corporations and their 250,000 foreign affiliates account for most of the world's mining, oil, industrial capacity, technological knowledge, biotechnology and international financial transactions. They harvest much of the world's wood and most of its paper, grow many of the world's agricultural crops, whilst processing and distributing much of its food. TNCs hold 90 per cent of all technology and product patents worldwide and are involved in 70 per cent of world trade. More than 30 per cent of this trade is 'intrafirm' ie between units of the same corporation.[5]

At the same time, free trade agreements like GATT and NAFTA have created a global environment in which TNCs and banks can move capital, technology, production sites, goods and services freely throughout the world, relatively unfettered by the regulations of nation states or democratically elected governments. Through these processes, TNCs have effectively secured a system of rule and domination in the new world order.[6]

Because of such power, any threat to TNCs is sometimes seen as a threat to jobs. Although the combined sales of the 200 largest TNCs exceed the combined economies of all countries bar the biggest nine, they in fact only employ 18.8 million workers, less than 0.75 per cent of the world's workers.[7] Furthermore even these are being cut. The biggest European employer in the Top 200, Siemens, is planning to lay off 60,000 workers and nine of the top 59 US firms in the Top 200 laid off at least 3,000 workers in 1995: AT&T, Boeing, Lockheed-Martin, BellSouth, Kmart, Chase Manhattan, GTE, Mobil and Texaco. Between 1993 and 1995, global turnover of the top 100 TNCs increased by more than 25 per cent, but during this same period these companies cut 4 per cent of their global workforce of 5.8 million – over 225,000 people.[8] The accelerating numbers of mergers and acquisitions is increasing the labour shedding in TNCs.

## TNCs will Fight

TNCs are rightly seen as increasingly powerful entities, that use their economic and political power to influence trade and financial rules to their advantage, to threaten relocation if domestic laws or taxes aren't to their liking and that are often able to override the desires of local communities. They will use all their financial and political might to counter this form of localization, since it significantly undermines their power base. However, should citizens' movements persuade powerful groupings of governments in Europe and/or North America to use their political power to make the necessary changes in trade rules, they would find their politician's power to regulate these entities is often underestimated. The power centres of international business are still largely nationally embedded, even though many have subsidiaries throughout the world. Their controlling operations are therefore not beyond the reach of national and economic bloc regulation.[9]

Under the *Protect the Local, Globally* set of policies, these TNCs would no longer be able to play the trump card of international competitiveness as an excuse not to be bound by better working, environmental or tax regimes. Relocation becomes an empty threat as it means that the company is out of the market. Indeed, this would swing the pendulum of power back into the hands of governments who can make it clear that attempts to sabotage the process of localization could have its cost in terms of denial of future market access.

## NGOs Could Succeed Under Localization

Present efforts to curb the power of TNCs all assume ever more open borders will be the norm. This leads to a set of usually rather cautious approaches, ranging from calls to monitor TNC activity through to various, usually voluntary, codes of conduct and standards. Yet still central to the efforts of NGO's and churches has been the concept that eventually there should be rules governing the operations of corporations domestically and internationally.[10]

There have been a wide range of responses to examples of bad business practice. Inside developed countries, there have been demands by unions and communities threatened by a closure of a TNC branch that the government give it further 'corporate welfare' to stay. Where a TNC actually shuts up shop there have been demands that previous tax breaks and local government infrastructural support costs should be repaid. Less defensively, examples of pollution have been highlighted and the companies concerned shamed or forced into improving that specific aspect of their activities. The most celebrated case being the Brent Spar battle between Greenpeace and Shell over dumping oil platforms in the Atlantic.

However, under globalization, any really radical improvement in corporate social or environmental practise soon flounders. Adequate compliance is usually deemed impossible since changes would make the company uncompetitive, hence it might shut down or relocate. The most widespread example of this has been resistance to energy price increases to combat climate change.

In terms of the developing world, anti-TNC campaign's by citizens' movements both North and South tends to focus upon four areas: the product the company is producing (eg the anti-Nestles baby milk campaign); the worker's age or their conditions (eg the Asian football, carpets or toy campaigns); the involvement of businesses in supporting regimes deemed unacceptable (eg South Africa under apartheid or Burma today); and the adverse effects of the production process (eg Union Carbide's explosion in Bhopal or environmental threats, such as clear-cut logging and deforestation by Mitsubishi and MacMillan Bloedel).

The activists research, lobby, hold demonstrations, call for boycotts, demand the introduction of codes of conduct and insist on adherence to international standards. While these approaches have had some success in changing the behaviour of the specific TNC targeted, there has been very little significant change in the overall activities of TNCs.[11] Indeed the pattern of the companies' responses has tended to be denial, followed by a degree of admission of a problem, followed by lengthy discussions of the details of voluntary codes of conduct, then further arguments of the scope of the code along the supply chain, then finally discussions of the details of independent verification and monitoring.[12] The end result is often far short of the original goal.

## Some Successes?

There have been more potentially significant and encouraging developments. The cases brought against Thor Chemicals, Rio Tinto Zinc and Cape plc have paved the way for TNCs to be held legally accountable in England for injuries caused by their overseas operations.[13] The instances cover claims by individuals of ill health caused by asbestos exposure from the activities of Cape, mercury exposure by Thor and by uranium dust exposure by RTZ (now Rio Tinto). Each case rests firstly on the presumption that companies controlling hazardous substances owe a 'duty of care' to those people who it is reasonable to foresee would be affected by the companies' activities, and that a company is negligent if it does not protect them. The legal argument is that because the companies' operations are controlled in the UK, that is where they should face the legal consequences of their actions.

Such cases are highly complicated and despite the huge rise in FDI in recent years, most laws remain limited by the nation state's frontiers. Those international laws that are at present in place to create and regulate the global economy overwhelmingly address only the obligations on countries to remove barriers to free trade. Legal systems that would allow TNCs to be held accountable in the country where their headquarters are based for adverse activities occurring elsewhere are not yet firmly established. This illustrates how such legal systems have not yet been brought into line with the realities of the global economy and the huge power of TNCs.

However, these recent cases, according to the World Development Movement (WDM), do at least send three clear messages to TNCs:

- Head offices will be held responsible for their decisions which determine the actions of their subsidiaries.
- It is not acceptable for a company to operate low standards overseas if it knows that such practices would be considered dangerous at home.
- The English courts are prepared to hear cases pertaining to injuries overseas if this is the only way for justice to be achieved.[14]

Inevitably, the TNCs have embarked on a campaign to undermine these important legal precedents and derail the cases. Methods include attacking the funding for the claimants, targeting politicians sympathetic to TNCs and encouraging certain sections of the media to criticise the cases and discredit the claimant's lawyers.

Another encouraging advance was that a UK MEP, Richard Howitt, successfully steered through the European Parliament a report proposing a code of conduct for European transnationals operating in the developing world. The code, although only at this stage a proposal, embraces existing international codes and agreements on corporate behaviour and promotes a more ethical approach to business. It establishes minimum standards in areas such as labour conditions and the treatment of indigenous people. Most crucially is its insistence on a system for monitoring company compliance.[15]

A new approach – social accounting – is also emerging. This calls for companies to recognize their responsibility towards society at large. It includes the demands that:

- Company directors should be accountable to shareholders for their impacts on all the company's stakeholders, ie workers in the local community and any other communities affected by the production, use or disposal of the product.
- Companies should be required to disclose audited information on their social and environmental impacts – just as at present they are required to disclose financial information to protect investors
- Greater opportunities for shareholders to influence the direction and priorities of companies.

Measures such as these are being proposed and attempts made to quantify them under this umbrella of 'social accounting'. This generally leans heavily on the involvement of stakeholders which have been defined as 'any individual or entity who can be affected by an organization or who may, in turn, bring influence to bear.'[16]

Another measure being developed is social auditing, defined by one of its leading exponents, NEF, as assessing the social impact and ethical behaviour of an organization in relation to its aims, and those of its stakeholders. The attitude of Shell, whose activities have been severely criticized over recent years, was summed up by one of its executives who put it bluntly that: 'We'd already started looking at social auditing. But Brent Spar and then Nigeria were hugely catalytic – they took the process and put a red hot poker up it.' Such changes have been described by Shell as moving from a 'trust me' world to a 'tell me' to a 'show me'.[17]

On the other hand, the public appear less convinced. A Mori opinion poll in March 1999 found that the corporate world's approval rating was at a 30-year low. Small wonder that there is a rapid spread of appropriate terminology, with the pro-free market Institute of Directors even going on record that at least three-quarters of its members in large companies believe businesses should report on social and environmental issues.[18]

Exposure of appalling working practices in countries from Bangladesh to China by development groups like Christian Aid, Oxfam and the WDM and the targeting by like groups of named giants like Walt Disney and Nike have of course also had their effects. British companies have been prompted to join the Ethical Trading Initiative, which is also backed by the government's Department for International Development (DFID). This alliance of companies, NGOs and trade unions has as its base code the demands that employment is freely chosen, that freedom of association and the right to collective bargaining are respected, that working conditions are safe and hygienic, that child labour should not be used, living wages are paid, working hours are not excessive, no discrimination is practiced, employment is regular and their should be no harsh or inhumane treatment.[19]

# THE REALITY OF GLOBALIZATION

Based predominantly as they are on the core ILO's Conventions, these efforts face the same difficulties and potential for failure. These base-line ILO demands have been called for for decades, but the pressures from companies' pleading threats to international competitiveness as a reason not to introduce such standards, have in reality taken them further and further away from being the norm.

An example of the difficulties involved in trying to superimpose good practice upon the reality of globalization was encountered by the US equivalent of the Ethical Trading Initiative – the Council for Economic Priorities. This carries out audits of suppliers, focusing on the core issues of human rights, health and safety and equal opportunities involving discussions with trades union workers and local NGOs. They have so far carried out four such full audits, with three of the sites in China. Establishing even what is a sustainable living wage is very difficult in today's competitive world. A spokesperson explained that: 'One facility in China had 25,000 employees. If we'd have insisted on raising wages to the required standard right away, it would have put it out of business. We have to see what is practical now and what we can aim at the future.'[20]

Indeed, the pressures of international competitiveness have recently hit two of the corporate flagships for social responsibility. The Body Shop had to come to terms with falling share prices and 'the realities of international competition' and abandon manufacturing and cut head-office jobs. Although its founders Anita and Gordon Roddick remain co-chairman and insist that their ethical and environmental values will not be diluted.[21] Levis Strausss has had to relocate completely out of production in America because it can no longer compete with low-cost imports. Given this, it remains to be seen how long the company's mission statement can be upheld when it states: 'We will conduct our business ethically and demonstrate leadership in satisfying our responsibilities to our communities and to society.'[22]

## TNCs Can Be Brought to Heel by Localization

Big business has fought anti-slavery movements, Factory Acts, environmental laws and now human rights and social issues by claiming 'the business of business is business'. The fundamental shift that is required is an accounting process auditing the social and environmental impact as rigorously as those for measuring profits, followed by changes in behaviour in the light of these findings.

Today's reality is that once globalization is accepted, then all these campaigns can never adequately and fundamentally alter TNCs activities. The constraints that it is possible to place on actual TNC behaviour under trade liberalization are nothing like as rigorous as is required. Trade liberalization allows TNCs to use their financial muscle to counter constraints that significantly threaten their profits. They can hide behind commercial confidentiality to refuse the provision of information and to claim the problems are caused by their local suppliers, not themselves. Perhaps most tellingly, they can cite trade rules that don't allow commerce to be curbed because of the way goods are produced. Often their strongest card is the threat of relocation due to the need to be internationally competitive.

However, within the *Protect the Local Globally* framework, the activist's demands become much more feasible. Once the threat of relocation is effectively denied, once locally grounded provision of markets take place under the social, labour and environmental standards of the country concerned, then the TNCs become controllable. Chapter 12 on trade and aid rules explains how TNCs international involvement in the provision of minerals, cash crops and the like can also be dramatically circumscribed.

## Time to Shift the Campaigning Emphasis

This doesn't mean there is no purpose in campaigning today for constraints on TNCs. Neither is it to imply that campaigns against specific activities of TNCs haven't had successful outcomes. Shell was seriously troubled by Brent Spar and perhaps, most dramatically, the rejection by European consumers of GM foods have adversely affected Monsanto and other biotech TNCs. However, overall, the harmful activities of TNCs globally are rarely adequately curbed.

Though efforts by NGOs, consumers, unions and developing world movements to expose and pressurize TNCs to improve specific practices, agree codes of conduct, legal constraints and so on are praiseworthy, these approaches are likely to be far more effective if put within the context of policies to achieve a worldwide shift from globalization to localization. It is globalization that makes the achievement of ethical and environmental business practice and international norms an impossibility. However, such actions against TNCs will all be crucial in the transition to the *Protect the Local, Globally* form of localization.

> '*Control of TNC behavior must come from organized grass-roots activism, participatory governmental processes, the force of local and national laws, and the commitment to international agreements. In that context, corporate use of market mechanisms, "multi-stakeholder" processes, and sincere voluntary initiatives can be important: they cannot, however, replace regulatory control.*'[23]

In Part Three, the actual activities of TNCs to block social, environmental, and developmental advances will be looked at. But the conclusion for activists in these areas is the same as that drawn for those working to make TNCs more ethical and accountable. All their campaigning efforts will be strengthened enormously, and indeed can only really succeed, if all these issue-specific efforts are put within the context of demanding policies to ensure the shift from globalization to localization. These movements must debate this, and then act upon the results of their internal deliberations.

# Chapter 8

# Localizing Capital

## INTRODUCTION

*'It is often claimed that technological innovations in commu-
nications and computers have made financial liberalization
inevitable ... but technology is not destiny, at least when it
comes to economic policy. The new technologies could also
make it easier to monitor and regulate capital flows, if government had the will to use them to that effect.'*[1]

Global policy makers share a theology that the liberalization of trade
and investment will increase efficiency, raise human productivity and
eventually eliminate world poverty. Chapter 3 criticized the theory
behind the liberalization of investment and how it is embodied in
proposed treaties such as the MAI, and its revisions that formed part
of the plans for WTO's Millennium Round in November 1999.

This chapter considers the range of mostly palliative suggestions
on offer to cope with the present global economic crisis. It then
suggests a programme to control capital which prevents further liberalization, severely limits speculation, ensures money stays
predominantly local and that what money does leave countries for
foreign investment or aid has a *Protect the Local, Globally* approach.

In the golden age of the 1950s and 1960s the OECD countries
pursued policies of full employment and the building of stronger social
safety networks. What helped make this possible was a system of
national controls on capital movements and credit allocation. After
the war virtually all countries in the world, except the US, had extensive controls on capital outflows, inflows or both. An extreme case
was that of South Korea where 'violations of prohibitions on overseas
capital transfers were punishable by a minimum sentence of ten years
in prison and a maximum sentence of death'.[2] Since the government
was serious about enforcement, its controls were effective for decades.

However, today's globalization of financial movements and capital
investment has increased the power of transnational business and

finance to set a different agenda. Their demand is that the goal of full employment be replaced by that of controlling inflation and ensuring international competitiveness. Reducing controls on capital, and the increased pressures of globalization, were the means by which this dramatic shift in political and economic priorities occurred.[3]

The resulting unfettered money flows led to the 1998 destabilization of, firstly, the Asian Tigers, then increased financial instability globally. Despite the huge number of international conferences and ministerial meetings to tackle the crisis, no really significant blocks have been put on the flow of capital globally. There has therefore never been a better time to demand that capital remains predominantly where it is generated in order to fund sustainable development and create jobs. The alternative is to risk once again causing large-scale economic and social disruption and instability worldwide.

Although the present reality is that most of the economic and social pain caused by the recent crisis has been felt by the poor in developing countries, Eastern Europe and Russia, the richer countries have not escaped unscathed. The late 1990s financial instability is the first time economic events in the developing world have affected the financial security of developed countries since the Organisation of Petroleum Exporting Countries (OPEC) crisis in the 1970s. The G7 has mobilized some US$3000 billion as lender of last resort to major economies such as Mexico, Korea, Indonesia, Russia and Brazil, because of the threat to the increasingly interconnected international market system. This is illustrated by the fact that although advanced industrial countries still dominate the international financial and trading system, 48 per cent of global production and 55 per cent of world investment now takes place outside this group of rich countries.[4]

Yet, the greatest adverse effects are felt mostly by developing countries. The economic structure of most of them makes for dependence upon and vulnerability to international money flows. Their limited domestic capital markets mean that relatively small flows of foreign capital can have a disproportionate effect on prices, particularly those of government bonds and privatization issues, which tend to make up the bulk of traded investment items. Their firms, thanks to cheap credit from abroad influencing their investment strategies, tend to be highly dependent on borrowed funds. The swing from boom to credit restrictions have thus had a disproportionate effect upon production. Their populations in turn are vulnerable to economic disruption because so many of them live near the poverty line, unprotected by modern welfare systems.

Since the economic crisis of the late nineties affected both North and South discussions of the global financial architecture should necessarily involve the two-fifths of the world population living in countries that until recently were seen only as clients for development assistance. At present they are effectively excluded from this debate because of their lack of power in the rich-country-dominated global institutions such as the IMF, World Bank and WTO.

In the end, a return to national democratic control over the movement of capital is the key to providing the money for governments and communities both North and South to improve local livelihoods and social and environmental conditions.

## TODAY'S GLOBAL FINANCIAL CASINO

*'when the capital development of a country becomes a by-product of the casino, the job is likely to be ill-done.'*
John Maynard Keynes[5]

The global casino, as today's international financial market is often characterized, consists of traders gambling on minute market fluctuations that have no grounding in real economic activities. In 1980, the daily average of foreign trading was US$80 billion. Today, more than US$1500 billion (US$1.5 trillion) flow *daily* across international borders. Private financial flows to developing countries grew from US$44 billion in 1990 to US$2565 billion in 1997. Today 90 per cent of capital flows are speculative (eg based on movements in currency and interest rates), rather than productive in nature.[6]

This financial and trade deregulation was theoretically supposed to promise progress and well-being for all. In fact it has benefited the few; 447 billionaires now have wealth greater than the income of the poorest *half* of humanity. A mere 100 multinationals control one-fifth of all foreign-owned assets in the world.[7] Due to mergers and acquisitions this concentration of wealth and power is increasing.

### New Financial Architecture to the Rescue?

Most proposals for a new financial architecture focus on ways of making markets work more efficiently, stressing the need for greater transparency on the part of financial institutions, business firms, and government agencies, and for improved regulation and supervision of financial markets. Most of the burden of reform is placed on the debtor countries, requiring them to make fundamental, and usually damaging, changes in their domestic practices in order to be better prepared to handle massive inflows of foreign funds.

Essentially, the conventional new architecture proposals seek to make the world a safer place for the international capital flows. But no amount of transparency and supervision can eliminate the inherent information problems in international investments or prevent the herd mentality of global financial markets from destabilizing domestic economies.

So the official suggestions for a new financial architecture called for relatively painless changes, such as increased transparency and an intention to work together internationally to try and head off any repeat of 1998. What was more disappointing was that many of the suggestions from civil society also failed to contemplate a fundamental rethink in the end goal of economic policies. Their suggestions were of course more radical, including calling for more use of capital controls, curbing derivatives and offshore havens and a coalescence around what could be called a new NGO's 'GATT' – a General Agreement on Tobin Taxes.[8] Such suggestions were, however, very rarely put within the context of a different priority for overall economic management.

Not surprisingly once the worse appeared over, as Asian stock-markets rose and currencies became more stable, official complacency began to return. The US economy was stirred but not shaken, so optimism returned and thoughts of anything other than the merest of tinkering with the flow of the world capital was no longer perceived as necessary.

# A SOUTHERN PERSPECTIVE ON THE REAL CAUSES OF THE PRESENT ECONOMIC CRISIS

This section is based on a paper presented by Walden Bello for a conference in Bangkok in 1999.[9]

> 'For some, capital controls are not simply stabilising measures but are, like tariffs and quotas, strategic tools that may justifiably be employed to influence a country's degree and mode of integration into the global economy. In other words, capital and trade controls are legitimate instruments for the pursuit of trade and industrial policies aimed at national industrial development.'

> '...the new economic order is unlikely to be imposed from above in Keynesian technocratic style, but is likely to be forged in social and political struggles. This fire down below is likely to upset the best laid plans of the tiny elite that are trying to

*salvage an increasingly unstable free-market order by tinkering at the margins of the global financial order and calling it reform.'*

Walden Bello

Walden Bello, professor of sociology and public administration at the University of the Philippines, and the large number of other individuals and organizations that signed a *New York Times* article protesting against the 'Washington Consensus' approach to the handling of the Asian Crisis.[10] make the point that those who are actively debating this issue are, for the most part, still arguing within a paradigm of neoliberal economics. Yet it is this very approach that has been central to generating this crisis.

Devising a global financial order is not simply a matter of technical economics, but one that must be informed by values, and the main values and priorities of those who are managing this process are different from those of the majority. This process is, first and foremost, a question of power, and unless civil society brings its own priorities to this debate, what will emerge will simply be a global architecture that will benefit a very small global elite and continue to marginalize the vast majority of the world's peoples.

## Six Clarifications

Before discussing strategies being proposed for global financial reform, a few basic clarifications are needed.

First, the Asian crisis was not predominantly a product of 'crony capitalism'. What brought about the crash of 1997 was 'casino capitalism'. *The Economist* admitted that 'the economic pain being imposed [by global capital markets] on the ex-tigers is out of all proportion to the policy errors of their governments.'[11]

The IMF and the US Treasury, of course, continue to uphold the correctness of their approach to reforming domestic economic and financial arrangements. However, the credibility of this approach has been eroded by the way the IMF straitjackets have adversely affected economies and particularly the poor in, for example, Thailand, Indonesia and Brazil. The IMF itself has estimated that an additional 20 per cent of the population in Indonesia and 12 per cent of those in Thailand and South Korea will fall into poverty due to the Asian crisis.[12]

Second, finance has been the cutting edge of the globalization process. The integration of commodity markets via free trade and that of production systems via TNC consolidation have proceeded rapidly, but both processes have been outstripped by the integration of global capital markets under the aegis of London and Wall Street.

Third, finance has steadily gained ascendancy over industry and other sectors of the economy. This pre-eminence of the financial sector is related to the crisis of dwindling growth caused by deflation which has increasingly overtaken the real sectors of the global economy. This crisis has its roots in overcapacity or underconsumption, which today marks global industries from automobile to energy to capital goods. Diminishing, if not vanishing, returns in industry have led to capital being shifted from the real economy to squeezing 'value' out of the financial sector.

Fourth, differences in exchange rates, interest rates, and stock prices are much less among the more integrated Northern markets. The potential for greater gains has resulted in the movements of volatile capital between the capital markets of the North and the so-called big emerging markets of the South and Asia. Thus, while crises are endemic to the finance-driven global capitalist system, the crises of the last few years have been concentrated in the emerging markets. Since late 1994, there have been the Mexican financial crisis, the 'Tequila Effect' of this crisis in Latin America, the Asian crash, the Russian collapse, the pressure on the Brazilian currency, and the potential knock-on effect of the Brazilian crisis on the rest of Latin America.

Fifth, despite the global financial system's proneness to crises, finance capital is still allowed to operate, as Robert Kroszner describes it, 'in a realm close to anarchy'. The reason that deregulation at the national level has not been replaced by reregulation at the international level is because finance capital has accumulated tremendous political power over the last two decades. Finance capital was liberated from the straitjacket of the Keynesian economy by Margaret Thatcher in the UK and the Republican administrations of Ronald Reagan and George Bush. Yet it has been under the Democratic administration of Bill Clinton that financial interests have become paramount in the foreign economic policy of the US Government. Represented in the inner sanctum of Washington by former Treasury Secretary Robert Rubin (ex Goldman Sachs) and Federal Reserve Chairman Alan Greenspan (a former Wall Street consultant), the so-called Wall Street–Treasury Complex stands four-square against any serious financial regulation. The power of this lobby stems partly from the strength of the interests it represents, but even more from its ideology of market freedom, which it markets as applying not only to trade in goods, but also to the mobility of capital.

Sixth, the crisis of the developing countries of the South is not simply one of exposure to unregulated financial flows, and one that can hence easily be fixed with capital controls at both the global and national levels. The financial deregulation of their economies that has proven so devastating is simply the latest phase of a development model that they have had to internalize over the last two decades under the aegis of IMF–World Bank structural adjustment programmes. These have as their underpinning the concept that foreign markets and foreign capital are the twin engines of development.

Walden Bello concludes that '... the Mexican Crisis of 1995, the Asian Collapse of 1997, and the Latin American unravelling of 1999 were events waiting to happen to economies where liberalization of trade and investment had become equated with development, and where import substitution, trade policy, and industrial policy had been vilified as anti-development.'

The status quo still champions the indiscriminate integration of the South into the global economy and the over-reliance on foreign investment, whether direct investment or portfolio investment, for development. Yet, although the current crisis is wreaking havoc on people's lives throughout the South, it also gives these regions the best opportunity in years to fundamentally revise their model and strategy of development. Box 8.1 summarizes a developing country's position and is taken from Walden Bello's paper.

# A 'LOCALIST' DEVELOPMENT MODEL

To criticize capital market liberalization does not imply that all capital flows should be blocked. There is a desperate need for channelling more stable and productive long-term investments into the less developed parts of all regions of the world economy. These must however provide more equitable and sustainable growth in developing and industrialized countries alike, and have at their heart the protection and rebuilding of local economies. This is the opposite of what is at present on offer.

## Today's Status Quo

> *'In the simplest terms, international investment treaties create a broadly-defined list of investor rights to conduct business free from government oversight or regulatory control. This is accomplished by explicitly prohibiting an extensive catalogue of government policies, laws and programs. To guarantee that governments respect these new limits on their authority, these treaties also include very powerful and secretive legal enforcement mechanisms that can be invoked by any foreign investor.'*[14]

## Box 8.1 Changing the Development Model

Comprehensive, integrated formulations are few and far between, but the following ideas, proposals, or visions are being actively discussed throughout East Asia.

While foreign investment of the right kind is important, growth must be financed principally from domestic savings and investment. This means good, progressive taxation systems. One of the key reasons for the reliance on foreign credit and foreign investment was the elites of East Asia did not want to tax themselves to produce the needed investment capital to pursue their fast-track development strategies. Even in the depths of today's crisis, conspicuous consumption continues to mark the behaviour of Asia's elites, who also send so much of their wealth abroad to safe havens in Geneva, Tokyo, or New York. Regressive taxation systems are the norm in the region, where income taxpayers are but a handful and indirect taxes that cut into the resources of lower-income groups are the principal source of government expenditures.

While export markets are important, they are too volatile to serve as reliable engines of growth. Development must be reoriented around the domestic market as the principal locomotive of growth. Together with the pitfalls of excessive reliance on foreign capital, the lessons of the crisis include the tremendous dependence on export markets of the region's economies. This has led to extreme vulnerability to the vagaries of the global market and sparked the current self-defeating race to export one's way out of the crisis through competitive devaluation of the currency. This move is but the latest and most desperate manifestation of the panacea of export-oriented development.

Making the domestic market the engine of development brings up the linkage between sustained growth and equity, for a Keynesian strategy of enlarging the local market to stimulate growth means increasing effective demand or bringing more consumers (hopefully discriminating ones, that is) into the market via a comprehensive programme of asset and income distribution, including land reform. There is in this, of course, the unfinished social justice agenda of the progressive movement in Asia – an agenda that has been marginalized by the ideology of growth during the miracle years. Vast numbers of people remain marginalized because of grinding poverty, particularly in the countryside. Land and asset reform would simultaneously bring them into the market, empower them economically and politically, and create the conditions for social and political stability. Achieving economic sustainability based on a dynamic domestic market can no longer be divorced from issues of equity.

Regionalism can become an invaluable adjunct to such a process of domestic market-driven growth, but only if both processes are guided not by a perspective of neo-liberal integration that will only serve to swamp the region's industries and agriculture by so-called 'more efficient' third-party producers, but by a vision of regional import-substitution and protected market-integration that gives the region's producers the first opportunity to serving the region's consumers.

While there are other elements in the alternative development-thinking taking place in the region, one universal theme is 'sustainable development'.

The centrality of ecological sustainability is said to be one of the hard lessons of the crisis. For the model of foreign capital fuelled high-speed growth for foreign markets is leaving behind little that is of positive value. In the case of Thailand, 12 years of fast-track capitalism is leaving behind few traces except industrial plants that will be antiquated in a few years, hundreds of unoccupied high-rises, a horrendous traffic problem that is only slightly mitigated by the repossession of thousands of late-model cars from bankrupt owners, a rapid rundown of the country's natural capital and an environment that has been irreversibly, if not mortally, impaired, to the detriment of future generations.

In place of 8–10 per cent growth rates, many environmentalists are now talking of rates of 3–4 per cent or even lower. This links the social agenda with the environmental agenda, for one reason for the push for high growth rates was so that the elites could corner a significant part of the growth while still allowing some growth to trickle down to the lower classes for the sake of social peace. The alternative – redistribution of social wealth – is clearly less acceptable to the ruling groups, but it is the key to a pattern of development that will eventually combine economic growth, political stability, and ecological sustainability.

These and similar ideas are already being discussed actively throughout the region. What is still unclear, though, is how these elements will hang together. The new political economy may be embedded in religious or secular discourse and language. And its coherence is likely to rest less on considerations of narrow efficiency than on a stated ethical priority given to community solidarity and security.

Moreover, the new economic order is unlikely to be imposed from above in Keynesian technocratic style, but is likely to be forged in social and political struggles. This fire down below is likely to upset the best laid plans of the tiny elite that are trying to salvage an increasingly unstable free-market order by tinkering at the margins of the global financial order and calling it reform.'[13]

The status quo view of what form international rules covering investment should take is represented by the MAI. Negotiations for this began in 1995 within the 29-member OECD. The MAI would have been the world's first multilateral agreement establishing comprehensive and binding rules for investment, the provision of market access, legal security for investors and a 'level playing field' for international investment flows. Its proponents use the usual arguments that freeing the movement of capital will encourage economic development, create wealth and employment, help the transfer of technology and benefit developing countries. Enhancing competition is supposed to assist efficiency and productivity and is the most effective way of keeping production costs down.

The MAI was the subject of massive international opposition from grass-roots organizations, NGOs and trades unions. Their concerns centred around the adverse effects on development, environment and labour standards. The collapse in the Paris negotiations of the MAI in 1998 was due in a large part to this pressure on governments, although the eventual breakdown arose from the nature of the exceptions claimed by OECD members (particularly France and the US) rather than development issues as such. The call for greater liberalization in investment resurfaced at the WTO Ministerial meeting in Seattle in November 1999 and met with a similar range of opponents and arguments.

The basic arguments against the MAI, and the investment issues that the rich countries try to introduce into the WTO, are that they will make it mandatory for all WTO countries, both rich and poor, to give foreign investors the right to enter and establish themselves with 100 per cent ownership. Foreigners and foreign firms would also have to be treated as well (or better) than locals, and restrictions on the free flow of capital into and out of the country (and on the foreign firms' operations) would be prohibited.

In addition, in discussions at the WTO working group on investment, the rich countries have sought to give a wide scope to the definition of foreign investment, including not only FDI, but also portfolio investment (investment in shares and government stocks) and purchase of property.

The original MAI, and the new direction of WTO investment discussions, will mean that developed and developing countries will no longer be able to give preferences or protection to local investors, firms or farmers. They would thus face the threat of having their businesses wiped out by competition from the bigger foreign firms, or by being taken over by them. Also, the kind of restrictions that Malaysia and other countries place on inflow and outflow of portfolio or loan capital from abroad, and on foreign ownership of land and houses may also come under question.

## THE ALTERNATIVE INVESTMENT CODE

An Alternative Investment Code (AIC) is the *Protect the Local, Globally* alternative to the MAI and WTO investment rules. The intention of such a code is *not* to ensure the unimpeded international flow of capital and investment, but to have as its basic aim the regrounding of capital locally to fund the diversification of local, sustainable economies which have at their core the right to livelihood. The right to livelihood is a key human rights goal in this AIC. Other rights such as private property rights are contingent on fulfilment of this most basic human right.

Tony Clarke and Maude Barlow in a groundbreaking book pointed out that:

> '...*the UN Charter of Economic Rights and Duties of States provided quite a different framework for establishing a set of global investment rules. It was based on the assumption that nation states acting on behalf of all their citizens and the public at large, had the political sovereignty to regulate foreign investment. The Charter granted member nations the authority to supervise the operations of transnational corporations in their territories by establishing performance requirements.*
>
> *These performance requirements were to be based on the national development needs of the people of each country. While nation states were also granted the powers to "nationalize, expropriate or transfer ownership of foreign property", the charter called for the payment of fair compensation for expropriation.*
>
> *Although changes in the global economy over the past twenty years or so would require that modifications be made, the UN Charter on the Economic Rights and Duties of States contains many of the elements for modern, alternative approach to global investment rules.*'[15]

Bearing this in mind a fundamental rethink of the MAI could result in an agreement along the lines of Box 8.2.

## CONTROLLING CAPITAL AND INVESTMENT

> 'It is often said that computer technology would make such capital and investment controls impossible. Imagine however that the "rocket scientists" who deal in cybermoney wheezes like derivatives, saw the writing on the wall. Were they to be paid handsomely to use computers to control and localise money flows, then there would be a Porsche-jam in every national Treasury car park. Future attempts by regional groupings of governments to deal with development, environment and unemployment could then be transformed into being able to offer real solutions instead of today's impotent handwringing.'[16]

With barriers to trade being dismantled and international capital flows virtually unfettered, national treasuries have less and less control over their economic future. Money flies around the globe at the touch of a

---

## Box 8.2 Key Provisions of the Alternative Investment Code

*Purpose:* The AIC seeks to strengthen democratic control of capital and stimulate investments that benefit local communities.

*National Treatment:* Investments that increase local employment with decent wages, enhance protection of the environment and otherwise improve the quality of life in communities and regions within states which are parties to the AIC are encouraged. States are urged to give favourable treatment to domestic investors who further these goals and are prohibited from treating foreign investors as favourably as domestic investors.

*Most-Favoured Nation Status:* Provided it is not at the expense of domestic investors, states shall give preferential treatment to investors from other states which respect human rights, treat workers fairly, and protect the environment.

*Performance Requirements:* States may impose requirements on investors which further the goals of this code such as to:

- achieve a given level or percentage of domestic content, whilst at the same time ensuring that monopolies do not develop;
- give preference to goods produced locally;
- stipulate a minimum level of local equity participation;
- hire a given level of local personnel and respect labour and environmental standards;
- protect enterprises which serve community needs from unfair foreign competition.

*Standstill and Rollback:* No state party to the AIC can pass laws or adopt regulations that diminish local control of capital or that divert investors from giving priority to meeting local needs. Existing laws and regulations that give preferential treatment to foreign investors or encourage absentee ownership of community-based enterprises must be rolled back over the next decade.

*Dispute Resolution:* Citizen groups and community institutions are given standing to sue investors for violations of this investment code. All judicial and quasi-judicial procedures such as arbitration shall be fully transparent and open to public observation.

*Investment Protection:* Workers and communities play a vital role in the creation of corporate assets, and that role must be recognized and protected. Thus, expropriation of such assets to serve vital community needs is permitted and must take into account the interest of workers and communities in those assets. Similarly, restrictions may be placed on excessive repatriation of profits by foreign investors, and capital may not be transferred without indemnification of worker and community interest in such capital.[17]

---

computer key, when there should be adequate controls on the movement of the funds from banks and pensions, insurance and investments. These constraints would need to ensure the investment of the majority of funds in the locality where they are generated and/or needed, ie an invest-here-to-prosper-here policy.

Democratic control over capital is the key to providing the money for governments and communities to rebuild local economies and improve environmental and social conditions and job opportunities. As well as a Tobin-type tax on international capital transactions to curb currency speculators, broader re-regulation of finance capital is required. This would include controls on capital flows, taxes on short-term speculative transactions, tightening of easy credit that allow speculators to multiply the size of their 'bets' way beyond the cash required to cover them. Also required is a wide and coordinated attack on corporate tax evasion, including offshore banking centres. And equally important is the regulation of corporate investment in terms which impose some obligations towards affected communities.

Any one country proposing such controls on its own would immediately be punished by the markets. However, a regional grouping of powerful states such as the EU or North America would be a secure and lucrative enough market to ensure that those that control money wouldn't dare to leave the safety and security afforded by such a bloc. This pattern would then be attempted globally.

To prevent the threat of a capital strike or flight it is crucial that the constraints envisaged by any regional configuration of nation states be introduced over a stated timetable. Along with this would come tough confiscatory laws regarding the assets of those who have tried to evade localizing measures prior to the introduction of the legislation. Computer records of money movement should make this possible, using the methods at present used by institutions such as banks to track their own international money flows allied to lessons being learnt globally from hunting down laundered drug money, tax evasion, Jewish resources stolen by the Nazis and so on.

Once the threat of capital flight has been substantially lessened the taxation system can be changed progressively to reduce inequality and serve the needs of the community in general. Higher taxation of capital gains, green and land taxes, progressive taxes on income and lower taxes on labour all have a place in this transformation. Strict and transparent accounting rules would enable the phasing out of 'corporate welfare' for the undeserving wealthier sections of business. Payback periods need to be lengthened using penal short-term capital gains tax for shareholders who take early profits, but tapering to near zero for long-term shareholders

A bloc-wide 'Beat a Cheat' tax campaign cracking down on corporate evasion would require public disclosure of corporate finances, especially global taxes paid or avoided, and closing national and global tax loopholes. It could also penalize and eventually eliminate tax havens. Intra-corporate financial transfers, at present used to avoid paying national taxes (eg transfer pricing), would also be monitored and punitively taxed. After due warning, to allow diversification of the economies concerned and the reinvesting of deposits back to the country of origin, offshore banking centres would be closed down. This would be achieved by prohibiting domestic banking systems from honouring the transfers of offshore capital. Such measures would drastically constrain the ability of those controlling capital to evade national banking and investment laws and national taxes.

To keep capital local the influence of local banks on central bank policies must be strengthened to reinforce the significance of the local banking structure. This would encourage the rebuilding of local economies via smaller locally based banks, credit unions, LETS schemes etc. Insurance, pension, building society and endowment funds must be encouraged via legislative measures and tax breaks to invest in the local. And those who are the contributors to such funding must, in law, become more genuine owners of their own savings and deferred wages. Civic bonds could be another mechanism to attract funds to local regeneration (see Chapter 5).

## Internationalism and Development

These policies must also incorporate an internationalist approach to make certain that they don't merely benefit the rich countries at the expense of the poor. Tax penalties will exist for foreign investments which didn't directly help the developing world or Eastern Europe to protect and rediversify their own sustainable local economies. Aid and trade rules must be changed to ensure a similar outcome, and the transfer of sustainable technologies must become the centrepiece of new aid regimes. The North itself must absorb the costs of protective patents, and the burden of royalties, so that the South can choose and afford the least polluting technologies.

This is the opposite of the last few decades, when trade and aid programmes have pushed a 'growth by exports' model of development. This has been facilitated by the conditions demanded for debt repayment and by the rich countries' desire for cheaper imported products. The resulting overproduction by Southern producers has reduced their earnings and ability to repay their debts. Structural adjustment programmes, reducing even the most meagre levels of health, education and infrastuctural work, have still been relentlessly pursued.

# DETAILED STEPS TO LOCALIZED ECONOMIES

## Change the Terms of the Debate

1 Shift the elite debate about minor controls on capital to a public debate about the necessity to ensure that capital flows and investment is used to rebuild sustainable economies worldwide. Make clear that to overcome the powerful vested interests of banks and TNCs that these changes will have to be introduced in powerful groupings of countries, perhaps firstly in the EU. Then it is crucial to ensure that other less powerful regions can move along the same path.

2 Make clear the feasibility and the steps involved in this approach – firstly to ground capital and secondly to break it up and tax it for social and economic benefits leading to more localized economies.

## Grounding Capital

1 Make clear that to control capital, the constraints on finance initiated by the regional bloc of nation states will be introduced over a stated timetable, with tough confiscatory laws on the assets of those who have tried to evade the measures prior to the introduction of the legislation.

2 Reintroduce exchange controls.

3 Governments need to reassert control over fiscal policies (ie tax and public expenditure) by re-regulating finance and banking and the role of the central banks. Emphasis must be put on investing locally. Introduce 100 per cent reserve requirements on demand deposits to limit the ability of banks to create money and give governments greater control over the money supply (see Appendix 2). Reregulate finance capital to stabilize financial markets, reintroduce exchange controls and make capital owners more responsive to the general needs of the local economies.

4 Attack speculation by:
   – The introduction of a Tobin-type tax which taxes domestic and global foreign exchange speculation. Taxes on short-term speculation (to take a risk in business through which it is hoped to make a profit) and arbitraging (making a profit at very little risk from the known difference in value of various assets), such as a purchase tax on stocks, bonds, foreign currency and derivatives.
   – Tightening terms for easy credit, reign-in devices for hedging (protecting against possible loss by buying investments at a

fixed price for delivery later) and derivatives (a tradable security, ie paper asset, whose value is derived from an actual or expected price of an asset, such as ordinary bonds or shares, commodities or currencies) that allow speculators to multiply the size of their plays many times.

- Setting higher margin requirements for purchasing bonds and other financial instruments on borrowed money. (A margin is the proportion of the value of a transaction which traders have to deposit to guarantee that they will complete it, this is set at a price sufficient to protect the seller against loss if the buyer cannot complete.)
- Restricting the use of derivatives to the genuine market-hedging needs of multinational commerce by requiring that the issuing banks have cash or easily cashable assets in reserve to back up these contracts.

## Changing the Taxation System

Once the threat of capital flight has been substantially lessened by the above, then the taxation system can be changed to reduce inequality and serve the needs of the community. These measures are:

1   Less taxation on labour, which induces job cuts in order to be competitive.
2   Higher capital gains taxes and progressive income taxes. Lower the cost of capital and lengthen the payback periods. Introduce penal short-term capital gains tax for shareholders taking early profits, tapering to near zero for long-term shareholders. Give preferential tax breaks to income earned through productive work compared with the returns from simply holding money.
3   Better credit assessment techniques with incentives to lenders to develop closer relationships with their local industrial customers and community businesses.
4   Audits of impartially prepared accounts, following a transparent set of rules, providing a proper measure of company worth and allowing comparison of performance over time or with other firms; these to provide the information to ensure proper corporate taxation and the phasing out of 'corporate welfare'.
5   Ecotaxes. The phasing in of energy, resource, pollution and waste taxation will generate huge financial resources for the transition to a sustainable local economy (see Chapter 10).
6   Severely limit tax evasion by forcing public disclosure of corporate finances, especially global taxes paid or avoided; closing national

and global tax loopholes; penalizing and eventually eliminating tax havens; monitoring and actively working to stop intra-corporate financial transfers used to avoid paying national taxes (eg transfer pricing); penalize downsizing or relocation for profitable corporations by taxation or where legally relevant by dechartering.

## Encouraging Local, Long-term Investment

The measures to encourage local long-term investment are:

1 Provide higher tax breaks for longer term investment in the local economy, tax penalties for foreign speculation unless it directly helps to protect and rediversify the local economy where the investment is occurring.
2 Central banks at national level would have the power to influence directly the structure and profitability of local banks such that they encourage the rebuilding of local economies. To help fund the transition it would reintroduce reserve requirements to support its interest rate policy (thus limiting the money that can be loaned) and regulate the markets in a wider public interest rather than that defined by the markets themselves. Encourage smaller locally based banks, credit unions, LETS schemes etc. Introduce tax breaks for the breaking up of big financial enterprise into the optimum size for providing finance for local investment, using local knowledge with an end goal of maximizing the number and range of local businesses.
3 Encourage savings by creating a public agency to act as a financial intermediary collecting longer term deposits and channelling them to lending institutions such as commercial banks and a network of local development banks.
4 Channel insurance, pension, building societies and endowment funds via legislative measures and tax breaks to invest in the local. Float civic bonds for local regeneration.
5 After due warning to allow diversification of the economies concerned, close down offshore banking centres where capital hides from banking and securities laws or from national income taxes. This to be policed by prohibiting national banking systems from honouring the transfers of offshore capital.

## International Steps

Measures that will be necessary internationally to foster localization are:

1   Following consultation with developing countries the OECD should devise international competition rules (with a localist rather than free market agenda), which break up monopolies in big capital institutions and TNCs (see Chapter 9).

2   Reform the terms of international trade to ensure more balanced flows of commerce, such that it is used only for investment, goods, technology flows and services that rebuild local economies. At the trading bloc and international level, supranational authorities are likely to be needed to allow the world to have predictable exchange rates that reflect economic realities for what trade remains between countries. Blocs and countries need to be able to manage their economies themselves, making what they consider to be the right trade-off between inflation, growth and employment.

3   To aid the transition for Eastern Europe and the developing world, the level of foreign exchange needed to adjust their regional economies towards localization will need to be agreed. This will require an extension of the IMF system of Special Drawing Rights, so they can convert their own currency into hard currency. Aid, structural adjustment policies and trade rules must be changed to ensure the transition to increasingly diverse and sustainable local economies.

4   Reduce inequality and increase demand within local economies. To achieve this, raise wages on the low end as rapidly as possible by making ILO laws mandatory domestically and requiring trade between nations to honour labour rights.

5   Forgive the debtors – ie initiate a general write-off of bad debts accumulated by the poor countries provided that the money that would have been used as debt repayment was clearly used for social improvements within more localized economies.

6   Reform the objectives of central banks so they will support a pro-sustainable growth regime for local economies instead of thwarting it.

7   Set the conditions under which foreign investment can take place, including setting conditions of location, employment, domestic representation on Boards of Directors, sourcing, public account-ability and taxation.

8   Change intellectual property laws to only allow for incentives for research and development, not to create protected information monopolies. Where there is a conflict between an exclusive private interest and a community interest, the community interest should prevail.

9   Refocus national economic agendas away from long-distance trade and international competitiveness, towards the priority of employ-

ment and improvements in the social and physical infrastructure and the environment. This, along with the rebuilding of local economies that will be its result, should be the defining issue for domestic policy.

## Chapter 9

# A Localist Competition Policy

*'Beginning with Adam Smith, market theory has been quite explicit that the efficiency of the market's self-organizing dynamic is a consequence of small, locally owned enterprises competing in local markets on the basis of price, quality, and service in response to customer-defined needs and values. No buyer or seller may be large enough to influence the market price individually.*

*By contrast what we know as the global capitalist economy is dominated by a few financial speculators and a handful of globe-spanning megacorporations able to use their massive financial clout and media outreach to manipulate prices, determine what products will be available to consumers, absorb and drive competitors from the market, and reshape the values of popular culture to create demand for what corporations choose to offer.'*[1]

There is an understandable unease that once there is protection for local business providing goods and services on a national level or for a geographical bloc, then the quality of such safeguarded provision could decline. Also there is a concern that the pressure to innovate and the adherence to standards, rules and laws could lessen and hence consumer choice and satisfaction would be eroded by a kind of Eastern European bureaucracy and inefficiency. It is therefore vital to retain the positive sides of competition, ie the need to produce high-quality goods or services, but on a more level, more local, playing field.

Under the *Protect the Local, Globally* form of localization, pressures to provide the best product and services, will take into account national labour, social and environmental regulations. There would not be the downward pressure on such standards that comes with the need to compete with businesses abroad. However, this does not mean that advances in ideas, product design or manufacturing from other parts of the world will be denied other nations by this localist approach. The utilization of the best new ideas and technologies found abroad will be facilitated by the technological and information flows encouraged under localization's trade and aid rules (see Chapter 12) and by joint ventures or licenced production with such innovators. These will of course be domestically based.

Competition law must also cover the smaller amount of international trade that will remain. This trade will be based on what goods and services can clearly be produced domestically given relevant technologies versus a produce like bananas for which temperate climatic conditions would make, say, glasshouse production prohibitively expensive and probably environmentally questionable. The competition laws will discriminate in favour of countries with localist domestic competition laws. These measures will help ensure that the materials or goods traded will be produced with minimal pollution, with workers and social conditions being continuously improved and with the local economy, and communities from where the export derives, being strengthened. However, a local economy cannot ensure that competition won't be undermined by local patronage networks (eg freemason's or even the local rotary club). However a *quid pro quo* for such a more protected economy will be to clamp down on such damaging practices by local firms, particularly through maximum openness in business practice.

## THE IMPORTANCE OF COMPETITION

For most economists, competition policy attempts to facilitate the efficient allocation of resources. The ultimate result, according to Adam Smith in his championing of the benefits of competition within nations and of free trade among nations, is to 'render the annual revenue of the society as great as possible'.[2] From vigorous competition is supposed to flow pricing that sends the right signals to market participants. This in turn, it is claimed, fosters efficient resource allocation through pressure forcing suppliers to manage their operations tightly, ie at minimum unit cost. It also provides an incentive to introduce superior new products, and production processes, because only through innovation can a firm outpace its peers and realize competitive profits.

As was seen in Chapter 2, such a theoretical world is a long way from the real one. In international trade in particular the different economic strengths of governments and the increasing power of TNCs, means that the theoretically positive aspects of local competition does not exist in practice. The reality is one of dominant TNCs incursions into national economies, a reduction in the range of goods and services provided within countries and hence an increase in long-distance trade.

Another aspect overlooked by competition theory is that 'efficiency' in the real world's markets tends to be a narrow and inadequate concept. It often excludes costs which do not fall on market participants, but instead are borne by governments, taxpayers or citizens or the ecosystems. Such 'externalities' include unemployment, social impacts and environmental degradation.

# GOVERNMENT COMPETITION POLICY

When barriers to trade were high, governments and citizens could sharply distinguish international from domestic policies. International policies dealt with at-the-border barriers, such as tariffs and quotas, or responded to events occurring abroad. Domestic policies were concerned with everything behind the nation's borders, such as competition and antirust rules, corporate governance, product standards, worker safety, regulation and supervision of financial institutions, environmental protection, tax codes and the government's budgets. Domestic policies were considered as matters about which nations were sovereign with little regard to other nations. Localization will gradually reintroduce barriers to trade so this situation will require many of the measures used by governments before the 1980s and 1990s to be adapted and reintroduced.

## Competition and Industrial Structure

Government competition policy can be concerned with the structure of industries, or with the behaviour of firms within them. Governments can favour monopolies such as the UK postal service, or regulate private involvement in areas such as telephones, telecommunications, television and transport. Restrictions occur via monopoly legislation and in the UK the setting up of the former Monopolies and Mergers Commission (MMC), now the Competition Commission. In general, governments have, since the war, tried to limit cartels, unless like the most successful version, OPEC, it is perceived to benefit the government concerned.

Cartels are a formal or informal agreement between a number of firms in an industry to restrict competition. Cartel agreements may provide for setting minimum prices, setting limits on output or capacity, restrictions on non-price competition, divisions of markets between firms either geographically or in terms of type of product, or agreed measures to restrict entry to industry.

Cartels are only usually condoned by governments where they benefit either their immediate coffers, as in OPEC, or when they want them to contribute to national industrial policy goals by favouring exporters. Domestic producers also enhanced their profits by participating in international cartels with sellers from other nations. In the 1930s, Britain's Imperial Chemical Industry (ICI) agreed with du Pont not to sell in the US, Central America and Venezuela, while du Pont ceded the UK and most of the British Empire (except Canada) to ICI. The amount of cartelized trade – including activity not registered with national authorities – appears to have dropped considerably since the 1930s, when it is estimated very crudely, from 30–50 per cent of world trade was subjected to some degree of cartel control.[3]

Cartels still exist of course. Nowadays they are not usually condoned by governments and this tends to mean they are more subtle and may often be difficult for competition authorities to identify. They may be based on very 'informal understandings' under which companies do not trespass on each other's territories. In July 1998, the US Justice Department had 25 grand juries investigating international price-fixing cases in industries as diverse as vitamins, glass and marine equipment. It is estimated that cartels are transferring billions of illegal dollars from consumer to corporate coffers.[4]

## Competition and the Behaviour of Firms

Governments have legislated against various practices thought to inhibit competition, including retail price maintenance (RPM), exclusive dealing (an agreement between the producer and a distributor of certain goods that one will trade only with the other), and refusal to supply (refusal by producers to sell their goods to all applicants, which can inhibit competition between distributors). In the UK, the Office of Fair Trading (OFT) is responsible for enforcing these rules.[5]

Their limitations are illustrated in Box 9.1, taken from a paper by Tim Lang, which details the increasing concentration – in one sector – the food system.

## International Competitiveness Inhibits Fairer Competition Laws

*'The Government must promote competition, stimulating enterprise, flexibility and innovation by opening markets.'*
Tony Blair[6]

*'To make markets more competitive we will strengthen the Office of Fair Trading, consider the case for reform of merger*

## Box 9.1 Not a Nourishing Monopoly – Increasing Concentration of Ownership in the UK Food System

In the UK, with the ending in 1965 of RPM – a system whereby food manufacturers could stipulate to retailers what price their goods would be sold at – power passed from manufacturers and farmers to retailers. By the mid-1990s, four chains accounted for at least half of all food sold. Fifteen multiples (defined as having ten stores or more) owned 83 million square feet of sales area out of the national stock of 127 million square feet. Viewed by size of outlet, the sales area owned by these 15 multiples was in the form of just 7250 shops, whereas the 44 million remaining square feet in the national sales area was provided by 51,324 other shops, almost all of them small independents and specialist shops.

The national food retail picture is of a small number of giant concerns dwarfing a large, but dwindling number of small shopkeepers. Retail analysts no longer debate whether there will be retail saturation but when. One source, for instance, anticipates saturation in 2004 or 2005. Retailer power stems not just from market share, but because the retailer mediates between producer and consumer, sets standards through rigorous contract specifications and translates consumer lifestyle into food products. UK retailers have also developed 'own label' markets, in which they subcontract to unbranded manufacturers for the production of their own brand of foods which are then sold at prices lower than branded goods. Own-label products now account for 45 per cent of all food sales in the UK. With such scale, one can appreciate how retailers' specifications and contracts are so important to would-be providers.

As own-label sales have grown, partly due to their higher profit levels for the retailers, conflicts have erupted with both farmers and giant global branded goods. This has been particularly strong over soft drinks (notably colas in the early 1990s), ice creams and other highly advertised goods and over fresh meat. Following the price collapse after the BSE crisis of 1996, upland farmers saw their prices drop by about half in a year. Yet it was quickly noticed that meat prices to consumers did not drop similarly. Unprecedented conflicts emerged with UK farmers blockading ports, demonstrating violently outside supermarkets and putting great pressure on government to act. In mid-1998, an inquiry was set up by the OFT, the UK's anti-trust body which has never issued a critical report on the supermarkets. The inquiry reported in 1999 and as a result the government referred the issue to the Competition Commission to report in spring 2000. Such episodes illustrate the tensions within the food system following the emergence of retail power. This dynamic presently dominates much of the UK and European food systems.

Although researchers into chain management suggest considerable integration, particularly in new product development, between retailers and manufacturers, few doubt which sector carries the cards. UK supermarket multiples are now the UK's largest private-sector employers. Their employee numbers have risen as independent shopkeepers have declined. Described as flagships for the service sector economy, modern supermarkets are, in some respects, purveyors of the self-service economy. The consumers travel more and service themselves. In latest technological self-scanner till developments, shoppers check themselves and make the low-paid checkout operator redundant.

While there can be no doubt that there is considerable control over food on the part of state and particularly commercial interests, there are immense problems for those who dominate food systems. Even for today's giant food businesses, uncertainty rules. An estimated 10,000 new products are launched in the EU annually of which only 10 per cent survive a year. Ready-to-eat food is now the norm.

The daily reality of tensions between manufacturers and retailers and the complexity of contracts and balancing margins and costs are considerable. Whole sectors like the liquid milk business are being changed radically in a matter of a few years. In the UK, doorstep delivery of milk has been a tradition since industrialization but in a few years, consumers are following the US model of purchasing milk at the supermarket. Such tensions and changes are inevitable and pose genuine commercial risks for investors.

The current phase of globalization is characterized by concentration at national, regional and international levels. The UK food industry is one of the most concentrated in Europe. Three companies in 1995 – Unilever, Cadbury Schweppes and Associated British Foods – represented two-thirds of total capitalization in UK food manufacturing. Yet these companies compete on the world stage and their plant investment decisions involve comparisons between locations able to serve the whole European market. Of the top 50 European companies, 19 are British and British companies are second only to those of the US in the level of their FDI in other countries (Heasman 1997). Although the UK is concentrated, half of the world's top 100 food sector companies are US owned. Currently, the top 200 groups worldwide have combined food and drink sales of £700 billion – broadly half the world's food market. Private estimates by industry anticipate that the global food industry will come to be dominated by up to 200 groups which will account for around two-thirds of sales.

*Source:* Lang (1999)[7]

---

*policy, step up the pressure for economic reform in Europe, press for the removal of barriers to international trade and oppose unnecessarily burdensome regulations from whatever source.'[8]*

*'The UK is one of the world's most open economies. Our aim is to maintain this position.'[9]*

Britain's national economic policy, under the previous Conservative government, was to increase its international competitiveness through inward investment. Thus the country was promoted to foreign investors as a low-wage deregulated 'enterprise zone' with a relatively pliant workforce. In a 1995 brochure, the government's Invest in Britain

Bureau (IBB) highlighted the country's 'Pro-business environment' specifying 'labour costs significantly below other European countries' and assuring potential investors that 'no new laws or regulations may be introduced without ascertaining and minimizing the costs to business'. It continued:

> *'The UK has the least onerous labour regulations in Europe, with few restrictions on working hours, overtime and holidays... there is no legal requirement to recognise a trade union. Many industries operate shift work, and 24-hour, seven days-a-week production for both men and women.'*[10]

The New Labour Government is not always so blunt. It has for example introduced a minimum wage and some improvement in labour legislation such as the employment relations bill giving new rights to unions. However, as can be seen from the above quotes, it still continues very much with the priorities of the previous government in terms of supporting pro-big business and the overriding need to be internationally competitive. This had affected its competition policies in a number of ways. If the powerful Competition Commission set up by New Labour finds that a merger raises no concerns for the public interest, then the government has to accept this recommendation and can take no action. If an adverse finding is announced then the government can either accept or reject this, and either accept the remedies proposed or choose their own. The government retains a veto solely over mergers involving national security – such as the £7 billion plus takeover by British Aerospace of GEC's Marconi defence business.

One of the most potentially controversial of mergers in terms of its implications for wider social issues was the takeover in June 1999 by Wal-Mart of the UK supermarket chain Asda. In the previous March, company executives paid a 'courtesy call' to Tony Blair. One of the big stumbling blocks to Wal-Mart's takeover was thought to be the government's desire to curb the building of new large shopping centres. Since 1996, British planning regulations have sought to confine superstores to town centres. In 1998, after sustained lobbying by Tesco and the British Retail Consortium, the government abandoned plans to tax out-of-town parking places.

The Competition Commission is looking at planning laws stopping new retailers from entering the arena with lower prices. It was also reported as 'hard to believe' that Tony Blair would have told Wal-Mart executives at his meeting with them that the UK planning restrictions were 'non-negotiable', and so Wal-Mart 'appears to have calculated that it can change the law'. The company's US stores are vast and so have to operate almost exclusively out of town. Its biggest stores stock 10 times as many items as the biggest supermarkets in Britain. Should such an out-of-town planning moratorium go, this will further threaten small retailers and make far harder the government's hopes for an integrated transport policy.[11]

Another example of how competition policy can damage smaller shops and consumer choice concerns the OFT. The UK 1998 Competition Act gave 20 per cent extra resources to the OFT to deal with cartels and restrictive behaviour. Much attention has been paid to the high prices that the supermarkets are perceived to charge with their control of more than half the food sold in the UK. Yet the OFT is putting pressure on independent chemists for their price maintenance on over-the-counter medicines. Their present price support stops them being taken over by supermarkets, thus ensuring a wide diversity of supply. This will not be maintained if the OFT is merely driven by considerations of the lowest price levels. Small bookshops have already been adversely affected by the ending of the Net Book Agreement.

## PROTECT THE LOCAL, GLOBALLY COMPETITION POLICY

The crucial goal of such competition policy is a series of measures which discriminate in favour of environmentally and socially enhancing domestic production:

- To ensure production is as diverse and efficient as possible a limit should be set for market share of products by any one company.
- New firms should be encouraged by grants and loans to enter the marketplace. This guarantees the local competition needed to maintain the impetus for improved products, more efficient resource use and the provision of choice.
- The transfer of information and technology globally should be encouraged by new global aid and trade rules (see Chapter 12) to improve the efficiency of local competitiveness. The key to such an approach has to be sustainability and diversity.
- A range of government competition regulations concerned with the structure of industries, or with the behaviour of firms within them, including: favouring monopolies if advantageous to localism (eg the post office); breaking up cartels; retail price maintenance, retained if supporting local economies (eg protecting small chemists); minimum wage; and employment legislation.

### Tackling TNCs

Competition policy must ensure that large companies do not use their power to prevent competition in the market. As companies get larger they have an increasing ability to dominate the market, fix prices via monopolies and form cartels which push local firms out of business. Most competition policy takes place at the national level, but the global activities of TNC require specific action that eventually will need to be coordinated at the economic bloc level and internationally.

TNCs are used to setting up branches in a range of countries to get access to regional markets, and adapting their products for differing areas. Their operations are controlled centrally to ensure maximum profitability. Thus, in the transition to the end goal of localization, a major question for competition policy is how to ensure the activities of TNCs are steered to this end, rather than to exhorbitant international profit levels. Part of the answer will lie in the limitation of market share of any one entity; another will be to ensure fair competition when TNCs get involved in national joint ventures or franchising (ie the licensed use by independent firms of a business system and brand name for which a royalty is paid).

The requirement for strict transparency and disclosure rules to prevent TNCs from transfer pricing will be of key relevance. This concerns transactions between firms and their branches, subsidiaries or affiliates in other countries. By using suitable transfer prices a TNC can shift overall profits between different parts of the same business and where a government has high taxes and rigorous rules, the profit is registered as low, zero or a loss thus depriving governments of the taxes they are owed. It may also be advantageous to minimize profits in a country more likely to attract criticism or the attention of regulators.

Actual figures for this activity are inevitably hard to find. However, in 1990 a US Congressional Committee calculated that just 36 TNC's had used transfer pricing to avoid paying US$100 billion in US taxes in the 1980s. A survey of the 12 major Japanese TNCs manufacturing in the UK showed the average taxation to turnover was 0.4 per cent. Thus, the Japanese companies paid only £44.1 million in taxes, against a turnover of £11.2 billion. A sample of 33 well-known UK companies showed that in the same year they paid 3.8 per cent. One calculation suggests that the UK Government lost £380 million from these 12 TNCs in 1992 alone.[12]

Where there is a competitive market in similar products produced domestically then blatant cheating through transfer pricing becomes more apparent. Even if a TNC involvement in the local market was via a joint venture it would still be competing with domestic competitors and so any transfer pricing would be easier to detect.

## UN Suggestions for International Competition Policy

The United Nations Conference on Trade and Development (UNCTAD) produced a set of principles and rules for the control of restrictive business practices that was passed by the UN General Assembly in 1980. These were subsequently strengthened in a follow-up resolution in 1990. The 1980 report was also used as the competition policy in the non-binding Draft United Nations Code of Conduct on Transnational Corporations.[13]

These UN rules and codes all suffered though from the overarching acceptance of 'the benefits that should arise from the liberalization of tariff and non-tariff barriers affecting international trade'. They also called, albeit with an emphasis on developing countries, for 'Promoting the establishment or development of domestic industries and the economic development of other sectors of the economy' and 'Encouraging their economic development through regional or global arrangements among developing countries.'

With localization as the overarching end goal, the details in these documents, no matter how flawed some of their premises may be, could still be a basis for the practicalities of setting up effective national, regional and international competition policy. The proposed UN measures covered:

- principles and rules for enterprises, including transnational corporations;
- principles and rules for states at national, regional and subregional levels;
- international measures:
- international institutional machinery;
- consultations;
- technical assistance.

## Chapter 10

# Taxes for Localization

*'Fiscal policy: the use of taxation and government expenditure to influence the economy, it can be used both to influence the level of aggregate demand in the economy, and to change the incentives facing firms and individuals so as to encourage or discourage particular forms of activity.'*[1]

*'Public finances are one of the best starting points for an investigation of a society. The spirit of a people, its cultural level, its social structure, the deeds its policy may prepare – all this and more is written in its fiscal history, stripped of all phrases. He who knows how to listen to the message here discerns the thunder of world history more clearly than anything else.'*[2]

The debate about taxation's role in ensuring a decent quality of life needs to be broadened. In the last 20 years, tax rises have been thought of as bad and as too much revenue diverted to an inefficient 'nanny' state. What needs to be reasserted is that taxes are socially necessary, but their effectiveness is determined by how they are raised and what they are used for. They should provide incentives to improve environmental standards and funds to restructure the economy in a sustainable and more equitable way and to enable society to do things that otherwise could not be achieved by individuals.

## DIFFERENT TYPES OF TAXES

Direct or progressive taxation (ie on income and capital) in principle shifts resources from the richer to the poor, and is therefore a commendable thing. But in practice:

*'A policy of increasing direct taxes, even where the money is used exclusively to reduce it for others, appears to lead to enormous problems in the political market place... It worries people trying to manage the household budget, who imagine it*

*will hit them wherever the actual cut-off is; it has become associated with putting a cap on aspirations... the redistribution it represents seems to many to be an attack on hard workers and achievers in favour of lazy good-for-nothings...'[3]*

Direct taxes are also easier to evade and avoid than indirect taxation.

An indirect tax is a tax on spending on goods and services, eg value-added tax (VAT) on energy, or taxes on alcohol and tobacco. The term indirect is used because it is usually assumed that the tax will be paid by the consumer, rather than the firm immediately responsible for paying it. In reality, the degree by which such a tax can be passed on depends on the level of demand and whether the supplier, such as a state energy company, has captive customers dependent on one source. The other major form of indirect taxation is a sales tax, normally a fixed percentage of total sales for some classes of goods and services.

It is thought that the public may therefore be happier to pay indirect taxes than direct ones. (However, when direct tax rise proposals are linked to public concerns like health or education there is considerable support.) In the UK, resistance to a VAT rise on fuel did cause outrage and was reversed. Other indirect taxes, which less obviously hurt pensioners and the very poor, such as those on insurance and holiday flights, have provoked less opposition. The public appears not to be strongly against indirect tax mainly because it is a less obvious deduction from their basic pay. They also feel that expenditure taxes have a choice element, since in many cases the taxed item doesn't have to be bought. In addition, if people can be convinced that the tax influences behaviour in a way they generally approve of, such as tobacco and green taxes, less hostility is felt.[4]

Polls in the EU and the US have found that 70 per cent of people support the idea of green tax reform once it is described. In a 1998 US poll conducted by Friends of the Earth (FoE) 71.5 per cent were in favour of cutting taxes from income and payrolls and putting them on fossil fuel energy sources, with support cutting across party lines.[5]

Of course this is not an argument against direct taxes, which are a crucial source of government funds and potentially the most efficient way to promote more equality. Also, care must be taken because indirect taxes can hit the poorer sections of society disproportionately and could be inflationary (see below).

## Taxes for Localization

Ecological taxes on energy, other resource use and pollution would help pay for the radical economic transition towards the *Protect the*

*Local, Globally* form of localization. They would be environmentally advantageous and could allow for the removal or reduction of taxes on labour and limitations on direct taxation. Competition from regions without such taxes would be minimized by the reintroduced tariffs and controls explained in Chapter 6. For the environment in general, relocalization would mean less long-distance transportation and energy use and resulting pollution. Also, any adverse environmental effects would be experienced locally, thus increasing the pressure, impetus and potential for control and improved standards.

The environment will be better protected under this system than under any attempt to put minor environmental constraints on liberalization of trade. Today's system inevitably sacrifices adequate local environmental protection measures, as they are deemed to make a nation uncompetitive. Industry's ability to use this argument to block proposals for relatively anodyne increase in energy taxes in the EU, the US and Japan is testament to this process. Similarly, meaningful steps towards dealing with global warming at the various international meetings of the climate convention have been curtailed by arguments about threats to competitiveness.[6]

## RESOURCE TAXES

Most serious environmental threats arise from the economy's failure to value and account for environmental damage. Because those causing the harm do not pay the full costs, other parts of society and the planet have had to bear them, for example pollution from fossil fuel use in power stations or cars. By taxing products and activities which pollute, deplete or otherwise degrade the environment, governments can cause some environmental costs to be taken into account in commercial or private decisions. Each individual producer or consumer then decides how to adjust to the higher costs. Such taxes are what economists call 'corrective taxes'. They improve the functioning of the market by making prices reflect an activity's true cost. If the undesirable act costs more, there will be an incentive to reduce the amount of undesirable acts that happen.

The other advantage of resource taxes is that they can provide enormous amounts of revenue quite quickly – particularly an energy tax. Such a tax need not be dramatic in the first stage, but its continued increase can provide both growing revenue and the signal to society that the sooner it changes the better. One suggestion from Professor von Weizsäcker of Essen University is the introduction of Ecological Tax Reform whereby taxes would involve a steady price increase of some 5 per cent annually over some 30 to 40 years for fossil fuels and nuclear energy, as well as for other 'problematic natural resources ... to provide strong and enduring incentives to invest in new technologies geared to reducing significantly the energy and raw material inputs per given unit of output'.[7]

An energy tax would have other localist benefits. The increased financial costs of transportation and the lessening of dependence on imported energy, with the shift to local renewable energy sources and energy efficiency, would speed up the trend for regional self-reliance. Most governments raise the bulk of their revenue by taxing income, profits and the value added to goods and services. While convenient to collect and often serving a crucial redistributive purpose, they are thought to distort the economy to some extent by discouraging work, savings and investment. Taxing resource use, such as energy, changes behaviour by taxing the bad and part of the revenue generated can then be used to ensure that taxes on the good (eg labour and investment) aren't increased or are even decreased.

## How Resource Taxes Help the Environment

Energy taxes will not only ensure the shift towards localization, they will play a key role in tackling the world's greatest environmental threat – climate change. To understand the scale of changes necessary to prevent this process reaching disastrous proportions[8] it is necessary to consider one of the few scenarios radical enough to significantly improve the situation.[9] This scenario achieves greater than 50 per cent fossil fuel reductions within 30–50 years, calls for global carbon emissions to be halved from current levels by 2030 and down by 70 per cent by 2075.

The main changes would be in buildings, which would use less than 20 per cent of current average consumption, transport systems with car efficiency approaching 100 miles per gallon (Imperial) and widespread mass transit systems in cities, and the development of biofuels for transport and products formerly made from chemicals. Industrial processes and machinery would also have huge improvements in their energy efficiency.

Taxes to help achieve this would include carbon taxes on fossil fuel use in power stations and transportation, road pricing, capacity-kilometre tax for efficient lorry space use, increased company car taxation, car tax to reflect fuel efficiency and parking tax.[10]

Resource taxes can also help phase out other economic activities that contribute to climate change, such as logging of old growth forests, the production of chlorine-based ozone layer depleting chemicals, and agrochemicals. The extent of the tax and the rate at which it increases over time will depend on the rate at which the activities in question must be phased out.

Other resource taxes range from quarrying and other mining taxes, to encourage more efficient use of raw materials, landfill taxes and packaging taxes to discourage over-packaging, agricultural input tax for discouraging fertilizer and pesticides as would water pollution taxes. The latter also encourage the shift to more organic agriculture.

One of the best examples of a successful resource tax is the water pollution levies in the Netherlands. Starting in 1970 these gradually increased charges on emissions of organic material and heavy metals into canals, rivers, and lakes. Between 1976 and the mid-1990s, emissions of cadmium, chromium, copper, lead, nickel and zinc into waters managed by regional governments plummeted 72–99 per cent, primarily because of pollution taxes. The demand for pollution control equipment has also resulted in the country becoming a leading exporter of such technology.[11] The United States, Australia and Denmark used taxes on CFCs to help their phase-out by 1996. This was achieved in less than a decade, as required by the 1987 Montreal Protocol to protect the ozone layer.[12]

### Other Taxes

Other ways of raising taxes include a land-rent tax and a Tobin Tax. The land-rent tax on the area of land owned, perhaps differentiated by use, would raise money and would, within a democratic planning system, encourage a more efficient use of land. It would also increase the likelihood of housing at present kept empty being brought into use.

The Tobin Tax, which is a key part of controlling capital (see Chapter 8), is named after the Nobel Laureate Dr James Tobin, who first proposed it. It is a tax on international currency transactions, estimated to be in the order of US$1.5 trillion per day. A tax of merely 0.25 per cent would yield US$250 billion annually. (The United Nations estimates that US$225 billion per year would eradicate the worst forms of poverty and environmental destruction.)[13] Even if the tax reduced the volume of transactions, which is a desirable goal, it would still yield considerable sums during the transition period to localization.

## How Resource Taxes Could Create Jobs

The transition to more environmentally sustainable local economies would have huge job-creating potential. Examples include improving energy efficiency of most of the building stock, developing renewable energy sources on a substantial scale, increasing public transport and making agriculture organic and hence more labour intensive. The resource taxes would be a major funding source for such a labour intensive transition, particularly if they also cut taxes on labour.

A study by Cambridge Econometrics modelled the effects on jobs between 1997 and 2005 of recycling the revenues from green taxes to reduce employers' payroll tax, ie National Insurance Contributions. The main elements of the package were a commercial and industrial energy tax, a waste-disposal tax, higher fuel tax, a quarrying tax, reform of company car tax and an office-parking tax. The result was a reduction of carbon emissions by 9.5 per cent in 2005. Reduction in other emissions of key pollutants included from road transport, 19 per cent; iron and steel, 18 per cent; chemicals, 12 per cent and other industry, 10 per cent. There was also a substantial reduction in the amount of waste produced, total waste production falling by 16 per cent in 2005.

This package resulted in 717,000 extra jobs by 2005. Official unemployment fell by 300,000, the discrepancy being because not all those who fill the new jobs are registered as unemployed. Two thirds of the new jobs are full-time. Health and social work gains 141,000 jobs, business services 91,000, education 61,000, and construction 50,000. Employment in manufacturing also increases substantially.

Instead of all the green tax revenue going to cut payroll tax, another model allowed for some money to be used to mitigate the effects of tax rises. This approach cut the standard rate of VAT to help low income households, and offset some of the increased cost of motoring, and also reduced business rates to help small businesses; 576,000 jobs were still generated. Of course, all such modelling has to be treated with a degree of caution, but does show the overall potential of resource taxes to help tackle unemployment, whilst generating substantial environmental improvements.

### The Role of Regulations

Regulations play an important role in ensuring that resource taxes achieve the desired results. To change behaviour requires, for example, efficiency standards, subsidies and public education campaigns. But the advantage of taxes over just regulations is that they can prompt the development of technology and processes which may go far beyond standards set by any regulations. Regulations often soon become too weak, and require enormous political effort to upgrade.

# REDIRECTING SUBSIDIES AND ENCOURAGING MORE BENIGN TECHNOLOGIES

A mixture of taxes, redirection of subsidies and legislation can change the direction of research and development (R&D) as well as speeding up the use of existing technology. This in turn can reduce the price, increasing demand and so on in a virtuous circle. This approach can cut out the most inefficient and dirty technology, which causes a disproportionate amount of pollution, while rewarding clean technology.

Successful examples of better energy use from all over the world, documented by the International Energy Authority, the Dutch Ministry of Finance and Rocky Mountain Institute[14] detail a package of policies to result in a dramatic reduction of fossil fuel use:

- Introducing energy taxes which reflect the damage caused by energy use, with recycling of tax revenue to reduce labour taxes and provide investment incentives for energy efficiency, co-generation and renewable energy.
- Removing all remaining subsidies for fossil fuels and nuclear power, estimated by the OECD to be US$215–235 billion per annum.
- Removing the wider range of market barriers to energy efficiency and renewable energy.
- Setting tough minimum efficiency standards for buildings, appliances, industrial processes and vehicles.
- Introducing local and national government purchasing programmes for energy efficient equipment and renewable energy technologies.
- Shifting energy R&D away from fossil fuels and nuclear power towards energy efficiency and renewables.

## Goodbye Fossilized Subsidies

Using amongst other things the constant argument of the need to be internationally competitive, the fossil fuel lobby has been able to misdirect between an estimated US$200–300 billion per annum.[15] In the 1995–96 US election cycle for example, oil and gas companies gave US$11.8 million to congressional candidates to protect tax breaks worth at least US$3 billion over the period. If the US national security cost of oil, via the maintenance of oil-rich regimes friendly to the west, are taken into account the subsidy reaches US$57 billion per year, or approximately US$9.19 per barrel of oil used in the US.[16]

A commitment to the phase-out of fossil fuels would allow the shift of these vast subsidies onto renewable energy. Public transport could be hugely expanded globally if the, at least, US$500 billion a year estimated to be spent on highways for the motor industry, were redirected.[17]

Another huge source of damaging subsidies are the aid agencies such as the World Bank, other multilateral development banks and bilateral agencies. They subsidize OECD companies to fund large-scale fossil fuel power stations, environmentally destructive infrastructure projects like large dams, and highways through forested areas. In Eastern Europe, the European Bank for Reconstruction and Development is bailing out beleaguered international nuclear industry by continuing to fund new nuclear power stations. This despite the fact that since 1948 this failed technology, and its R&D, has been subsidized to the tune of US$34 billion.[18]

## Technological Forcing

Redirecting technological progress such that more is done with less is a key environmental goal and is made more possible by the tax policies of localization. In the words of Amory Lovins:

> '*In the past, progress was the increase in labour productivity... resource productivity is equally important and should now be pursued as the highest priority... [this is] not the same as doing less, doing worse or doing without. Efficiency does not mean curtailment, discomfort or privation.*'[19]

Lovins maintains that resource productivity can – and should – grow fourfold, ie the amount of wealth extracted from one unit of natural resources can quadruple. Numerous scattered instances already exist and have come from skilled scientists and technologists, city planners and architects, engineers, chemists and farmers. He has gathered 50 detailed examples worldwide including super fuel-efficient cars, highly energy-efficient buildings, household appliances, lights, office equipment, motors, air conditioning; ultra efficient recycling and reusing of materials ranging from demolished buildings, wrapping plastic through to water; and local food production to reduce transport and highly efficient train and bus systems. The policies of localization would allow these instances to be much more widely spread.

Such leapfrogging of old and inefficient infrastructure is particularly relevant to the developing world and Eastern Europe. In the former, less of their capital is sunk in inefficient infrastructure, and in the latter public transport and much of their agriculture are less far down the energy and resource wasteful route than the rich countries. What is required by both is for radical improvements in their manufacturing and services, such as the examples above. It is key that aid policies (in conjunction with regulations, resource taxes and resource efficiency producing subsidies) facilitate these improvements.[20]

# MAKING HIGHER RESOURCE TAXES MORE ACCEPTABLE

High energy and other resource taxes are unlikely to be politically feasible unless some of the tax revenue is spent on ways to lessen any adverse effects.

## Protecting the Poor

To protect the poor, whose energy bills are highest relative to their incomes, some revenue from energy taxes can be steered into welfare benefits or into a flat-rate energy allowance (a certain amount of energy obtainable at a guaranteed low rate). Also, with the potential for overall direct taxes to be lowered, or not increased, it might be more politically palatable to raise taxes on the rich, and lower those on the poor.

All this depends very much on the structure of such taxes and can be compensated for to a degree by exemptions (such as VAT on food), or by giving the poor 'free' allowances (eg each person having a VAT-free allowance of fuel). Compensating funds can be provided by making items that feature more in the budgets of richer people subject to higher rates of indirect tax. The Institute for Fiscal Studies has shown how a carbon tax can be used to offset negative results for the poor by spending a lot of the money raised on services that improve the quality of life for the lower income groups.[21] This could involve grants for insulating houses and putting in more efficient heating systems.

Indirect taxes can also be used for benefits in kind, that is to provide things that are disproportionately useful and used by poorer households such as public services like health, housing and education. This plus the other *Protect the Local, Globally* measures to maximize domestic provision, would help reduce national deficit problems by reducing the needs for imports of energy or goods. It is always the poor who bear the brunt of the normal strategies used to cope with these deficit problems, ie higher interest rates, value added taxes and cuts in social infrastructure and services.

Finally, it is often assumed that environmental issues in the North are predominantly a middle-class concern. Although that might be true of many of the spokespeople and full-time workers for the environmental NGOs, it is certainly less true when looking on the ground, where poor people suffer more. Pollution tends to be concentrated around industrial sights, not in the leafy suburbs. Waste disposal facilities are more likely to be in poorer areas.

Nowhere is this more evident than in the US, where a wide-ranging grassroots Environmental Justice movement has grown out of increasing awareness that poorer communities, and in particular ethnic communities, live in the worst environments: 75 per cent of toxic waste in the southern US is disposed of in black communities, which make up 25 per cent of the population.[22]

Although environmental issues affect everyone, they do not affect everyone equally. Thus tax measures which improve the environment are likely to be a of disproportionate benefit to the poorer areas, provided the above compensatory measures are also taken into account.

## Curbing Inflation

One of the major objections to energy and other resource taxes is that they will cause prices to rise and be inflationary. The most effective way to counter this is to use some of the funds for cuts in income, payroll and corporation tax, or for guarantees for the period of the energy tax of no increase in such taxes. Reducing other taxes on spending, such as VAT, will also dampen any inflationary effect. Also, if governments announce well in advance plans for real energy prices to rise and stay up permanently, investors will bring forward investments to reduce energy and pollution bills. This process can be helped by some of the resource tax funds being used for subsidies for adapting to more environmentally efficient behaviour, and also to assist in the provision of less polluting substitutes, eg improved public transport or R&D into new technologies. All these measures have the potential to eventually stabilize or further reduce prices, once the transition is in place.

# Chapter 11

# Democratic Localism

---

'Civil society offers us a single civic identity that, belonging neither to state bureaucrats nor private consumers but to citizen's alone, recouples rights and responsibilities and allows us to take control of our governments and our markets. Civil society is the domain of citizens: a mediating domain between private markets and big government.'[1]

'My concern is not with capitalism but with civil society and what capitalism does to it, not with religion or ethnicity but with citizenship and how fundamentalist zealotry can undermine it. We need markets to generate productivity, work and goods: and we need culture and religion to assure solidarity, identity and social cohesion – and a sense of human spirit. But most of all, we need democratic institutions capable of preserving our liberty even in parochial communities: and capable of maintaining our equality and our precious differences even in capitalist markets.'[2]

Democracy in its broadest sense is now the dominant political process globally. In 1974 less than one third of the world's countries were democracies, by 1998 that proportion had risen to 60 per cent.[3] In this worldwide shift people are demanding a greater say in the way their governments are run. Demands for increased decentralization are often a part of this trend.[4]

Democracy should not just be considered as an electoral input over who controls the economy, but also in terms of access to participation in the economy and the development of individuals' and local communities' potential and capacities.

The Canadian Centre for Policy Alternatives has suggested that the goals for such an 'active democracy' should be:

- creating a strong industrial, commercial and service base to increase wealth, options and skills;

- building a comprehensive social infrastructure eg transportation, housing, communications, health, child care, education, environmental protection; this sustains and supports industry and commerce, but is also fundamental to removing barriers to universal participation;
- strengthening individual economic rights (eg the basic right to productive employment and livelihoods, education and training and culture);
- sustaining and rejuvenating the natural environment.[5]

A diverse local economy is the possible route for such an 'active democracy'. In terms of specific day-to-day involvement, to produce the maximum goods and services required as close to the point of consumption as possible will increase the likelihood of a wide range of people's active participation. This wider economic involvement needs to go hand in hand with wider political and democratic control and accountability at the local level. This will help ensure as broad as possible a distribution of the ensuing benefits. To use an environmental metaphor, it involves the stability of diversity as compared with globalization's move to the ever fewer providers of an economic monoculture. The recent rash of mergers and acquisitions involving banks, oil companies, IT companies, car producers and the like are the latest testimony to this latter trend.

Of course local control can be in the hands of the few rather than the majority, but there is more potential to curb such trends when control of the local economy is part of a global democratic localism. Today's situation, where democracy is harnessed to the requirements of globalization, is taking the world in the opposite direction.

## GLOBALIZATION'S THREAT TO DEMOCRACY

William Greider exposes how the 'triumphant dogma of free-market capitalism' has a comforting but misleading explanation for how:

> '...*industrial capitalism leads to democracy by a process of gradual evolution. This rationale, though not supported by history, provides a comforting refuge for policy thinkers in many leading nations... (it) is oblivious to the actual experience of industrial societies and the richly complicated social origins of political freedom. England, the United States, France and some other societies did evolve to systems of civil democracy and popular sovereignty, though the consolidation of*

*individual rights was tortuously slow and imperfect, spread across centuries and regularly advanced only by political upheaval and violent conflict... In Germany and Japan the rise of industrial capitalism did not lead to democracy, but to twentieth-century fascism. The repressive corporate states that emerged in those societies were able to supervise enormously productive economic systems without the bother of individual freedoms or electoral accountability.'*[6]

Destructive upheavals have often been the prerequisite for dramatic shifts to greater democracy. The French Revolution, the UK and US Civil Wars and the Second World War provide enough examples to prompt the need to learn from history. Likewise, increased internal inequalities, or threats from external aggression are a common historical precursor to democracy.

Today, the social damage is frequently caused by globalization. The rising inequality and insecurity experienced by most countries (see Chapters 14 and 17), particularly in the developing world and Eastern Europe, have contributed to the rise of external conflicts and internal upheavals. A dramatic example of this is Yugoslavia. Although often put down to historic ethnic classes, more careful examination has shown how the IMF's rigid structural adjustment policies provided the inequality, unemployment and insecurity that enabled demagogues like Milosovich to seriously damage a once relatively prosperous country.[7]

In addition, the environmental degradation that follows in the wake of producing the exports of ever cheaper minerals, timber, fish and cash crops is causing the number of environmental refugees to exceed those displaced by armed conflict.[8]

This is also the threat to the overall stability of the global economic system of globalization's reduction of effective demand. The need to be internationally competitive is reducing jobs through automation, relocation and curbed public expenditure (see Chapter 14). The only exception is a handful of richer countries, particularly the US, where the ability to go too easily into debt has kept consumer demand high.

Of course such trends might result in the kinds of backlash that could eventually result in greater democracy. However, such an end result is far from guaranteed and in any case will result in huge global upheavals and increased misery, before anything gets significantly better. The crucial lesson is to take these adverse trends as a warning and change direction to increase economic and political democracy now. Although the number of countries qualifying as democratic is increasing, the conditions for a growing number of their peoples are worsening. This is due in considerable part to globalization and the workings of its trade rules (see Part Three). The backlash to the insecurity inherent in this process has contributed to the rise of extreme-right political parties bent on stifling the democratic choices for sections of their populations.

There is though a growing worldwide realization that globalization's policies cause these problems. This understanding was in evidence in the massive protests at the WTO's Ministerial Meeting in Seattle at the end of 1999 and the calls for a halt to further liberalization and for the WTO's rules to be revised and reviewed.

However, the World Bank in its 1999/2000 World Development Report is stating the exact opposite. It equates the rise in trade liberalization with the rise in the number of countries now termed democratic. This trend and the move to decentralization that often accompanies it is now being defined by the World Bank as 'localization' (see Chapter 17). It asserts that: 'Localization is the push to expand popular participation in politics and to increase local autonomy in decision making.'[9]

The World Bank is adamant that trade liberalization is the best route to tackle the problems of the developing world and so its form of localization is an adaptation to globalization rather than the rejection of it in this book.

This is the general view of the official free market consensus. For them, democracy also requires trade liberalization for it to be nurtured by economic success. But the international status quo of multilateral banks, economic commentators and the OECD aid donors means that democracy is linked to a damaging set of measures. The reality is that countries have to reorganize their economies to allow ever greater penetration of foreign TNCs, strict curbs on social expenditure and the rise of a powerful strata in society, side by side with rising local inequality. This process ranges from gangster capitalism in Russia, to hi-tech billionaires in the US, to the takeover by foreign companies of sections of the Asian Tiger economies.

For democracy to result in an improvement in the social and economic lot of the vast majority, real local control over the direction, means and end-goal of the way the economy is organized, and who gains and loses from it, is required.

## DEMOCRATIC DEMAND

A broader involvement in the local economy – economic democracy – makes sense since it will increase the range of 'democratic demand'. It is not only crucial that the needs for goods and services be met locally to generate local work, but that people also have the money to obtain adequate quantities of them. 'Democratic demand' is essential to ensure that enough people are directly involved as consumers and producers so that the fruits of localization are both generated on an adequate level in the first place, and spread evenly enough to ensure such demand levels can be maintained. The environmental downside of such consumption is mitigated by the resource taxation programme (as in Chapter 10) and the fact that much of the work will involve face-to-face caring, personal services and cultural pursuits that do not rely solely on physical products.

## THE CITIZEN'S INCOME

A Citizen's Income (sometimes referred to as Basic Income) is probably the most fundamental route to economic democracy, in that it provides the wherewithal for an involvement in the economy as a matter of right. It is a modest payment payable to each individual as a right of citizenship, without means test or work requirement. Depending on its level it could replace all existing social insurance and assistance benefits with a single payment, paid unconditionally. Potentially it could result in huge savings in administration costs. It would also to some extent increase the demand level of the poorest. (For more details of financing the Citizen's Income and how it could become politically feasible, see Appendix II.)

A Citizen's Income would provide a measure of security, making part-time work and self-employment more attractive, allowing people to develop less rigid patterns of working more consistent with their own needs. It would thus help the economy move towards higher levels of employment. It would also help those desiring to enter higher education, training or retraining at any stage of their lives. The financial position of those unable to engage in full-time work because of caring responsibilities would also be improved, whether involving children, the elderly or disabled relatives.

Most pensioners who rely chiefly on the state pension are entitled to Income Support, but one million pensioners do not claim it and others are ineligible because they have saved a little capital or have small occupational pensions. The introduction of a Citizen's Income would alleviate poverty amongst the poorest pensioners without, according to the Citizen's Income Trust, 'incurring excessive budgetary expenditure.'[10]

A Citizen's Income would distribute economic power. Those in work would pay more taxes, yet the government wouldn't need to use so much tax revenues on today's wide range of benefits. To be effective in encouraging some into work and reducing the pressure on others to work so much or at all, it also needs the backing of sound public sector provision and competent government administration. The Citizen's Income must be seen as a reliable addition to personal or family budgets, and at the same time through, for example, adequate and affordable public health, education and transport, allow people to feel secure enough to review their decision on what form or amount of work they will seek.

A Citizen's Income would enable many people to work shorter hours and share jobs and allow the unemployed to be able to afford to seek work. In addition, the possibility of people working for less could help restore (in tandem with energy, resource and pollution taxation) the cost-effectiveness of good quality, more labour intensive, personalized production. Environmental taxes would remove the price advantage of centralized mass production and bulk transport, employment opportunities could be distributed, rather than centralized as at present. Thus, supportive government spending and a Citizen's Income would allow governments to meet their responsibilities for employment, transport and regional regeneration.

## DEMOCRATIZING THE POLITICAL PROCESS

*'Political marketing is the essential means to win political competition in democratic politics. In the information age it involves media advertising, telephoning banks, targeted mailing, image making, image unmaking, image control, presence in the media, staging of public appearances etc. This makes it an excessively expensive business, way beyond that of traditional party politics, so that mechanisms of political financing are obsolete, and parties use access to power as a way to generate resources to stay in power or to prepare to return to it. This is the fundamental source of political corruption... Those who survive in this world become politically successful, for a while. But what certainly does not survive, after a few rounds of these tricks, is political legitimacy, not to speak of citizen's hope.'*[11]

Announcing new measures in 1999 intended to control and curb political spending, the UK Home Secretary Jack Straw commented:

*'For too long public confidence in the political system has been undermined by the absence of clear, fair and open statutory*

> *controls on how political parties are funded. By providing honesty and openness to our political system, we hope to restore public trust and promote greater confidence in our democracy.*'[12]

Public support for, and hence eventual politician's acceptance of, the *Protect the Local, Globally* policies to achieve localization will probably result from the backlash against the adverse effects of globalization. However, the enthusiasm for such a radical change will need to be maintained. One method is for the fruits of such a transition to be seen clearly to work for the vast majority through the economic democracy of increased involvement in work. But it will also require an active political democracy to ensure that its advantages continue to accrue to the majority and are not usurped by the more powerful sectors of society.

This will require political transparency, not only of politician's policies, but also who funds them towards what ends. The corrosive effects of big money in politics can be seen at its most extreme in America. More than 16 months ahead of the November 2000 election the main Republican contender George W Bush had already raised US$37 million, mostly from business. Al Gore rushed to catch up, with Democratic fundraisers setting themselves the target of US$200 by November 2000.[13] Big business is the major source of such vast sums and, not surprisingly, they bring with their money their own self-interested policy agenda.

When the ceding of governments' power to free trade agreements and the agenda of big business and international finance is compounded by big political donations from vested interests, it is not surprising that confidence in the political system has been seriously undermined. This has contributed to 'why vote?' apathy resulting in ever lower election turnouts in the US and Europe.

Even in the UK the Conservative party raised donations of a staggering £106 million between 1992 and 1997 compared with £39 million for Labour and £9 million for the Liberal Democrats. Unlike in the US this is beginning to be addressed by the New Labour UK Government, who have proposed legislation which would cut political parties' funding to under £20 million for the year before the election. Public declaration of all donations over £5000 would be required and donations from foreigners banned. Political parties will still get free party political broadcasts and election mail. Buying TV and radio political spots remains illegal.

To overcome voter apathy and suspicion, the policies being proposed by politicians everywhere must be clearly seen to benefit the majority, both through democratic demand, furthered by localization, and strict constraints on political funding. This should provide confidence that their parties are not in the pocket of the already powerful, and so democracy on all levels should be permanently strengthened.

## Turning Politicians into 'Trustees'

Peter Brown in his thought-provoking book *Restoring the Public Trust* called for a trust conception of government.[14] This is based on the trustee's legal responsibility to preserve and enhance the assets of the trust, always keeping in mind the good of the beneficiaries – in the case of the political process, the democratic, social and economic rights of citizens. Trusts are set up because there is an asset to be managed for the benefit of someone, with the duties and privileges of the trustees clearly set out. Trustees have to act out of loyalty in the best interests of the beneficiary, not those of the trustees. They must not delegate the entire administration of the trust. They must provide the beneficiary with information concerning the trust, enforce claims on behalf of the trust and make the property productive.

Brown's political twist involves making any constitution and the laws, the documents and instruments of the trust. The assets are the natural resource base, the powers of the state to tax, to provide defence and 'the state's legitimate ability to foster the well-being of both its citizens and the community as a whole'. Politicians must act in the interest of the citizens, not their own; perform not delegate the duties of office, disclose information to the public; defend the assets of the trust from unjust interference, destruction or waste, and preserve and enhance the assets of the trust.

In the trust conception, taxes are an appropriate instrument by which government achieves its legitimate purpose. This is the opposite of the free market view of such taxation as a necessary evil that should interfere with the operation of the market place as little as possible.

At present, particularly in the US, the impartiality of current leaders cannot be trusted since they are 'for sale'. However, it has been calculated by the Congressional Budget Office that if candidates for both Houses of Congress received national funding of a maximum of US$200,000 to cover campaign expenses, then the total cost would be about US$175 million a year. The funds would come in part from general revenues and in part from fines levied against those who do not comply with campaign finance law. As Brown says: 'This is a low price indeed for trustees we can trust.'[15]

## CANADA – A CITIZEN'S PROPOSAL FOR CONCRETE DEMOCRATIC RENEWAL

'*Driven by the doctrine of international competitiveness, Canada's economy has been redirected to serve primarily the external demands of transnational capital rather than the basic needs of our own people. Through its extensive political machinery, Corporate America has been able to ensure that government economic and social policies are redesigned to consolidate this model of development. Despite all the rhetoric about cost-saving efficiencies, however, this corporate model has proven to be enormously wasteful in terms of both human and material resources.*'[16]

'*Once you accept the rules of the corporate model, you find yourself on a slippery slope from which there is no escape. Instead Canada needs to adopt an alternative, more democratic model which puts priority on the development of its citizen's capacities to build up the country's economy and society. According to this model, the democratic development of people's basic needs and their productive capacities would be the primary goal of the nation's economy.*'[17]

Canada's history is one of a mixed economy in which both the public and private sector were looked to as engines of economic and social development. However, in the 1980s and 1990s, Canada was pressurized and persuaded into emulation of the more free market economy of the US, first by the Canada–US Trade Agreement, then the NAFTA and finally via WTO rules. The resulting decline of democratic politics and the emergence of a 'corporate security state' reflect the experiences of many other countries.

The result has been that politicians have increasingly done the bidding of large corporations in what in Canada has become known as 'corporate rule'. The private sector is now prime engine of economic and social development with little government intervention or regulation. The public sector has been wrecked, plants shut down, businesses bankrupted and fish stocks and forests depleted.

Canada has a history of cross-country consultation and town hall meetings to discuss matters of national concern. In 1991–92, the Spicer Commission conducted such an exercise around issues of constitutional reform. The Commission's conclusion was that people wanted more democratic forms of representation, accountability and control over public institutions. This popular demand was due in part to people's sense that: 'traditional Canadian values are being usurped by anonymous market forces and that governments are doing nothing to deal with these.'[18]

## Battling the Undemocratic MAI

The run up to each free trade agreement signed by the Canadian government, saw an increase in local resistance. This culminated in a successful opposition to the MAI in Canada (and indeed across the world).

At the heart of the MAI battle had been a struggle for democratic participation and control. The original process that gave rise to the MAI was a highly elitist and authoritarian example of policy making. The basic components of the treaty were crafted in secret over a two-year period in the basement conference room of the OECD headquarters in Paris. The negotiators of 29 countries worked hand-in-glove with big business associations and leading corporate executives. No authentic citizen's movements were even consulted, let alone involved, during this period.[19]

This battle generated a debate in international citizen's movements about alternative strategies for reregulating global capital flows. Canadian activists initiated in late 1998 a cross-country MAI inquiry and search for alternatives.

The resulting document put democracy at the core of its demands. It stated that there is a need to develop a new framework for looking at investment rules, based on people's fundamental rights as citizens in a democratic society not as the MAI tried to do, to give corporations or investors rights to create 'a constitutional order for the global economy in which the rights of citizen's are subverted, or hijacked, by corporations.'[20]

The inquiry also concluded that the primary goal of economic development should be to ensure the basic democratic rights and needs of people in Canada and elsewhere, and the primary purpose of investment should be the democratic development of peoples.

## Corporation's Democratic Obligations

All industrial capital is the product of present and previous generations of labour, plus state support in terms of provision of physical infrastructure (including transport facilities and social support such as education). Also, in ecological terms, the energy and resources extracted are part of the common global heritage. To such 'stored social value of capital' it has been suggested should be added 'a social mortgage on all capital'. That is, that corporations have a debt, an obligation to invest capital in ways that serve the needs of the people and the planet that helped produce the capital in the first place.[21]

From these various public soundings of Canadian opinion a number of clear demands and suggestions have arisen. They could serve as a useful framework for citizens in all countries to adapt. Three prerequisites for the strategies (already covered in Chapters 7 and 8), include proper taxation of a corporation's real profits, curbing excessive speculation, and the grounding of local capital and production.

## Citizen's Participation and Control

In the process of this fundamental shift of power away from corporations to that of citizens, it is crucial that democratic control involves people having equal access to participation in the economy, that is economic democracy, and also political democracy in the form of concrete opportunities to develop their potential as citizens. People cannot participate effectively if their basic needs are not being met, ranging from limits on excess working time through to a sense of security about the future by, for example, access to education and training facilities. Given the desire to involve people as much as possible a number of new institutional mechanisms are required. These must encourage and maximize citizen's participation in defining development priorities and in planning economic, social and environmental initiatives, especially in local communities.

As the state moves away from serving corporate interests to prioritizing those of its citizens it will also be vital to overcome resistance from senior bureaucracies. New personnel must be given powers to override internal resistance and ensure that the government's plans for democratic reforms are speedily implemented. Concentrations of power in the old bureaucracy must be overcome by a powerful review board to coordinate the government's initiatives. Finally, the operating structures must be made looser and decision-making authority pushed to lower levels, with more citizen's access and decentralized services.

Exhortation and administrative reorganization is only part of what is required. It has been argued that the civil society movement in Canada has been engaged over the last 12 years in its free trade battles not only in an ongoing critique, but a rebuilding of both a democratic politics and a democratic economy.[22] The Citizen's MAI Inquiry, which the Council of Canadians organized, was essentially an exercise in the rebuilding of democratic politics via civil society groups. By the same token, the annual Alternative Budget process that the Canadian Centre of Policy Alternatives coordinates in relation to federal and provincial governments is essentially an exercise in the rebuilding of a more democratic economy. Both crucially develop community-based capacities, ie democratic localism.

## Dismantling Corporate Rule

To dramatically dismantle the corporate state and its mechanisms and influence will require legislative action to eliminate all forms of corporate financing for political parties and election campaigns; impose tight rules on big businesses lobbying and think-tank operations, whilst ensuring greater access to citizen's groups and their think-tanks.

There is also growing interest across Canada in the movement for community economic development (CED) which emphasizes strategies designed to employ local people to produce goods and services for local community needs. These enable citizens to participate in defining development priorities for their local communities, including job creation targets, housing priorities, health care needs, environmental safeguards, education requirements, cultural priorities and a range of related social objectives.

## Involving the 'Social Economy'

Finally, it is crucial that the democratic state should include a strategy that combines economic and social development by uniting the public sector with the 'social economy'. This includes voluntary associations, NGOs, cooperatives, mutual insurers and community economic development enterprises. The state, through the public sector, must play the major role in mobilizing and directing the resources needed to provide and distribute collective social goods in a fair, efficient and equitable manner. However, there is also a vital need to link economic, social and sustainable development initiatives to local community networks and grass roots citizen's movements. This will need some funding to strengthen such a social economy, whilst not undercutting the public sector. This could be achieved by a combination of direct and indirect government grants, and by setting up non-profit funding agencies at arm's length from the government with local stakeholders.

Although very tied to the Canadian experience, this example provides a structure for ensuring a more democratic transition to localization, and so should be relevant to other countries, with suitable national adaptations.

# Chapter 12

# Trade and Aid for Localization

For localization to occur new trade rules are necessary. The current trade rules are overseen by the WTO, which was established on 1 January 1995 representing the culmination of an eight-year process of trade negotiation, known as the Uruguay Round of the GATT. One hundred and thirty-five countries now belong to the WTO, and more continue to join. The WTO is based in Geneva, and is administered by a secretariat which also facilitates ongoing trade negotiations, and oversees trade dispute resolution. It aims to codify trade barriers, prevent increases in tariffs, and promote multilateral negotiations to lower tariffs. The central principles of the WTO, of liberalization, reciprocity, non-discrimination and transparency have already been outlined in Chapter 2.

A *Protect the Local, Globally* set of world trade rules would have completely the opposite end goal and principles. Instead of rules developed under GATT now policed by the WTO, these would be replaced by: The General Agreement on Sustainable Trade (GAST) administered by the World Localization Organization (WLO).

## KEY PROVISIONS OF THE GENERAL AGREEMENT ON SUSTAINABLE TRADE

The end goal of GAST is not to ensure the unimpeded international trade in goods and services, but to strengthen democratic control of trade, to stimulate industries and services that benefit local communities and rediversify local economies. Such a regrounding of production will provide the employment and tax base to allow the diversification of local, more equitable and sustainable economies.

**National Treatment:** Trade will be encouraged but states urged to give favourable treatment to domestic industry and services are prohibited from treating foreign goods and services as favourably as domestic producers.

*Most-Favoured Nation (MFN) Status:* Provided it is not at the expense of domestic goods and services, states will be allowed preferential treatment to goods and services from other states which respect human rights, treat workers fairly, and protect the environment.

*Performance Requirements:* States may impose requirements on foreign companies opening facilities within their country such as to:

- achieve a given level or percentage of domestic content, whilst at the same time ensuring that monopolies do not develop;
- give preference to goods produced locally;
- stipulate a minimum level of local equity participation;
- hire a given level of local personnel and respect labour and environmental standards;
- protect enterprises which serve community needs from unfair foreign competition.

*Standstill and Rollback:* No state party to the GAST can pass laws or adopt regulations that diminish local control of industry and services or that divert investors from giving priority to meeting local needs and existing laws and regulations that give preferential treatment to foreign companies or encourage absentee ownership of community-based enterprises must be rolled back over the next, perhaps, five to ten years.

*Dispute Resolution:* Citizen groups and community institutions should be able to sue companies for violations of this trade code. All judicial and quasi-judicial procedures such as arbitration shall be fully transparent and open to public observation.

There have been other suggestions for improving trade rules and these are summarized in Box 12.1

# WHY WTO RULES MUST CHANGE[5]

This section is written mostly in terms of how the WTO adversely affects the environment. Its adverse effects on employment, social issues, development, food security, animal welfare, culture and human rights are considered in Chapters 14–18, and a more detailed look at the environmental effects is in Chapter 19.

The WTO represents the most important element of an international corporate strategy to codify the rules upon which a global system of investment, production and trade depend. It enjoys broad

# BOX 12.1 CAN FREE TRADE BE IMPROVED?

Most of the changes to the WTO's rules at present being proposed are nowhere near as radical as the GAST. They have been categorized by Graham Dunkley in his comprehensive and insightful book[1] into three alternative trade perspectives: Managed Trade, Fair Trade and Self-Reliant Trade. The latter two usually entail 'non-economic' goals, alternative to those of both mainstrean Free and Managed Trade schools.

## Managed Trade

Managed trade shares many free trade goals and world views, but holds that intervention rather than unrestricted markets is the best route to hi-tech prosperity. It's strategies use tariffs and subsidies and systematic targeting and general planning. They don't include high tariff walls, see themselves as fair and transparent and that the costs of intervention with the market need to be regularly monitored. This approach is said to follow Keynes' idea that every nation has the right to a permanent domestic and trade intervention policy system, so as to ensure control of its own future in a planned way, with some possibility of insulation from the whims of markets and distantly controlled TNCs.[2]

Fair Trade and Self-Reliant Trade advocates believe that a free market world is economically, socially and culturally inequitable, the former advocating social constraints on trade and the latter favouring greatly reduced levels of trade for the sake of national autonomy.

## Fair Trade

Fair Trade is generally defined in the way used by many aid NGO's and ethical consumer groups. It concerns schemes that purchase goods or commodities from developing world producers at 'fair' prices, reflecting the need for a reasonable return. Increasingly, it is also concerned that the good or commodity be produced in a way that minimizes environmental damage, eg organic production of cash crops such as coffee, tea and bananas. It has been found that these projects greatly help developing world farmers and crafts people, increasing their incomes, autonomy and encouraging environmentally sound production methods. At present, this type of trade represents a minuscule 0.03 per cent of developing world exports.[3] However it is a growing 'niche' market with supermarkets recognizing that there are enough wealthier consumers willing to pay a premium for such goods.

Similar views also extend to trade to further improve human or labour rights and more recently animal rights. At present persistent abuses occur and in addition to the adverse effects for the victims, the fact that they can't effectively be challenged by the WTO trade rules means that attempts to improve national and international standards are undermined. Trading advantages can also accrue to the exploiting countries or industries.

## Enforcement of Standards

Avoidance of implementation of standards can be viewed by those trying to protect basic employment rights, human rights, animal rights or environmental standards as hidden subsidies in trade terms. Adherence to such standards generally implies dearer wages and higher product costs. Those countries not having or enforcing such regulations are therefore at an unfair competitive advantage. Fair traders with these concerns tend to call for one of three things. Firstly 'basic rights' system involving a selected but limited set of labour rights, usually based on the ILO's standards. Although these conventions have been signed by over 150 countries (more than in the WTO), they are often poorly enforced by member governments. The moderate International Confederation of Free Trade Unions (ICFTU) and some Asian trades unions favour this. The ICFTU proposes that all WTO members be required to ratify the key ILO standards relating to free association, bargaining rights, abolition of forced and child labour.

A second approach is to call for a 'social chapter' like that of the EU, requiring WTO members to grant a range of human, labour, social, and welfare rights. The third, more radical, version calls for a 'unit cost equalization' system based on the specification of minimum wages and conditions, though not actual wage rates. The aim being to minimize international 'unit cost gaps' as calculated on the basis of relative productivity and real wage rates. This is sometimes advocated in tandem with the unrealistic idea that developing world wages could be dragged upwards so as to generate markets for developed world exports.

Such systems would be enforced by sanctions such as withdrawal of trade concessions, tariffs against social or environmental dumping and anti-(social) dumping duties equivalent to the supposed hidden subsidy. (Such sanctions to be applied bilaterally, regionally or multilaterally. The latter perhaps through an addendum to Article XXe of GATT, which at present allows the banning of goods produced by prison labour.)

## Self-Reliant Trade

Self-reliant trade is not autarchy (or isolationism), neither is it self-sufficiency where some importation of necessities or exotics is allowed. Self-reliance 'seeks only to eschew heavy trade dependence for key capital, consumer, food, energy, cultural or social requirements'.[4] The latter goes some way towards the approach advocated in this book. Dunkley's view proposes a fusion of these approaches: a strategy of Managed trade, but one which incorporates international labour and social standards and which is directed at longer term self-reliance, along with other less growth-orientated, non-economic goals. An alternative world order centred around non-growth goals, less materialistic values and a reformed, UN-linked WTO could produce a more equitable, sustainable world without the need for 'deep integrated' globalism of the sort which may risk the sovereignty and diversity of societies.

It is however impossible to conceive how trade liberalization can be adapted in any meaningful way without fundamentally contesting international competitiveness and replacing it with trade localization as in this book (see Part Three).

support from many governments, founded on their faith that sustained, market-driven growth will bring them wealth and economic stability. What is absent from this is any notion of ecological limits, or addressing how the proceeds of growth will be distributed. Also missing is any real evidence to support these grand claims.

## The WTO and the Global Economy

Because it sets out a comprehensive set of rules intended to guide all aspects of global economic activity, the WTO will undoubtedly exert a profound influence over the future course of human affairs. *Indeed, it is not unrealistic to regard the WTO as representing effective world government for the first time in human history. There are several reasons that justify such an assessment.*

Historically, trade agreements were concerned with the trade of goods across international borders. But under the WTO, international trade agreements have been dramatically extended to include investment measures, intellectual property rights, domestic regulations of all kinds, and services. In other words, a great many areas of government policy and law that have very little, if anything, to do with trade per se. It would now be difficult to identify an issue of social, cultural, economic or environmental significance that would *not* fall within the ambit of these rules of 'trade'.

The WTO has powerful enforcement tools to ensure that all governments respect its limits on their authority. Any government found in breach is vulnerable to sanctions that are too severe for even the wealthiest nation to ignore. For example, in the first trade complaint to be resolved under the WTO, US Clean Air Act Regulations were deemed to violate WTO rules. The US was given two options – remove the offending provisions of its environmental statute or face retaliatory trade sanctions to the order of US$150 million a year.[6]

While previous trade agreements allowed for similar sanctions, they could only be imposed with the consent of all GATT members, including the offending country. Now, WTO rulings are automatically implemented unless blocked by a consensus of WTO members. Under the rules of 'cross-retaliation', sanctions can be applied to *any* aspect of the offending country's international trade – in other words, where it will be felt the most.

The convergence of these factors explains why the WTO is likely to emerge as the most important international institution ever to have been created.

## A Bill of Rights for TNCs

'Thus, when government consulted on trade matters, it looked exclusively to the business community; that is, large corporations with a substantial stake in international trade. Trade advisory committees, with very few exceptions, represented exclusive clubs for multinational corporations.'[7]

Because of the strategic nature of the interests at stake, trade negotiations have always been conducted behind closed doors, with little being revealed until negotiations are virtually concluded. Not only is there no public input or accountability, but many governments – particularly those from developing countries – are also left guessing about negotiations which take place almost exclusively in secrecy among a few key players.

When agreements do emerge, they are presented as an intricate and complex set of strategic compromises that will unravel should amendments be proposed. In this way, the normal processes of parliamentary or congressional debate are superseded. Law-makers are presented with a virtual ultimatum – accept the entire package of trade proposals or suffer the consequences of being isolated in a global economy.

Because trade agreements are negotiated in this way, they are preoccupied with the interests of large corporations and reveal virtual indifference to the impacts of these commercial interests on other societal goals, such as environmental protection, democratic processes, workers' rights, or cultural integrity.

## Freeing Corporations from Government Regulation

The WTO's goal is to deregulate international trade, with one important exception - the corporate protectionism of patent laws. Otherwise WTO rules seek to limit the capacity of governments to regulate international trade. They represent little more than extensive lists of policies, laws and regulations that governments *cannot* establish.

Some of these prohibit measures intended to regulate international commerce, such as controls on trade in endangered species or bans on tropical timber imports. But many others prohibit regulations that might only *indirectly* influence trade, such as recycling requirements, energy efficiency standards or food safety regulations. Other rules go even further by prescribing government measures that have nothing to do with trade – for example, prohibitions against government efforts to regulate the activities of foreign investors.

# DETAILED REWRITING OF RULES FOR A WORLD LOCALIZATION ORGANIZATION

The WTO is comprised of more than 12 distinct trade agreements. Among these, and forming the essential platform upon which the others are established, is the original GATT, first negotiated in 1947 as part of the Bretton Woods agreements that also established the IMF and World Bank. This is now known as GATT 1994, but throughout this text, simply as GATT. Other agreements of critical importance from a social and environmental perspective include:

- Agreement on Technical Barriers to Trade (TBT)
- Agreement on Sanitary and Phytosanitary Standards (SPS)
- Agreement on Trade-Related Aspects of Intellectual Property Rights (TRIPS)
- Agreement on Trade-Related Investment Measures (TRIMs)
- Agreement on Agriculture
- Agreement on Dispute Resolution

Each of these is now described briefly along with the changes that would be needed to them to meet the *Protect the Local, Globally* goal for the WLO.

## GATT 1994

The most important provisions of this core trade agreement can be found in four articles, as follows.

### Article I – Most-Favoured Nation Treatment

The MFN rule requires WTO member countries to treat 'like' products from a WTO member as favourably as it does from any other member. In other words, discriminating against foreign producers is prohibited.

This rule raises serious doubts about the validity of international environmental agreements, which actually require that less-favourable treatment be accorded to countries if, for example, they are not living up to their obligations under these environmental conventions. As a recent WTO case involving banana trade between several Caribbean islands and Europe illustrates, the MFN rule also prohibits the use of special trading relationships to support development assistance programmes to poorer nations.

Under the GAST rules of the WLO, this would be changed to the following:

*Provided it is not at the expense of domestic goods and services, states shall give preferential treatment to goods and services from other states which respect human rights, treat workers fairly, and protect the environment.*

### Article III – National Treatment

The National Treatment rule requires all trading parties to treat 'like' products of member nations as favourably as it treats its own domestic products. Thus, under the WTO it is unlawful for governments to discriminate against goods because of concerns about the destructive or unethical processes that may have been used to produce or harvest them. By the same measure, it is unlawful under these rules for governments to favour goods on the grounds that they are the product of more sustainable or humane systems of production.

When the principle of National Treatment or MFN status is applied to foreign investors – read corporations – the result spells disaster for efforts to foster domestic economic development. Often TNCs are given more rights in deciding *how* a nation should develop than that nation's government. Moreover, these rules abdicate to international market forces the critical role of allocating precious and often non-renewable natural resources.

This would be changed under the GAST rules of the WLO to:

*Trade controls that increase local employment with decent wages, enhance protection of the environment, ensure adequate competition and consumer protection, and otherwise improve the quality of life in communities and regions within states which are parties to the WLO are encouraged. States are urged to give favourable treatment to domestic industry and services which further these goals and are prohibited from treating foreign goods and services as favourably as domestic producers.*

### Article XI – Elimination of Quantitative Restrictions

Under this article, WTO members cannot limit or impose quantitative controls on exports or imports through quotas or bans. But duties, tariffs and other charges are allowed. This is also problematic from an environmental perspective. Consider the implications of such a rule when applied to such measures as an export ban on unprocessed resources such as raw logs; or as an embargo against the export of agricultural commodities from a country suffering food shortages; or as a prohibition against trade in endangered species; or as a ban on the export of hazardous wastes to developing countries.

This would be changed under the GAST rules of the WLO to:

> *Provided it is not at the expense of domestic goods and services, trade controls via quotas, bans, duties, tariffs and other charges on exports or imports should give preferential access to goods and services going to and coming from other states which in the process of production, provision and trading respect human rights, treat workers fairly, and protect the environment.*

### Article XX – General Exceptions to WTO Rules

This allows, provided it is not arbitrary or unjustifiably restrictive, the adoption or enforcement of measures to protect public morals, to protect human, animal and plant life or health, or the natural conservation of exhaustible natural resources.

This would be extended under the GAST rules of the WLO to:

> *Article XX exemptions should allow trade intervention for a wide range of purposes that further sustainable and more equitable localization, eg sanctions against human rights violations; 'red tariffs' for the enforcement of labour rights and other 'social clause' questions; 'green tariffs' for the maintenance of environmental, food, health, animal rights standards; enforcement of ecological and labour rights treaties; cultural protection, primarily the allowance of discrimination in favour of local films, TV programmes and publications; and centrally community preservation, to facilitate the local economy within regional development.*

### Agreement on Technical Barriers to Trade

In the jargon of international trade law, *all* environmental standards and regulations are, *prima facie*, considered technical barriers to trade. The actual provisions of the TBT agreement are detailed and complex, but reduced to bare bones, it establishes:

- An international regime for harmonizing environmental standards that effectively creates a ceiling – but no floor – for environmental regulation.
- A detailed procedural code for environmental law-making, and regulatory initiatives that would be difficult for even the wealthiest nations to meet.

At present, when nations fail to observe GATT's rules, they are vulnerable to international trade complaints and sanctions and the TBT rules have emerged as important new weapons for challenging government regulatory initiatives. Canada has recently relied upon TBT rules to challenge asbestos regulations in France.

This would be changed under the GAST rules of the WLO to:

*All international environmental and social standards and regulations are considered as effectively creating a floor for governing the conditions for trade between WLO members. Any country with higher levels should experience positive discrimination in terms of trade. Poorer countries for whom such standards are at present too expensive should receive financial aid to help them improve their standards, and once setting a future date for such improvements, should experience positive discrimination in trade terms.*

## Agreement on Sanitary and Phytosanitary Standards

The provisions of this oddly-named agreement are very similar to those found in the TBT, but deal with laws and regulations that concern food and food safety, including pesticide regulation and biotechnology. As with TBT rules, the SPS has proven a useful device for undoing government regulatory initiatives that are unpopular with large corporations. As interpreted by the WTO, the SPS also precludes the 'precautionary principle' as a justifiable basis upon which to establish regulatory controls when the risks warrant action, even in the face of scientific uncertainty about the extent and nature of potential impacts.

One casualty of this particular agreement has been efforts to negotiate a Biosafety Protocol to the Biodiversity Convention, with various countries, mainly the US, threatening WTO trade action should the Protocol require that host countries first consent to transborder shipments of genetically modified organisms. This agreement also seeks to remove decisions about health, food and safety from national governments by delegating them to international standard-setting bodies such as the Codex Alemantarius – an elite club of scientists based in Geneva. Because of its location and composition, Codex is an institution that is singularly inaccessible to all but a handful of international corporations and business associations that are capable of maintaining delegations in Geneva. Codex standards often fall substantially short of those established by jurisdictions closer and more responsive to the interests and views of consumers and health advocates.

This would be changed under the GAST rules of the WLO to:

*All laws and regulations that concern food and food safety, including pesticide regulation and biotechnology, are considered as effectively creating a floor for governing the conditions for trade between WLO members. Any country with higher levels should experience positive discrimination in terms of trade. Poorer countries for whom such standards are at present too expensive should receive financial aid to help them improve their standards, and once setting a future date for such improvements, should experience positive discrimination in trade terms.*

*The 'precautionary principle' is a justifiable basis upon which to establish regulatory controls affecting trade when the risks warrant action, even in the face of scientific uncertainty about the extent and nature of potential impacts.*

## Agreement on Trade-Related Aspects of Intellectual Property Rights

By attaching the prefix 'trade-related' this agreement transforms an entire domain of domestic policy and law into one that is subject to WTO regulation. The essential thrust of TRIPS is to compel all WTO member nations to adopt and implement patent-protection regimes.

This virtually provides US and EU multinationals with global patent rights which can now be enforced by retaliatory trade sanctions. The rights of indigenous communities to genetic and biological resources that are held in common are ignored. The result is to facilitate the appropriation of the genetic commons by corporate interests which can then demand user rents from the communities that should be the proper 'owners' of the genetic resource.

This would be changed under the GAST rules of the WLO to:

*Global patenting rights should not override the rights of indigenous communities to genetic and biological resources that are held in common. For products, fees should be able to be levied to cover the cost of development, plus a reasonable level of profit, but such patenting rights must have a limited timeframe and fully reimburse the parties whose knowledge contributed to the patented entity.*

## Agreement on Trade-Related Investment Measures

TRIMs sets rules for investment in the production of global goods and services. While this investor-rights agenda is constructed on the same platform of National Treatment and MFN treatment that is common to all WTO agreements, it goes much further in two critical ways. The first is to allow individual investors virtually unqualified access to international enforcement mechanisms that may be invoked by them directly against nation states. It would be difficult to overstate the implications of this radical departure from the norms of international treaty law which, with the exception of international human rights, has never created rights even for the benefit of individuals, let alone multinational corporations.

In other words, under NAFTA and MAI prototypes, for the purposes of enforcement, foreign investors are accorded the same status as nation states. The other critical departure of this proposed investment regime from the norms of international trade law is to be found under the heading *Performance Requirements*, which actually *constrain* the implementation of domestic investment regulation, even when applied only to domestic investors.

This would be changed under the GAST rules of the WLO to:

> No individual investor may use international enforcement mechanisms that may be invoked by them directly against investment regulations of the nation states. The implementation of domestic investment regulations shall not be constrained by trade rules, provided that the former improve social and environmental regulations domestically and further such advances in trade relations.

## Agreement on Agriculture

The vision expressed by this WTO agreement is of an integrated global agricultural economy in which all countries produce specialized agricultural commodities, and supply their food needs by shopping in the global marketplace. Food is grown, not by farmers for local consumers, but by corporations for global markets. This is a disaster for the food security of poor countries, as subsistence farms are lost to export producers, but is also extremely problematic for environmental and food safety reasons.

The globalization of food production and trade requires that agricultural commodities be transported long distances, and be processed and packaged to survive the journey. In addition to sacrificing quality and variety for durability, this requires enormous inputs of energy. In fact, when account is taken of all energy inputs, global food production and trade probably consume more fossil fuel than any other industrial sector. Thus international agricultural trade policies are likely to substantially increase greenhouse gas emissions and make climate objectives much harder to achieve.

Other important aspects of the WTO agenda for agriculture can be found in the agreements dealing with food safety standards and biodiversity (SPS and TRIPS). Together, these agreements set the stage for the next Green Revolution – the one that spreads biotechnology, in the form of genetically modified (GM) foods, across the world.

This would be changed under the GAST rules of the WLO to:

*All countries should be encouraged to reach maximum self-sufficiency in food. They should only export and import for the end goal of helping move towards maximum sustainable local production, whilst fostering rural regeneration. Trade in food not being able to be grown domestically should be obtained where feasible from neighbouring countries. Long-distance trade should be limited to food not available in the region. Those countries providing food exports should use the funds to increase their own level of food security and in a way that benefits rural communities.*

## Agreement on Dispute Resolution

Under the WTO's Dispute Settlements Body any member nation can challenge any other member's country's laws if they might be viewed as impediments to trade under WTO rules. Prior to the WTO, trade dispute resolution was a matter for negotiation and compromise. While trade panels could pass judgement on whether countries were in breach of their obligations, compliance ultimately depended upon the willingness of each member-state to accept their rulings. Retaliatory trade sanctions could only be imposed against an offending nation *with its consent*. With the creation of the WTO, the requirement for that consent has been removed and trade panel rulings are legally enforceable virtually as soon as they are rendered.

Enforcement under the WTO means recourse to the most potent remedies that exist under international law – retaliatory trade sanctions. Moreover, by the norms of conventional legal processes, WTO dispute resolution takes place with blinding speed. Cases are routinely heard, decided, appealed and resolved within a year of being brought. It is the effectiveness of its enforcement regime that ultimately accounts for the enormous influence that trade rules will now exert over the decisions of governments.

A review of WTO rulings on environmental or conservation measures reveals two consistent and common themes. The first is the expansive interpretation given to rules that limit government options that might, even indirectly, interfere with trade. The second is the exceedingly narrow interpretation given to trade provisions that might create space for environmental exceptions to the free-trade orthodoxy. This has spelled disaster for every environmental or conservation regulation considered by a trade dispute panel. *None* has survived the encounter and, in every case, trade panels have found several grounds on which to rule against the environmental regulation.

This would be changed under the GAST rules of the WLO to:

> *If any of the above rules were used by one member state to challenge another, for not furthering the* Protect the Local, Globally *agenda, then a well-researched case would need to be made. This would then be taken to the WLO. This is the successor to the WTO, which instead of implementing the GATT rules, would instead adjudicate using the* Protect the Local, Globally *rules of the GAST.*
>
> *Citizen groups and community institutions are given standing in such hearings as well as having the ability to sue companies for violations of this trade code. All judicial and quasi-judicial procedures such as arbitration shall be fully transparent and open to public observation. At the end of this process trade sanctions on the inter-governmental and inter-regional trade still occurring shall be brought to bear to enforce the internal national changes required under GAST.*

## DEMOCRATIZING THE WLO

The WLO will doubtless keep the same Geneva headquarters and many of its staff, since much of the work of guiding trade will remain the same, it will be the shift of the fundamental rationale to localization which will be the overriding change. It will only occur once the powerful blocks of Europe, North America and to a lesser extent Japan decide to replace globalization with localization.

As *Protect the Local, Globally* becomes the end goal of all the world's trading blocks, there is likely to be pressure to relocate the new WLO if not geographically, then at least to a more internationally democratic setting. Graham Dunkley suggests that any changed WTO 'be placed under the general supervision of the UN Economic and Social Council as was originally proposed for the International Trade Organization (ITO), and be given a wider, more stabilizing role, ie to fill the gap which many think the demise of the ITO has left'.[8] (The 1948 proposal for an ITO included wide measures for trade liberalization, but also included the facilitation of government policies for economic stability and full employment, fair labour standards at work; and general assistance for developing countries. Its disputes settlement mechanism was to be enforceable through the UN-affiliated International Court of Justice and was to be located within the Economic and Social Council of the UN. The Havana Charter, as the 1948 ITO formation document became known, had been initially signed by 54 nations representing 90 per cent of world trade. However in the US there was so much opposition due to fears of reduced national sovereignty that President Truman never presented it to Congress, thus effectively killing off the ITO disciplines as the IMF and World Bank have done from the outset.[9])

More direct NGO representation is envisaged, as is the replacement of the IMF with an International Central Bank. This would function much as Keynes proposed by providing a world trading currency, partially reregulating exchange rates, exercising mechanisms for reducing national trade surpluses and perhaps levying a Tobin type tax on speculative capital transactions. The World Bank would be replaced by a development body providing modest development programmes, encouraging localist schemes, relevant technology and skills exchange and arranging commodity price stabilization schemes, particularly during the transition to the *Protect the Local, Globally* approach. An environmental authority to ensure that what trade occurs furthers environmental protection and a similar one covering labour and human rights, culture and media regulation would also be set up.

Dunkley doesn't see such a structure as world government *per se*, but a cooperative system based on nation states (decentralized internally where desired), these being linked by international negotiation, coordination and mutual aid rather than centralized bureaucratic administration. Three broad alternative goals for society and the world system are suggested: social justice consisting of adequacy and equitability in matters such as sustenance, health care, civil liberties, and gender rights; sustainably organized systems, entailing an economy which preserves eco-systems, biodiversity, landscapes etc; and cultural integrity, the evolution or maintenance of intellectual and belief systems which are compatible with the other two goals, are stimulating and are respectful of worthwhile traditions.

The difference between Dunkley's approach and that of *Protect the Local, Globally* is that this book explicitly rejects the basic tenets of free trade and the overriding insistence of the need to be internationally competitive.

## 'AID FOR LOCALIZATION'

*'Debt, terms of trade, and increasing loss of control on the movement of capital flows, labour conditions and other crucial factors for (economic) development means greater global inequality and severely undermines the ability of aid to contribute to poverty eradication.'*[10]

Such an assessment is inevitable if aid takes place, as it does today, within the construct that globalization is inevitable and the best that can be done is to ameliorate its excesses. Those concerned about development have calculated that a billion people can be brought out of poverty if US$20 billion was found, but it isn't.[11]

There have been some steps in a more useful direction recently, eg the questioning of the purpose of aid prompted by France's debt forgiveness of Honduras and Nicaragua following Hurricane Mitch in 1998.[12] The UK wants the moratorium they have granted to be conditional on measures to relieve poverty. The World Bank is talking of the need to link aid more to the meeting of basic needs. This, like the case of capital controls, can be built on to shift the discussion towards an emphasis on aid for the end goal of local economic rejuvenation.

However, the general trend in neo-liberalism has been very much in the opposite direction. The *Guardian* newspaper asked 'what's the difference between Zambia and Goldman Sachs?' The answer is that 'one of them is an African country that makes US$2.2 billion a year and shares it among 25 million people. The other is an investment bank that makes US$2.6 billion and shares it among 161 people.'[13]

Aid for Localization shares the usual view of aid that to be effective it must enhance the capacities of the poorest, their education and skills, their health, their ability to control their own lives, and their opportunities to develop secure livelihoods. Such end goals have been consistently supported by the majority of people in the industrialized world.[14] It also meets the criteria of helping to empower people to improve their own lives and overcome the worst aspects of absolute poverty. It will however have the additional overriding condition that all such investments must lead to the rebuilding of local economies in the developing world and Eastern Europe. These regions have a much

higher percentage of the population in rural areas than OECD
countries, particularly the developing countries.

### Aid for Local Agrarian Reform

A key aspect of aid must therefore be to address the need for agrarian
reform. This is so crucial since land and agriculture is so fundamental
to the livelihoods of so many poor people. In Brazil for example, 42
per cent of privately owned land is not being farmed.[15] Aid can be
used to further land reform via help to set up systems of compulsory
or voluntary purchase, land ownership ceilings or land taxes.[16] Reform
however needs to be wider than just land reform and be used for the
broader end of furthering agricultural organization, including rural
development measures such as improvement of farm credit, farm input
supply, marketing and extension services.[17]

This should help stem the flow of people from rural to urban areas,
thus easing the enormity of the task of creating adequate livelihoods in
cities. The key here will be to enable the transition from the present
situation where they require enormous concentrations of food, energy
and materials, to one where such resources are provided more from
within the city, or local surroundings. This will generate a huge amount
of employment. Other areas for aid to help pump prime livelihoods in
poor cities are energy conservation and efficiency and the increased
use of renewables; waste reduction and recycling materials to decrease
imports into the city; building long-lasting structures with work and
home in proximity; efficient public transport systems and more urban
food production on allotments, in gardens and urban farms on former
wasteland.[18]

Grass-roots groups, people's organizations, trade unions, NGOs
and business interests must be helped to come together as part of civil
society to put pressure upon and interact with the state to effect such a
transition to localization. Whether such aid comes from government or
via NGOs, experience shows that working with local groupings to
achieve community-based improvements requires an emphasis on the
participation of local communities, and on enhancing the capacities of
the poor. It has been found crucial by Oxfam and others that this 'starts
by listening to the poor themselves, recognizes the role and needs of
women in the development process, and considers environmental implications and the sustainability of project initiatives.'[19]

Without such an approach the unequal power inherent in the donor-
recipient relationship can mean that local priorities can be unduly
influenced and local capacity undermined. This is less likely with the
localism approach since it does not share the problems of all govern-

ment and the majority of NGO aid, that they take place within the framework of acceptance of less barriers to trade. Thus, the best efforts for people on the ground are completely swamped by the conflicting national macro economic policies to curb public expenditure.

## Aid for Transfer of Technology and Information

In the transition to localization, and once it is achieved, it will be crucial to ensure that every encouragement is given to the transfer of technology, information, management and other key skills. The block to such transfers at present is that where higher tech products or production processes are required by poorer countries they are not in a position to pay the licence fees to cover the transfer and cost of the patents. Companies need to protect these initial investments to stay in R & D, though this is not to claim that the patent dues of some companies, particularly drug companies aren't far too high.

The answer would be for the export of such technology to be pooled where possible with a number of countries to lower the unit licence and patent fees. Where such a technological transfer would benefit the rediversification of sustainable local economies, the cost would be met by aid either as a grant or to be repaid once the product is sold. Rigorous evaluation of what would be a fair return on the patent or for the relevant technology or the information flows would be carried out to ensure the best use of the aid money.[20]

On the question of management, skills and data flows, once the costs had been agreed and evaluated, these too should be paid for by aid for localization funds. These funds could either be given on a bilateral or multilateral basis.

## Less Debt and Less Aid Needed

Much of what people think of as aid is in fact loans. Add to this the other kinds of borrowings that governments choose or are urged to do on infrastructure, arms, luxury goods and so on then the enormity of the debt problem soon becomes evident. However, the whole question of debt reduction and repayment being much more linked to poverty eradication is now being couched in more radical terms thanks to the campaigning of coalitions like Jubilee 2000.

Debt relief during the global transition to localism must be accompanied by a system of incentives for earlier and deeper debt relief for countries willing to make commitments to poverty reduction and increased self-reliance, particularly for the building-up of rural infrastructure. Such well-targeted debt relief would make the OECD's stated goal of halving those living in absolute poverty by 2015 far more likely. At the same time it would help reduce the dependence on aid itself, an aim of the OECD's *Shaping the 21st Century* which called for measures 'that foster self-reliance in which countries and people are less in need of aid'. This will require cooperation between debtor governments, donors and civil society and transparent and account-able structures for administrating such a transition.

Once localization is the norm then countries that have been given debt relief will be an economic path that will minimize their need for further borrowing. It will also allow them to generate surplus wealth to eventually repay whatever smaller level of loans will have been incurred in the transition to, and maintenance of, localization.

The transition from GATT to GAST will not be cheap and devel-oping world and Eastern European countries will require financial aid to pay it. It has been estimated that developing countries exporting to the OECD countries in 1980 would have incurred pollution control costs of at least US$5.5 billion if they had been required to match US standards. These figures are relevant, since although less will be exported under localization, it will still be its eventual aim to foster as high environmental standards as possible.

During the transition one approach could be tariffs on the imports of goods that don't meet national environmental standards, with the funds being recycled for investment to improve the environmental levels in the poor countries concerned. On a multilateral level, commodity agreements could incorporate an Environmental Fund for the same purpose, jointly administered by the parties to the agreement.

Poorer countries dependent on primary exports could impose a social and environmental export tariff on their goods, to be used for domestic programmes for increasing infrastucture for basic needs and environmental programmes. Importers should require such a tariff to ensure market access, so that a country that adopted such measures wasn't undercut by nations without such an environmental approach.

*Part Three*

# How Localization Might Come About

*Chapter 13*

# Growing Opposition

There is already widespread resistance to globalization that can be built upon. There is also a growing literature of the large number of people and groups strengthening their local economies.[1] The greatest spur to consideration of such radical local alternatives at the governmental level will be the need to respond to global economic upheavals and the deflation, the job losses and inadequate consumer demand that will come in its wake. Equally crucial in shaping a different localist imperative amongst politicians will be the pressure that the politically active can bring to bear. This must shift from fighting for different improvement to adding to that task the demands for an overarching change to localization. The key spur to this change could be the realization that this is the only route to their achieving their issue-specific aims. Some mixture of the above forces could then begin to work together for this fundamental change from globalization to localization.

## THE GROWING BACKLASH AGAINST GLOBALIZATION

In the US in November 1997, for the first time in 60 years, an expansion of free trade – the Fast Track legislation to extend the NAFTA – failed in Congress. In April 1998, the OECD had to call a six-month halt to the negotiation of the MAI, due to international opposition. In October 1998, the MAI was abandoned within the OECD, although moves to relocate it to the WTO met similar determined resistance internationally. Attempts to change the IMF's charter to extend its jurisdiction to the liberalization of capital movements also met stiff opposition in the US Congress.[2] At the Third Ministerial meeting of the WTO in Seattle in November 1999, thousands of protestors joined developing country delegates calling for a 'revise and review' approach to trade rules. The collapse of the talks was the biggest set back for globalization to date. A predominant call was for a halt to further trade liberalization and a fundamental review of the direction of trade and investment, such that it benefited the majority and actively protected the environment.[3]

Resistance is not centred on the rich countries, nor is there just concern from the poor in the south. In India, the BJP Government had stood on an anti-globalization and pro-Swadeshi (increased self-reliance) programme.[4] Although they have watered down such plans, in government there is substantial sympathy for this approach in India. In early May 1998, hundreds of thousands of peasants, agricultural labourers, tribal people and industrial workers from all regions of India demonstrated against the WTO, its neoliberal policies and demanded India's immediate withdrawal from the WTO.

## THE BEGINNINGS OF THE RISE OF PROTECTIONISM

In a statement issued after emerging from a meeting with steel industry and its unions, President Clinton warned America's trading partners he would not tolerate 'the flooding of our markets' with cheap imports.[5]

In the UK, women textile workers threatened with redundancy made the following comments:

*'Too much cheap stuff made abroad'*

*'Surely they can do something to stop work going abroad'*

*'Government should stop it'*[6]

As the true economic situation worsens for the majority, the desire to protect national economies is on the increase. The WTO's 1998 Annual Report expected that protectionist pressures will increase in 1999 as the crisis-hit economies of Asia step-up exports to kick-start recovery. US, Brazil, Mexico, and Australia are instanced as countries toughening anti-dumping or anti-subsidy rules and notes pressures on the US and EU among others to block unfair imports in sectors such as steel and textiles.[7]

In the steel sector, US producers, led by US steel and Bethlehem Steel backed by the United Steelworkers Union of America, have filed demands for anti-dumping action against Brazil, Russia and Japan. Before the case was heard steel companies had taken full-page newspaper advertisements pressing President Clinton to take action to safeguard American jobs and profits. Eurofor, the European steel producer's association, has asked the European Commission for anti-dumping actions against several Asian countries.[8]

While such responses are understandable, it is crucial that talk of protectionism be put within a new context. One-sided protectionism, ie attempting to protect yourself whilst still hoping to gain more foreign markets, is both unfair and self defeating. The *Protect the Local, Globally* policies in the previous part of the book offer a way for protected and diverse local markets to be the future growth source, not an unbalanced dependence on winning external markets in competition with a whole range of other countries.

Whenever such a radical change is called for, the general response is to say that globalization is unstoppable. Yet it is time to update UK Prime Minister Harold Macmillan's salutary warning of what rocks a government: 'Events dear boy, events', and to take into account the growing threat to the onward march of globalization: deflation.

## GLOBAL DEFLATION AND JOB INSECURITY

'The collapse of the global marketplace would be a traumatic event with unimaginable consequences. *Yet I find it easier to imagine than the continuation of the present regime.*' [emphasis added]

George Soros[9]

'*One does not have to be an expert in economics to see that the world economy cannot continue with all nations expanding exports and constricting the ability of their workers to buy imports.*'

Jeff Faux, US Economic Policy Institute[10]

'*If you cut wages, you just cut the number of your customers.*'

Henry Ford[11]

Robert Reich, President Clinton's former Secretary of Labour, warned that the seeds of depression were sown in the late 1920s when demand began to fall and sales of homes, cars and consumer durables declined, and there was a resulting fall in commodity prices and industrial production. Today, he asserts, we are entering a similar era. Even before the Asian currency crisis, world prices of food, steel and other commodities were falling. Reich asserts that 'a large, unco-ordinated global contraction is underway. We are experiencing only the beginnings'.[12]

Robert Reich and George Soros are not the only establishment figures expressing public concern about the way the present global economy is organized and the consequences of continuing in its present direction. The South East Asian crisis has merely added to concerns about the lack of constraints on capital flows, currently spinning stock markets into record highs and catastrophic lows. Unease about this has been voiced by, amongst others, Peter Sutherland, the first head of the WTO and in publications such as *Business Week*, the *Wall Street Journal* and *The Financial Times*.[13] The present economic system is being stretched by an excess of goods in the market place and an insufficiency of purchasing power to consume them. The spectre of global deflation, similar to that which led to the crash in the 1920s, is still a serious prospect.[14]

The lifting of controls on international capital movements over the past 25 years has been paralleled by a succession of international financial crises. Gerald Corrigan, former President of the New York Federal Reserve Bank, now with Goldman Sachs, observed that 'By any standard, the frequency and consequences of these events are simply too great'. The IMF reports that 36 of its 181 members suffered one or more system-wide banking crises from 1980-95, and that 108 others had one or more periods of 'significant banking problems' defined as 'extensive unsoundness short of crisis'. The frequences were similar for both developed and developing countries. The numbers have of course risen significantly since 1995.

Environmentally things are worsening in most parts of the world. Small farmers have had to make way for intensive agriculture for exports. Wood and fish exports are increasingly destroying forests and collapsing fisheries. Polluting industries move to countries where environmental regulations are lax and labour cheap. Developed countries that used to be in the vanguard of environmental protection, such as Germany and the US, are now putting the needs of being competitive before any 'green' transformation of their economies.

Asia has witnessed currency collapses, bank insolvency and soaring unemployment. Despite some recent recovery, the overall situation for the majority is much worse than the pre-crisis level. Yilmaz Akyur, the chief economist of UNCTAD and one of the first economists to predict the Asian crisis back in 1996, warns that the financial system is inherently unstable; '… economies are recovering, the people aren't'.[15] To bring 'stability', the IMF has enforced policies which have hurt local businesses and reduced subsidies for the vulnerable. The result is rising social unrest and hardship, ranging from riots to brutal repatriation of those migrant workers deemed surplus to requirement. In Latin America, there is rising unemployment in Brazil and falling real wages throughout the continent. In Africa, with the exception of a relatively buoyant but increasingly unequal South Africa, the picture is predominantly the same:

> '*Asia's financial and economic crisis has lowered the continent's takeup of imported commodities and caused a slowdown in the global economy that is feeding through to lower demand. Commodity prices have plummeted over the last six months... the world price of both rubber and copper has fallen by around 20%. Rubber earns foreign exchange for Liberia, the Ivory Coast, Nigeria, Cameroon, and Congo DR (formerly Zaire) while copper revenues now account for more than 90% of Zambia's foreign earnings.*'[16]

In Europe, most economies suffer intractably high levels of unemployment by post-war standards. Their mixed economy model of growth with relatively adequate social provision is under threat. Europe's structural adjustment policy is policed by the convergence criteria of the European Monetary Union (EMU). This imposes a deflationary monetarist logic of reduced public expenditure in the major labour-intensive areas of public service provision and infrastructure renewal.

Along with EMU's reduction of public expenditure goes globalization's pressure for tax reductions for corporate activity. EU governments are played off against each other to continue reduction in corporate taxes. There is thus a pattern of rising tax burdens on labour alongside falling revenues from capital, companies, and the rise in numbers of the self-employed. The final twist is that trade liberalization has increased continental and international competition with countries with lower social and environmental costs.

This leaves the global importer of last resort, the US. Its economy is buoyant on the back of a soaring stock exchange, but when economic gravity results in its eventual fall, the result will be less investment, less taxes and rising unemployment. Since the Asian crisis the US has increased its imports from the devalued Asian exporters and the latter's capacity to absorb US exports has declined. Americans have been paying for this far more out of consumer credit than wage earnings. The US levels of personal credit debts are the highest in the industrial world and Reich argues that these are approaching the limits of what their economy can sustain. If this bubble bursts the whole world economy will be affected.

Perhaps the final wake-up call leading to a dramatic reform of the world's financial system will come should the US dollar collapse, rather than decline. The layoff of 24,000 workers at Boeing was a warning that in the end what happens to earnings and profits cannot be divorced from stock market performance. Establishment commentators like *The Economist* have warned of the 'bubble economy' and noted that:

> '...the climb in (US) share prices... shows neither that the
> market is correctly valued nor that the bubble is a figment of
> our imagination. History shows that markets do overshoot
> and that bubbles can persist for some time – indeed that is
> their nature. It also shows that the bigger the bubble gets, the
> greater the excesses it creates in the economy – and the bigger
> the bang when it eventually pops.'[17]

This analysis was shared by a report by Steven King, an economist
with Economic and Investment Strategy arm of the bank HSBC. He
commented that:

> 'The US bubble is likely to burst through a combination of
> rising interest rates and a falling dollar... This combination is
> likely to deliver a slowdown in growth through 2000 and
> raises the risk of outright recession in 2001. The rest of the
> world will not be immune. Falling US equity prices and a
> weaker dollar will create new problems for both Japan and
> Euroland, increasing the dangers of outright global reces-
> sion.'[18]

Profits in the US's 'miracle economy' have been dropping for the past
year and are now declining at an annual rate of 6 per cent. America is
also running a vast and expanding current account deficit funded by
inflows of foreign capital. This money is attracted by rising US asset
prices, which in turn are helping to fund excessive consumption.
Should international confidence weaken then there could be a
movement by global money out of the US. This could be the trigger
for a run on the dollar. In the words of the *Guardian*'s economics
editor Larry Elliot:

> 'What would be the policy implication of this? Obviously, in
> the short run, a dollar currency crisis would be utterly disas-
> trous, since it would choke off European exports and do
> immeasurable damage to the prospects of Japanese recovery.
> But in the longer term, the global crisis may have to arrive in
> America's backyard before anything serious is done to reform
> the world's financial system.'[19]

# Chapter 14

# Globalization – Destroying Jobs, Increasing Deflation

*'Empirical evidence tends to show that trade liberalization may
entail non-trivial adjustment costs for certain groups.'*
WTO Annual Report 1998[1]

This chapter considers in more detail the point made in the previous
chapter of why the continuation of globalization will lead to more
decline in demand and hence deflation (ie a reduction in economic
activity due to falls of output, wages, prices etc)[2] and, in turn, increasing high unemployment and underemployment.

At the beginning of 1999, according to the ILO there were 150
million people fully unemployed worldwide and up to one billion
underemployed (a third of the world's labour force). In the words of
ILO Director-General Michael Hansenne: 'the global employment
situation is grim, and getting grimmer.'[3]

## RELOCATION, AUTOMATION AND PUBLIC SPENDING CURBS

At the heart of global deflation and its reduction in levels of demand is
the threat to adequately paid employment worldwide. Industries and
services have relocated to countries where labour costs and environmental protection are lower than in their country of origin. (TNCs also
move to gain access to domestic or regional markets.)

TNCs push for new trade agreements based on fewer constraints on
the movement of firms and capital, goods and technologies. The resulting cheap labour competition and threatened further relocation increases
pressure on secure and adequately paid jobs. At the same time, manufacturing (and an increasing part of the service sector) is driven down a
path of ever more automation and 'downsizing' of its workforce.
Increased job losses far too frequently result in redeployment to lower

## Box 14.1 Employment Losses

A US study of the employment record of five large corporations, all of whom were active proponents of the NAFTA, showed that all had made workers redundant through automation, relocation and mergers and aquisitions. AT&T, Allied Signals, Proctor and Gamble, Kimberley-Clark and Zenith have all been highly profitable and have become highly 'efficient' by being leaders in corporate downsizing. The companies have laid off nearly 80,000 workers in the last five years, particularly since the passing of NAFTA. AT&T laid off 4000 workers during NAFTA's first year and the next year, 1995, they announced they would eventually lay off 40,000 workers. They have expanded in both Mexico and Canada. Zenith Corporation announced in December 1996 that it was laying off 1200 workers, a quarter of its US workforce. Today about 12,000 of Zenith's 18,100 employees are now in Mexico.[4] The mergers and aquisition mania of late 1998 involving huge TNCs in the oil, finance and the automobile sector has already resulted in tens of thousands of job losses. 'Career Vitality', an expert on short-term contracts in the UK financial sector, estimates that up to 80,000 permanent and contract jobs could be lost in the City as a result of such mergers.[5] Perhaps most symbolic of the loss of relocation of jobs once thought secure for the Northern working class was the transfer of cloth cap production from Leeds in the UK to China in an effort to remain competitive.[6]

paid, part-time, more insecure work, or simply to unemployment. For example, see Box 14.1.

Moreover, the push to attract and keep private investment in national economies has led to a shift of welfare away from funding public provision of basic needs towards corporate welfare. Yet the areas where substantial new jobs could be created which can be neither automated or relocated are in the sectors of infrastructural renewal and face-to-face caring. These require some measure of underpinning by public money, even if the final service is delivered by the private sector. Yet this avenue is being blocked increasingly by the international economic orthodoxy of personal and corporate tax cutting.

In the OECD, the decline in the concept of 'a job for life', has been a blow particularly to middle-class consumers. Heightened job insecurity comes at the same time as growing fears about inadequate pension provision. This may lead to an increase in savings and lower consumption which is already happening in Japan, where the government has been unable to persuade its people to spend their way out of a recession.

The result of all these trends will be rising unemployment due to the continued slowing down of growth in consumer demand. (This was the experience after the late-1990s Asian crisis, even though economic activity has picked up somewhat in some countries since.) Yet the real tragedy is that there is absolutely nothing on the political, economic and business-policy horizon which will do anything except tinker with microeconomics policies. Making a few workers better qualified is little comfort when there is falling demand for the jobs they could do. Pursuing macroeconomic policies which only makes employment figures worse will rightly test the credibility of all the employment policies governments pursue.

Of course, the status quo view is that in countries like the US and UK the employment situation is improving. This is seen as vindication of the so called 'Anglo-Saxon' model which emphasizes reorganizing the economy to be open to foreign investment, encouraging retraining to increase employability and 'flexibility' (ie a watering down of labour rights) in working practices.

Closer inspection of the official unemployment figures shows that in the US they are a gross underestimate of the real levels. No matter how few hours a person works they are counted as being in full employment, large numbers of people aren't on the official lists of those looking for work and lastly an incredible 2 million Americans are in prison and hence off the job market.

In the UK, where unemployment is significantly lower than in Europe, there is increasing underemployment that is not featured in the official statistical snapshots of unemployment. 2.9 million 'economically inactive males' are reportedly hidden from the official count, mostly in the old industrial heartlands.[7] The flexibility emphasis in the UK has generated increased insecurity, short-term contracts and part-time work. Even those with permanent contracts both in blue and white collar jobs have seen their job insecurity rise markedly in the decade to 1997. More than 60 per cent of employees claim that the pace of work and the effort they have to put into their jobs have increased. UK full-time workers now have the longest hours in Europe, with 30 per cent of male employees working over 48 hours per week. Moreover job insecurity and work intensification are associated with poor health and tense family relationships. Ironically, a 1999 OECD study showed that there was no relationship between inflexible labour markets and unemployment.[8]

## Relocation

Globalization's reductions in barriers to trade in goods, services and capital has led to more relocation of industry and services, often from higher labour cost countries to lower ones. To give an idea of the range involved, the pay rate per hour in manufacturing in 1996 in Germany was US$14.7 per hour, in the US US$12.8, in Japan US$12.4. In South Korea US$4.8, in Hungary US$1.7 and in China 35 cents.[9]

Recent counter-trend developments which have seen investment by Asian TNCs into developed countries like the UK have been to provide guaranteed access to the European markets. This is now threatened by fallout from the Asian crisis and firms such as Hyundai and Mitsubishi have already announced that they are pulling out of sectors of European production altogether.

Relocation worldwide has also been greatly helped by a sharp decline in shipping costs caused mostly by containerization. Before this became widespread, port turnaround times were up to three weeks, today they are 24 hours. Before containerization the cost of sea freight was 5–10 per cent of the value of the consignment; it now stands at 1.5 per cent.[10] With oil prices still relatively low and the lack of any international taxation on aviation fuel, air freight is also cheaper.

The majority of world trade is intra-OECD. This is often quoted as a reason to downgrade the effects of relocation on levels of employment or business decisions. The move is real however, and Professor Adrian Wood has calculated there has been a loss of jobs equivalent to 9 million person years from North to South in recent years.[11] Unfortunately, a North–South job transfer is not the same as a North–South wealth transfer. Most of the profits are held by global corporations, and are repatriated as dividend payments and to predominantly Northern tax havens.

Across the industrial world, pressure to reduce real wages and downsize labour forces has been a hallmark of policy since the late 1970s. It is heightened both by competition from low-waged, but increasingly high-skilled exporters from the Asian economies and China, and by the actual or threatened relocation of industries to lower-waged, less regulated economies. Following the implementation of NAFTA in 1994 around one-third of a million US jobs were estimated to have been lost. General Motors employs 74,500 workers in 54 factories in 27 Mexican cities, most of them close to the border, at gross wages of 70 cents an hour. Hours after NAFTA was signed, General Motors informed Detroit Steel of Indiana that it was shifting spring production to Mexico to save 40 cents per spring. Goodyear tires has shifted production to Mexico as has Johnson Controls and Osram Sylvania plans to follow. By 1997 there were 517 new factories set up in Mexico since NAFTA began.[12]

In Europe, the French Senate's finance committee has already argued that much of the present unemployment in France is the direct result of the siting of factories in developing countries where wages are a fraction of those in France.[13] A survey of 10,000 large and medium-sized western German companies found that one in three intend to transfer part of their production to Eastern Europe or Asia, because of lower wages and laxer environmental standards.[14] Of course, companies often find it useful to threaten relocation to improve their bargaining power with governments, unions and local communities.

Meanwhile, chemical companies like ICI, Bayer and Ciba are shifting bulk capacity to Asia, partly because it was until very recently a booming market, but mainly because the latest plant can be run by local labour. According to Bayer, labour costs in Taiwan are 21 per cent of those in West Germany; those in Singapore are 20 per cent and those in Hong Kong are 16 per cent.[15]

Relocation also occurs between Western Europe and Eastern Europe in the search for cheaper labour. Electrolux shut its Luton factory which was its largest producer of vacuum cleaners and transferred to other European centres in 1999, with 650 job losses. The production of small refrigerators for caravans has been moved to Hungary.[16]

The high-tech future of information technology is often seen as the growth industry for the richer countries, which will somehow compensate for job losses in more traditional areas. However, relocation of high-tech services such as computer-based accountancy and ticketing have been transferred by Swissair to India and British Airways to the Caribbean. Some airline maintenance has also been transferred from the EU to Turkey and the US to Puerto Rico. Indeed a wide range of companies, including London Transport, now have software work done in Bangalore, India, where wages can be a tenth of the cost of a software engineer in the OECD.[17]

A Washington DC suburban hospital transferred its medical records, typing and filing via modem to Bangalore, India. The salary in the US is US$25,000 per year, compared with US$3,000 per year in India. The trend to transfer such 'back office' operations, from insurance actuaries to airline reservations (American Airlines is the largest private employer in Barbados), has led governments in the Philippines, Barbados, Ireland and other nations to form development corporations to encourage US service providers to relocate there.

Companies that created Silicon Valley, such as Advanced Micro Devices and Hewlett-Packard, have also been shifting employment to low-wage countries. Many US technology companies now contract with computer programmers in Bangalore, where workers holding PhDs in computer science are paid US$9,000 annually. IBM hard drive disk business, which started in the US and Western Europe, moved to cheaper labour markets since it took off. According to the Wall Street Journal: 'IBM plans to establish this new site as a joint venture with an undetermined Asian partner and use non-IBM employees so that it will be easier... to move to an even lower-cost region when warranted.

Moving from higher cost regions in Asia cuts in half the cost of assembling the disk drive.'[18]

Of course not all industries and services will relocate. However, if enough do, this introduces a sense of discipline to the workforce, such that they limit expectations of better wages and conditions.

## China – the Ultimate Bottom Line

China and a number of Asian countries were until the set-back of the Asian crisis, the major destination for developing world investment controlled by Western and Asian multinationals. The usual argument for such relocations is that they will raise wages in these new countries. This will then enable those countries' citizens to purchase from the country that has lost the jobs, thus providing new work. The thing that is rarely realized is that the geographical site of the relocation is often short term, which adds to the downward pressure on already low wages.

The special economic zones in China were originally served by 30 million migrant workers. In just five years factories are already relocating just north of these zones. This now gives them access to the 80 million floating population of migrant workers looking for jobs.[19] In overall employment terms, China plans to cut 4 million civil servants and 150 million jobs possibly to go from 'inefficient state enterprises'. Add to these over a 100 million peasants who have moved from the land in search of jobs[20] and this is hardly a recipe for rising wages and conditions, let alone social and environmental stability.

Chinese efforts to join the WTO will be a colossal mistake for the majority. Its entrance to the WTO will increase its unemployment. Cheap food imports will worsen an agricultural decline in a country which has already seen the largest rural–urban migration in human history. These numbers will ensure a permanent cheap labour force whose products will undercut workers in other developing countries as well as in the North.

Of course there will be more affluent consumers in China – an estimated 200 million. Coexisting with these, however, is expected to be a labour pool of around 1.2 billion workers, whose numbers will keep wages low. With technology transfer and automation they will be able to beat OECD competition and increasingly dominate the markets in Europe and the rest of the North in a huge range of goods. China is not inviting transnationals in merely to meet the demands of perhaps 200 million comfortable consumers. They want to be self-reliant, but they also want an increasing share of world export markets, particularly in the higher tech areas. Shougang Steel has become so expert in computerized production techniques that it won a contract to install the control systems for a US steel maker.[21]

## Asia Comes West

Not all relocation is from the OECD countries. To gain proximity to the European market Japanese and then Korean and other Asian companies set up factories predominantly in the UK. Although initially seen as a job-creating advantage, there has been less technology transfer or the setting up of local suppliers than initially expected. As more and more of these companies have shut or scaled down their investments there is questioning of whether this is a sensible policy to continue.

A huge amount of 'corporate welfare' in the form of grants and tax breaks were spent on these firms rather than being invested domestically. The fundamental lack of control over decisions inherent in such foreign investment has been illustrated in the fallout from the Asian crisis. The Korean group Hyundai mothballed plans for a £2 billion semi-conductor factory, expected to have created 2000 jobs in Scotland. Korea's Samsung also froze a £450 million investment near Newcastle that was due to employ 3000 people making microwave ovens, computer monitors and faxes.[22]

## Corporate Welfare

The potential for relocation is increasingly used as a reason to pay, not just to attract a foreign firm, but to keep existing ones where they are. In 1995 New York City awarded more than US$30 million each to Morgan Stanley and Kidder, Peabody and Company in response to their threat to move elsewhere. The State of California and the City of Anaheim, reportedly spent US$800 million on roads and other improvements to keep Disneyland there. In 1997, Chrysler won concessions totalling US$232 million (US$47,000 per job for each job retained) for a Jeep assembly plant in Toledo.[23]

Perhaps the most audacious instance is that of Liberty Orchards, who make fruit and nut concoctions Aplets and Coplets. In 1997 they asked the town they are sited in, Cashmere, Washington to convert itself into a marketing arm of the company, including changing the city's road signs and its official stationary to read 'Cashmere, Home of Aplets and Cotlets'. The company also proposed that the city sell to them the city hall and float a municipal bond to fund a tourism campaign featuring the company.[24]

The amounts of money spent by all countries to lure in foreign companies, or keep existing ones, inevitably means that tax money won't be spent on local needs. Worse than that, the companies demand that their own tax is minimized under threat of relocation, so the local treasury is doubly disadvantaged.

## Mergers and Acquisitions Frenzy

More and more foreign investment is not in new factories, but in the form of cross-border mergers and acquisitions (M&As) where TNCs take over or merge with companies that already exist. Of the 1997 world FDI total of US$400 billion, 85 per cent, ie US$342billion, was in the form of cross-border M&As. In the case of FDI flows to the developing world, cross border M&As represent roughly two thirds of all FDI, ie US$96 billion out of a total of US$150 billion.[25]

These M&As lead to job losses through post-acquisition rationalization, where the new, bigger company has two sets of employees and so gets rid of duplicated staff. This process led to the closure of 60 manufacturing, administrative and distribution sites by merged pharmaceutical companies SmithKline & French of the US and Beecham of the UK,[26] and 25,000 job losses in the case of power plant manufacturer ABB.

The WTO admits that 'Firms have increasingly relied on outsourcing across national frontiers as a means of cutting costs and increasing efficiency.' In these cases, foreign investment is almost certain to lead to job losses. Yet even when M&As are undertaken for reasons of genuine expansion, rationalization will often lead to job losses.[27]

1998 was known as the year of the 'mega-merger' with more than 12,500 deals totaling more than US$1.6 trillion – an all time record for merger and acquisitions. Most of these mergers were in the financial and telecommunications sectors and many were cross-border in nature. These two service sectors are the ones that have so far undergone the most WTO deregulation via the General Agreement on Trade in Services (GATS). The WTO describes the GATS Agreement as 'the world's first multilateral agreement on investment' since it covers 'not just cross-border trade, but every possible means of supplying a service, including the right to set up a commercial presence in the export market.' 'Commercial presence' means that corporate service providers have a new right to enter WTO member markets and compete against and acquire domestic companies. Furthermore, the widespread firings of workers deemed superfluous by mergers is a major factor in the soaring stockprices of the resulting mega-companies. Personnel cuts show up in balance sheets as savings, thus boosting their net worth.[28]

## *New Technology – Nirvana or Automatic Unemployment?*

Supporters of globalization frequently argue that the relocation threat is an over-stated one and that threats come more from automation. The point is that both trends are job threatening. Arguments about the what percentage should be allocated to each are a diversion. Trends in automation are now occurring in every sector as corporations, financial institutions and the public sector are able to restructure and utilize the full benefits of new technologies. These benefits are also transferred with companies should they at the same time choose to relocate. Another link between relocation and automation is that resistance to the latter will be less when compliant non-unionized labour forces can replace more unionized workforces.

Automation can be a boon to ridding the workplace of dangerous or tedious toil. It becomes a bane when it results in stressful work practices, and where no alternative jobs are found for those displaced, which is what is occurring as the pressures of international competitiveness interact with automation and new technologies.

In manufacturing, robotics or other technical improvements are harnessed to the huge quantities of marketing information analysed by ever faster computers in order to reduce costs and labour. 'Just-in-time' inventory techniques plus 'cycle timing' of different numbers of workers required assure bursts of activity as companies mobilize to fill orders. This is followed by slower periods when a smaller, core, full-time workforce is sufficient. Gillette spent US$100 million during 1995–98 to adjust output on an hourly basis in its 60 factories worldwide. Just-in-time inventory is being wedded to just-in-time workforces. The US Bureau of Labor Statistics figures show that the number of Americans on the books and employed through temp agencies or 'personnel supply services' grew by 400 per cent from 1983 to 1995, from 619,000 to 2,459,000. The Bureau projects that by 2005, more than 3.5 million Americans will fall into this category.[29]

Such technologies can also result in 'management by stress', where production is sped up deliberately and workers are required to identify weaknesses in the process. Changes in design and procedures are then introduced to increase the pace and performance. The ever-increasing pace of production creates its own casualties. Worker stress under these conditions has reached near epidemic proportions in Japan.

As Jeremy Rifkin, points out, management too is subject to the new combination of management systems and new technology. Layers of middle management are eliminated to make structures more 'computer-friendly'; organizational pyramids are flattened and work teams created. Such re-engineering typically results in job losses of more than 40 per cent in a company.[30]

When employment in manufacturing sectors was hit by restructuring, new technology was a key factor. The political response was that the decline of employment in the old industries would be compensated by a growth of the service sector. Over the last 40 years, this may have had some validity. But today's new technology is eliminating service-sector jobs in finance, retail and office work on an enormous scale. Most of the recent cut-backs in the US have been in the service industries, such as banking, insurance, accounting, law, communications, airlines, retailing and hotels. US banking and savings institutions were projected to lose 700,000 jobs in the seven years up to the end of the century.[31] In the UK, the current wave of building society and bank mergers follows a similar pattern.

The previous UK Government's assault on the state – particularly local government – seriously undermined public sector employment prospects and current financial orthodoxy shows little sign of significantly reversing this trend. In the US the Clinton administration announced its intention to 're-engineer' the government, using many of the same management practices and new information technologies that have been introduced in the private sector. 'Re-inventing' government may create work in consultancies, but merely adds to middle-class insecurity.

A chilling calculation was carried out by Hans-Peter Martin and Harold Schumann, who worked out what will happen in the key European job sectors of banking, insurance, telecommunications, airlines and the civil service should they follow the same automation trends of the world leaders in their areas. They concluded that a further 15 million white-collar and blue-collar European workers could lose their full-time jobs in the coming years.[32]

## Structural Adjustment and Public Spending

*'For good or ill, an unforgiving capitalist process is driving wealth creation. It has become increasingly difficult for policy makers who wish to practise, as they put it, a more 'caring' capitalism to realize the full potential of their economies. In a less competitive world, when trade barriers were higher, governments were able to construct social safety nets and engaged in policies intended to redistribute income. But today, as a result of falling trade barriers and new technologies, international competitive pressures are narrowing the choices for economies with broad safety nets: The choice is of accepting shortfalls in standards of living, relative to the less-burdened economies, or loosening the social safety net and acquiescing*

*in the greater concentrations of income that seem to be associated with our high-tech environment.'*
Alan Greenspan, Chairman of the<br>US Federal Reserve Board[33]

Public expenditure is still a major funding source of the job generating sectors that can neither be automated or relocated. Often relatively well-regulated work and secure, it can range from teaching, health and care for the elderly to the building or refurbishment of homes, schools, hospitals and public transport. Public expenditure, if not the entire source of funds, can often be the pump primer of such activity through grants, loans and training provision. Friends of the Earth has calculated that up to half a million jobs could be created in the EU's manufacturing, retail and service sectors through installing energy efficiency technologies in homes and industries in the EU. Over a million jobs could be created if just half of the EU's renewable energy potential were put into place and if there was greater investment in the rail system.[34]

The developing world has experienced the pressures to curb levels of taxation and public expenditure for decades through structural adjustment programmes (SAPs). Eastern Europe has followed. Both are under pressure from the IMF, World Bank and the WTO. Dramatic cuts in public expenditure and services have reduced the living standards for the vast majority, and distorted economies away from meeting basic needs towards the goal of exporting in order to pay off development debts.

The EU is now experiencing its own SAP – Economic and Monetary Union (EMU). Its convergence criteria impose a deflationary monetarist logic of reduced public expenditure in the major labour intensive areas of public service provision and infrastructure investment. Hand in hand with EMU's reduction of public expenditure goes globalization's pressure for tax reductions for corporate activity. EU governments are also played off against each other to continue reductions in corporate taxes. There is thus a pattern of tax burdens on labour alongside falling tax revenues from capital, companies, and the rise in numbers of the self-employed.

Worse still, the whole of Europe has become caught up in pressures for new subsidy systems which support corporate activity. This emergence of a corporate welfare state has displaced priorities from the personal welfare state. This is the price nations are constantly told they must pay to remain competitive in the global economy.

Common to all the examples of orthodox solutions to unemployment is the concept that it is the role of governments to order their economies to partake with increasing effectiveness in the world economy.

Proponents of this 'beggar your neighbour' system constantly assert that these measures are really succeeding in delivering prosperity and are the key to tackling unemployment. Yet despite some impressive GDP growth figures, the fruits of globalization are unevenly shared. Its supporters argue that one day the process will provide enough growth to enable governments to direct the necessary resources adequately to tackle environmental and social problems, including unemployment. In any case there is, most establishment commentators agree, no alternative.[35]

Yet employment is often a required end result of most of the changes and campaigns of the politically active. The fact that globalization undermines employment through relocation, automation and public expenditure curbs has to be allied to the fact that it also undermines the potential for the huge range of activists to obtain their end goals, which in turn would generate more work. This, and the need for such campaigns to be recontextualized within a localization framework in order to have any real hope of significant success, is the theme of the rest of the chapters in Part Three.

# Chapter 15

# A Localist Wake-up Call to Political Activists

The establishment of free trade agreements has already created substantial new obstacles to progress in areas of labour and human rights, culture, environmental protection, food safety regulation, species protection, resource conservation and development. It is also serving to 'chill' further regulation because of fear of contravening WTO rules by, for example, eco-labelling[1] and using trade measures to curb toxic products or protect biodiversity.[2]

Four and a half years of the WTO's operation has produced ample evidence that – as predicted by critics in 1994 – it has undermined health, safety and environmental standards, human rights advocacy efforts and democratic accountability in policy making worldwide. At the same time, the vaunted economic benefits have failed to materialize for the majority.[3]

The WTO has consistently insulated big business and industry from social responsibility. For instance, it has enabled Chiquita Banana to 'rent' the US Government in its effort to undermine crucial economic development strategies of tiny, banana-producing nations (see Chapter 17). This to increase its already dominant share of the European banana market. It allowed the Venezuelan gasoline industry to evade high-standard clean air regulations in the US. It has assisted the US Cattlemen's Association in defeating an EU public health law banning growth hormones overwhelmingly supported by European and US consumer and health groups, as well as by the European public. There have been an increasing number of controversial rulings in which the WTO dispute settlement body has upheld corporate interests over those of people and the environment.

## LOCALIZATION – THE ROUTE TO NGO SUCCESS

If critical social, developmental and environmental objectives are to be achieved, the end goals of trade rules must be changed to protect and rebuild the local economy. This could occur within the World Localization Organization (WLO) described in Chapter 12. This will be a difficult challenge, but not unlike the struggle waged in the early decades of this century for workers' rights and conditions and the most recent struggle for environmental protection and conservation goals. That change in conditions occurred by informing and then mobilizing group interests and eventually public opinion. In the process, policy development and law-making processes were generally made more open, democratic and accountable.[4]

There are two important reasons to be optimistic. The first has to do with the potential for developing a deeper understanding of the underlying causes of the social, employment and environmental crisis. A host of social and environmental issues can be recognized as symptoms of a more profound and systemic problem – unsustainable economic, resource and trade policies. For example, while pesticides, or even a particular pesticide, can become the target of a national environmental campaign, little attention has been paid to the agricultural policies that make the continued use of pesticides inevitable. Of course, regulating pesticides, protecting species, creating parks and controlling pollution are important goals – but it is now necessary to move beyond the symptoms to tackle the root causes of these problems.

The second reason for hope has to do with the need for binding international agreements to confront global economic and social problems, such as deflation and structural unemployment, as well as environmental problems, such as climate change and biodiversity loss. In this regard, the WTO's structure, but not its end goal, could actually be a *model* for such social improvements and international environmental agreements (provided it was transformed to the WLO of Chapter 12).

This is because the WTO reveals that when governments are persuaded that a new direction is crucial, they *will* sign on to forceful, proactive and effective international agreements. Economic theories, pushed by TNCs, have caused politicians to sacrifice the best interests of the majority of their voters, for a set of policies that benefit the already dominant minority interests. The challenge, of course, will be to force these same governments to undergo a mindwrench to change direction and adopt similarly enforceable international agreements. This time they must be to achieve the goals of global economic and ecological security, rather than to guarantee the narrow interests of large corporations and foreign investors. Governments do not change on their own. What will be required is a similarly dramatic shift in approach by the politically active to force such a dramatic shift in policies of governments.

# REASONS FOR ACTIVISTS NOT ACHIEVING THEIR OVERALL AIMS

The term 'activists' is used here in its very broadest sense. It encompasses people's movements, national and international NGOs, local activists, trades unions, non-TNC business groupings and politicians. All these groupings concentrate on their own issue-specific priorities, using the tried and tested tools of research, direct action, public education, media coverage, lobbying and proposals for legislative change. At their core, very many of them are seeking to return power from a dominant minority to the majority.

Such groupings can point to successes, but a cool appraisal of the number of victories versus the number of setbacks or failures is salutary. The march of globalization continues onward via trade rule changes, privatization, deregulation and perhaps most damaging the acceptance by most politicians and many activists of Margaret Thatcher's most enduring legacy – the TINA syndrome of 'there is no alternative'.

What tends to be lacking in all these issue-specific solutions is discussion of what appealing fundamental idea, with its concomitant political policies and steps, would be required to replace the dominant free market theology. This new vision must bring about a fundamental change in the *overarching context*, such that the disparate campaign and social goals can be achieved.

Too often those working for social change claim that there is no one solution to solving all their problems. This is a fundamental error that is not made by the dominant forces preventing the changes the activists seek. They have a very clear and constantly repeated TINA mindset to globalization and international competitiveness.

Activists must consider whether they should have an equally all-changing, overarching demand, and whether their campaigns should have one overriding feature. Globalization is the major *roadblock* to their aims, and it is only through the *roadway* of something like the *Protect the Local, Globally* form of localization, that their priorities and those of their supporters can be met. In this way they will constantly contribute to the rejection of this dominant paradigm and its replacement by the localist one.

To begin to counter this process at a time when globalization is being increasingly questioned, will require discussion of a roadmap for localization. This is what is suggested in the *Protect the Local, Globally* set of policies in this book.

## The Fundamental Flaw in an Activist Approach

Most individuals and groups working for political and social change tend to want similar basic demands. They want more money and resources for their specific concerns, better laws and regulations to achieve them, and a decentralization of political power so that local economies can gain control over their activities (see Table 15.1 below). When the first two are campaigned for they inevitably run up against 'international competitiveness' used as the reason why more funds can't be allocated to whatever project is requesting it (since it will raise the tax base, and hence deter domestic or potential incoming business and investment). The regulation proposals invariably falter under the opposite pull of deregulation, the purpose for which is again to make countries or areas more competitive.

Fuelling this downward spiral of increased subjugation to international competitiveness are the processes of structural adjustment and foreign direct investment. On the other hand, any call for real decentralization of political power to enhance local needs works against 'comparative advantage', ie the necessity to prioritize the politics of every economy in order that they provide the cheapest exports.

Those fighting local battles against this process are sometimes successful, most activists however increasingly face defeat in the face of continued financial rectitude, deregulation and the threatened flight of capital and business. Those campaigning for political parties suffer the same fate as their previously left/centre groupings move to the right and to the acceptance of the inevitability of the free market.

Activists fighting their issue-specific campaigns (eg employment, food security, social needs, community regeneration, the environment, development) have to consider making central to all their campaigns the recognition that they can never achieve what they fully want without challenging the need to be internationally competitive.

As is detailed, in Chapter 6 the *Protect the Local, Globally* policies consist of having a goal of maximum self-reliance nationally and regionally in a way that ensures increased sustainable development.

To recap, this route to localization consists of seven interrelated and self-reinforcing policy areas, which are the themes described in Chapters 6–12. In summary, the basic steps are:

- Reintroduction of protective safeguards for domestic economies.
- A site-here-to-sell-here policy for manufacturing and services domestically or regionally.
- Localizing money such that the majority stays within its place of origin.

**Table 15.1** *Issue-specific Solutions for World Problems*

| Problem | Suggested solutions |
|---|---|
| Unemployment and automation | Workers' rights, worksharing, voluntary work and retraining |
| Hunger, declining numbers of small farmers, more intensive farming, unsafe food and cruelty to farm animals | Land redistribution, fewer cash crops, organic farming and animal welfare |
| Environmental degradation and endangered species | Clean production, reuse, renewable energy, minimal resource use and habitat protection |
| Overconsumption | Voluntary simplicity |
| Taxing labour | Taxing resources |
| GNP accounting | 'Real Welfare' measurement |
| TNCs and corporate welfare in industry, services and the media damaging local economies, | Rebuilding and funding local industries and services for local needs |
| Capital flight | Grounding money locally and local currencies |
| Growing inequality, poverty, racism and declining social provision and rights | Resources for local basic needs via local control of the indigenous people's economy |
| Increased migration and refugees | Stabilize, rebuild and improve local conditions |
| Spread of less-treatable disease and pests | Less hi-tech medicine and less unnecessary travel and trade |
| Centralizing and damaging technology | Appropriate technology for sustainable development |
| Declining real power of elected governments | Regaining democratic control of the local economy |
| Free market aid and trade rules | Aid and trade for maximum local self-reliance |

- Local competition policy to eliminate monopolies from the more protected economies.
- Introduction of resource taxes to increase environmental improvements and help fund the transition to *Protect the Local, Globally.*
- Increased democratic involvement both politically and economically to ensure the effectiveness and equity of the movement to more diverse local economies.

- Reorientation of the end goals of aid and trade rules such that they contribute to the rebuilding of local economies and local control.

Given the strength of the theology of the free market this localization approach has the potential to reduce campaign groups' short-term credibility with those they are used to lobbying. This is without doubt a problem for those activists who measure success in incremental changes to present legislation. However, given the track record of so few really significant NGO successes, such groups are in any case lacking real credibility through their inability to bring about the substantial changes they have been set up to achieve.

It is obviously vital to continue demanding campaign-specific solutions. That is what the groupings are set up for, usually with considerable public support. However the route to achieving their demands could also be viewed as starting points for considering a more radical approach. To really achieve their end goals, campaigns need a supportive political and economic *context*. This must allow their limited, if valuable, successes (plus their as yet unfulfilled demands) to be achieved. Not however, just in a few highly publicized instances, but for these triumphs to be allowed to be replicated such that they become the norm.

## Now is the Time for Localization

At the end of the Second World War in the rich countries as a whole there was a seismic shift. The collapsing effective demand in the Great Depression and its resulting war led to an emphasis on a massive channeling of national resources into improved social infrastructure, health, education and rebuilding economies with an end goal of full employment and economic security. As general standards of living improved from the 1960s onward, new campaign concerns developed with growing public support. These included concerns about third world poverty, human rights, racism, women's rights and the environment.

As the world economy worsened for the vast majority, particularly through the 1990s, concerns shifted back to questions of personal security in terms of job permanence, increased crime, community and family breakdown. Nowhere was this more pronounced than in the world's richest country, the US.

The widespread acceptance of the free trade orthodoxy has meant that for both activists and the general population in all the OECD countries there has been a retreat from demands or expectations of large-scale changes from the political process. The involved have concentrated on issue-specific, fragmented campaigns, while the numbers going to the polls drop, reflecting public cynicism about politicians' willingness to change things.

Hopefully nothing as appallingly dire as the Great Depression and its resulting world war is round the corner. Nevertheless, there are some chilling echoes that if not heeded in time could result in similarly fundamental changes. Outside of the US, the picture is mostly one of inadequate economic activity, falling permanent jobs and high unemployment. This is resulting in an overall decrease in demand levels and job losses through relocation, automation and curbed tax levels, as described in Chapter 13. The instability caused by the Asian crisis has not been effectively tackled and more such global economic upheavals appear inevitable.

The time appears to have arrived when an economic rethink of the enormity and positive outcome last seen after the Second World War is long overdue. Such a U-turn will occur if it is perceived to be the only way for the huge range of the politically active to achieve their issue-specific campaigns. They can then move from campaign-specific isolation to seeing the mutual advantage of forging themselves into effective alliances. For motives ranging from morality to self-interest, a fundamental change away from globalization towards localization is the way to success for most issues. The strength of such a coalition is that it would range from issues that are of wide and immediate public, business and political concern (such as jobs and declining demand levels, education and health), to more local issues, eg declining shopping centres. It would also encompass crucial concerns that lose out in times of economic insecurity, such as the environment and reduction of global poverty and inequality.

The new unified mantra chant needs to emerge from this huge grouping, ranging from international NGOs to local community groups, from small and medium-sized businesses to unions, from food activists to the culturally concerned. Activists must assert that their campaign demands can only be realized through a move away from distorting national economies to achieve international competitiveness, towards protecting and rebuilding local economies. It's time to lay TINA to rest.

The remaining chapters in Part Three look at major issues of public and activists' concern and argue the case that substantial success is only likely within the context of the overriding shift to localization.

## Chapter 16

# Failure to Adequately Challenge Globalization – Social Services, Unions and Culture

## SOCIAL NEEDS CAMPAIGNING

Many activists campaigning for domestic improvements in basic social needs such as health, education, housing, transport, pensions, poverty alleviation, disability rights, gender issues and racism still look to more government expenditure as the solution. Examples of such demands for increased public expenditure that have appeared in the UK press over a few weeks serve to illustrate this:

- Tackling poverty through some higher benefits – an extra £4–5 billion annually.
- Universal provision for frailty and disability for the elderly – an extra £1 billion annually.
- Adequate funding for an integrated transport system – an additional £3–5 billion in each of the next three years.
- Upgrading London Underground – £7 billion.
- Long-term health care for the elderly in homes – an additional £1.2 billion annually.
- Investment needed to tackle run-down council estates – up to £20 billion.
- Even the £21 billion extra the government has allocated to health over the last three years will not solve its basic problems, spending on healthcare in Britain at 6.7 per cent of gross domestic product (GDP) is the lowest in Europe, other countries spend between 7 per cent and 10.4 per cent.
- Starting salary for university lecturers needs to rise from £15,500 to £20,000, for a professor from £35,000 to £46,500.

During the same period, uncosted demands were made for more funds to raise 3 million children out of poverty. Claims were also made for more money for health inequality, for parental leave, for information technology provision for the 'information poor', for housing schemes for care in the community, for high-cost drugs for the mentally ill, and for pay rises for midwives.

There is an implicit assumption in those social needs campaigning that if they can lobby, pressurize or embarrass the government enough, then resources and the improvements in legislation they require will come. Far too often all that occurs is the best groups at this technique manage to gain some more funds, but often at the expense of increased funds that might have gone to another sector. Because of their history of seeing such improvements through a domestic lens, they appear often to fail to take into account that governments are under huge ideological and big business pressure to curb public expenditure. In the EU, the single currency explicitly sets targets of overall levels of public expenditure.

One example of a domestic social issue campaign that did understand these wider pressures was that of a group called the London Health Emergency. They realized that the financial straightjacket required to join EMU had resulted in strict curbs on public expenditure in the run up to its date of coming into operation on 1 January, 1999. Since then the levels of public expenditure have been taken out of the hands of elected governments, and are governed by the European Central Bank.

Although the UK hasn't joined the single currency it has kept its public expenditure in line with the 'convergence criteria' of those that did join. These stipulate that inflation must be kept low at around 3 per cent, the public debt of a country must not be more than 60 per cent of the country's GDP (the total annual wealth generated by the country) and that government borrowing deficit of each country must not be more than 3 per cent of that country's GDP.

These monetarist policies (ie controlling inflation through regulating the money supply) have also given birth to the private finance initiative (PFI). This allows private sector companies to design, build and operate public sector facilities, like hospitals, for profit. This is a way of limiting public expenditure today to keep within the single currencies convergence criteria, but having to repay far more money to the private financiers. Building a £40 million hospital wing under the PFI can cost up to £500 million over 30 years. Since public expenditure is already constrained tightly, these repayments further cut into public services. The *British Medical Journal*, not an entity known for sensational statements, was nevertheless moved to go on record in July 1999 with an editorial that described the PFI as 'perfidious financial idiocy, that could destroy the NHS'. It asserted, in what was described as a closely reasoned analysis, that PFI hospitals are being built in the wrong places, that payment for them is sucking money out of the NHS front-line services and providing an incentive for more pay beds.[1]

The London Health Emergency group is clear that:

> 'The only appeal (of the PFI) for the government is that the cost of the hospital does not appear as an immediate lump sum in the public expenditure figures. Capital advanced by the private sector as a PFI transaction is not counted as public sector "borrowing" requirement, although the hospitals will effectively be paying off a high-cost mortgage for decades to come. This enables the government to stick within the single currency straight jacket... The cheaper alternative, building hospitals with public money financed through government borrowing is ruled out by the Maastricht criteria.'[2]

However, such a broad analysis is the exception rather than the rule. The majority of social needs activists have failed to take into account adequately the pressures of globalization on public expenditure and hence their hopes for achieving their demands. Such matters may have been touched upon during internal discussions within such organizations, but they haven't been made a part of their public campaigning.

Other areas of political activism have had to take more account of events outside their country. This includes those concerned with the environment, the developing world, food, employment, human rights, culture and animal welfare. The WTO has used trade rules against the campaign goals of all these sectors. The response of many of the groups involved has been to try and call for very specific changes to the overall neoliberal rules that do not challenge the thrust of trade liberalization.

The clearest example of such an approach can be found in certain groups campaigning for labour rights, environmental issues and animal rights, considered in this and the following chapters.

## LABOUR RIGHTS AND UNIONS

When the WTO held its first Ministerial Conference in Singapore in December 1996 the International Confederation of Free Trades Unions (ICFTU) proposed that:

> 'The contracting parties agree to take steps to ensure the observance of the minimum labour standards specified by an advisory committee to be established by the WTO and the ILO, and including those on freedom of association and the

*right to collective bargaining, the minimum age for employ-
ment, discrimination, equal remuneration and forced labour.'*

This proposal was an attempt to tie the enforcement mechanism of the powerful WTO, whilst giving the far weaker ILO responsibility for determining whether a country complied with labour standards. The WTO rejected the idea of a social clause and instead asserted:

> *'We reject the use of labour standards for protectionist
> purposes and agree that the comparative advantage of
> countries, particularly low-wage developing countries, must be
> in no way put into question.'*

Indeed the then Director General, Renato Ruggiero, clarified that any cooperation with the ILO would be limited to information exchange, such as whether ILO programmes ran afoul of international trade rules.[3]

Despite this rebuff, international and regional trades union organizations still repeat the same demands. The ICFTU and TUAC (the Trades Union Advisory Council to the OECD) still make the same calls despite correctly analysing the impotence of international trades unionists to defend an ever worsening position for organized labour worldwide in face of the onward march of globalization:

> *'However, because of globalization it is increasingly the case
> that "high road" companies are being undercut by unscrupu-
> lous "low road" companies. Here, trade union rights are
> suppressed and an atmosphere of fear pervades the workplace...
> hundreds of trades unionists and workers fighting for the right
> to organize are murdered each year while many more are
> detained, subjected to violence and intimidation or simply
> sacked... a new TUAC survey has painted a worsening picture
> of the labour standards situation in multinational enterprises
> operating within and beyond the OECD... there is a growing
> tendency whereby governments use labour standards as part of
> their incentive packages to attract investors ... such as
> Bangladesh, Namibia, Pakistan, Panama and Zimbabwe where
> the existence of trades unions is openly banned, or as in the case
> of Malaysia severely circumscribed... the reality is of continuing
> abuses to gain a short-term comparative advantage.'*[4]

Yet despite such a realistic appraisal of the reality of globalization's effects on workers, the same author Roy Jones, Senior Policy Advisor to the TUAC can still assert that:

> *'It bears repeating that when trades unions talk about core labour standards we are talking about human rights that are enabling rights. We are not talking about wage levels, or other prescriptive labour market mechanisms that would undermine comparative advantage of developing countries.'*

A mere two sentences later however he adds:

> *'...as regards the issue of comparative advantage developing countries in particular should consider what the inclusion of China would mean for them within a WTO devoid of enforceable labour rights.'*

The whole purpose of the WTO is to enforce comparative advantage. Even if in the absurdly unrealistic concept that China should introduce labour rights it would still undercut most competitors with low wage levels, which the trades union movement specifically demands not be covered in WTO rules. It has already been shown in Chapter 14 that foreign and domestic exporters based in China are relocating internally for even lower wages. That and the over 100 million people leaving the land and joining those made unemployed due to the modernization of the public sector are likely to keep wage levels very low indeed.

It is time for a fundamental rethink by the unions. It is hardly in the interest of Chinese workers, whose conditions are worsening, of workers in other developing countries being undercut by China or trying to pay even less to undercut it, for the movement supposedly protecting them, the international trades unions movement, to hang onto such an oxymoronic approach. For workers and their unions in the OECD and Eastern Europe it is similarly self defeating.

In 1992, presidential candidate Clinton expressed concern over what he considered to be the serious threat that NAFTA posed to the incomes and future job-security of American workers. He noted the failure of the agreement to include enforceable labour standards, and recognized that TNCs could take advantage of 'their ability to move money, management, and production away from a high-wage country to a low-wage country'.[5] Influenced by growing domestic opposition to NAFTA, Clinton adopted two parallel side agreements: the North American Agreement on Environmental Cooperation (NAAEC) and the North American Agreement on Labour Cooperation (NAALC).

The NAALC, allowed for labour complaints to be dealt with by the imposition of trade sanctions on matters relating to child-labour, minimum-wage violations, and health and safety regulations.[6] However, if the violation is considered to be a 'technical labour standard', the only sanction available is one of consultation; 'at no time can any technical labour standard violation ... lead to a trade penalty'.[7] (A 'technical labour standard' violation might include such issues as forced labour, labour protection for children and young persons, minimum employment standards, etc) Additionally, a fundamental set of labour principles, such as the freedom of association, the protection of the right to organize, the right to bargain collectively, and the right to strike, are exempt from all other enforcement mechanisms except consultation.

By the end of 1997, the NAALC had completed only five public reviews of complaints initiated by labour unions and human rights organizations. These complaints, involving more than two-hundred workers, have not resulted in any reinstatements or compensation, regardless of illegal dismissals, harassment and intimidation by employers;[8] and which, for many independent trade union supporters, has resulted in capture, torture and assassination.[9] The reality of course is that the key to Mexico remaining an attractive investment is the continued repression of independent trade unions; the prevention of free collective bargaining. This is what ensures that Mexico does not lose its competitive advantage, as neither wages nor conditions are permitted to improve.[10]

## A Localist Approach for Unions

If trades union demands were couched within the internationalist approach inherent in the *Protect the Local, Globally* policies for localization, then the position of workers everywhere would have a real chance of improvement. No longer would countries from one geographical part of the world be undercut by exports from cheaper labour countries, if such goods and services can be produced domestically. No longer could companies or investors threaten to relocate if wage levels and labour standards improvements were required. Businesses would not have access to this market unless they produced there and abided by national rules governing labour rights. Eastern Europe and the developing world will no longer have to compete ruthlessly – their future too will lie in local production.

The arguments that exports from the south and east to the OECD are needed for development of these poorer countries is simplistic. This does not help those seeking economic improvements for the majority, but those already powerful sectors seeking to pit country against country, and workers against workers (see Chapter 17).

The transition from globalization to localization is the real route to incorporating labour rights into domestic economies. What remains of long-distance trade will of course be based on market access dependent on the verifiable implementation of ILO standards. Comparative advantage needs to be replaced by local advantage, labour subjugation by labour rights.

## WTO – THE CULTURE VULTURE

*'Many countries view culture as their richest heritage, without which they have no roots, history or soul. Its value is other than monetary, they assert, and therefore, to commodify it is to destroy it. They say that culture is not just another product like steel or computer parts, and should not be included in trade agreements at all.'*

Maude Barlow[11]

The issue of culture and trade liberalization's efforts to harmonize cultural diversity is one growing in prominence. The right to protect it from the forces of globalization has become as important a fight as preserving biodiversity. Governments and peoples around the world are increasingly concerned about global cultural homogenization in which the world is dominated by American values and lifestyles, universalized through the massive US entertainment–industrial complex.

The entertainment–industrial complex sees culture as a business, a very big business, and one that should be vigorously advanced at the WTO. This industry combines giant telecommunications companies, movie studios, television networks, cable companies and the internet. These work together in a complex web that includes publishing, films, broadcasting, video, television, cable and satellite systems, mega-theatre productions, music recording and distribution, and theme parks. Mass-produced products of American popular culture are the US's biggest export, and US Trade Representative, Charlene Barshefsky, has said that she will be very aggressive in protecting them in WTO negotiations.

### History of Culture and Trade

In the 1920s, European countries began resorting to screen quotas to protect their film industries from an influx of American movies. The American motion picture industry responded by developing closer ties with the Department of State and American embassies; by the end of the Second World War, most European countries had overturned their laws. In 1947, compromise language was found at the GATT that lasted until the same countries and Canada started to impose protectionist polices regarding television.

In the 1970s, the US complained in the Tokyo Round of GATT negotiations that at least 21 countries were protecting their film and television industries and the problem surfaced again at the Uruguay Round in the 1980s. In 1990, a working group was established that dissolved in disagreement over whether member states had the right to subsidize their audiovisual industry.

The GATT agreement of 1994, which forms the basis of current WTO trade law, basically subjects culture to all the disciplines of the agreement, including National Treatment, Most Favoured Nation and the prohibition against quantitative restrictions. There are two small exceptions: a member country can establish or maintain some screen quotas under very limited conditions. But even this exception was to be subject to negotiations at the 1999 WTO Millennium Round and the US had said it wants it eliminated.

In spite of the limited nature of GATT protections for culture, European countries have become more, not less, protectionist about their culture in recent years. The European Parliament advocates curbs on foreign television programmes to keep out US sitcoms and game shows. France has recently added local content rules for radio to its many other protections. Ireland, Portugal and Belgium have placed quotas on their air waves and the UK is trying to revive its film industry, as British movies take up only 6 per cent of screen time.

There have been seven complaints concerning culture at the WTO between 1995 and 1998; of those resolved, all have had the effect of limiting states' rights to protect their cultural industries. In 1997, the US successfully forced Canada to abandon protections of its magazine industry, even though American magazines make up 85 per cent of all magazines available at Canadian news-stands. The WTO ruled that magazines are 'a product' subject to trade rules governing other products, and Charlene Barshefsky said the decision would serve as a useful weapon against Canada's protections of its film, books and broadcasting industries.[12]

When Canada tried another method to protect its magazines, introducing a law that would fine Canadian advertisers who place ads in 'split-runs' (US magazines like *Sports Illustrated* whose Canadian content is comprised of Canadian advertising), the US threatened massive retaliation. This amounted to US$4 billion against Canadian steel, wood and clothing under a clause in NAFTA that allows the US to retaliate against any sector, if Canada invokes its right to protect its culture.

Christopher Sands of the Center for Strategic and International Studies in Washington says the US is taking such a hard line with Canada for two reasons. The first is that any exemption for Canada will set a negative precedent for other countries, especially in the developing world where cultural protection is just emerging as an issue. Washington is willing to wage an all-out trade war about a sector that is essentially small because an example must be made of Canada if other cultural protectionists around the world are to be subdued.

Sands says that US negotiators are still angry at the role Canadian citizens and cultural nationalists played in rousing international opposition to the OECD's MAI. What further startled US policy makers was to hear these Canadian arguments echoed in Europe and even Asia. In an increasingly small world, ideas travel fast, and the Canadian concern that the MAI would lead to greater American cultural hegemony touched a cord around the world.

The other reason is that a huge, well-organized coalition has formed that links the US entertainment, media and IT sectors together in a common front to oppose cultural protection. Companies like Time–Warner and Disney have powerful friends on Capital Hill and in the White House and intend to get their way.

## WTO Millennium Round

The WTO Millennium Round was to launch new negotiations in the telecommunications sector, which includes all the new technology, including the Internet and Digital, so new cultural issues were on the table. As well, global negotiations on the deregulation of broadcasting were to begin 1 January, 2000, so this sector was expected to be discussed at the Millennium Round as well. WTO documents showed that areas for discussion included 'access and reciprocity to domestic and foreign markets', which could force countries to abandon public broadcasting and relinquish domestic controls, opening up their airwaves to takeovers by global entertainment transnationals.[13]

Ironically, although the push for this deregulation came from US corporations, the US Government has protected its own broadcasting sector in NAFTA and the WTO as being 'essential to national security.'

Finally, in a US initiative, the World Intellectual Property Organization (WIPO) was being brought under the jurisdiction of the WTO in time for the Seattle Millennium Round. This would mean that the WTO would now have the authority to rule on patents, trademarks, and, crucially for culture, copyright law. This would allow the US for example, to make good its threat to attack copyright legislation such as Canada's, that provides compensation to its own artists, writers and musicians for home copying that deprives them of royalties.

A number of countries, wary of the looming issue of culture at the WTO Millennium Round, have begun to meet to share strategy. Canada initiated a meeting in the spring of 1998 that was attended by the culture ministers of dozens of countries, including Greece, France and Mexico, and they agreed to meet again before the Seattle meeting. The US was not invited.[14] Such plans were not to be implemented as expected, due to the collapse of the WTO meeting at Seattle.

## A Localist Media and Culture

This issue provides the opportunity for a completely different sector of society, those involved with the media and culture in general, to be made aware of the adverse effects of trade liberalization on their interest. They could then be the forefront of a media campaign to halt these adverse developments and to consider how the *Protect the Local, Globally* approach would be to their advantage. It would protect their domestic market enough to ensure survival and national cultural diversity. Such security would not limit the flow of cultural ideas, but would limit the reduction of cultural diversity through the concentration of ownership and media power inherent in today's world-trading system.

Culture is of course a crucial component not just of films and books, but also an activity to ensure the maintenance of the diversity of life in its broadest sense. It also overlaps with the human development and environmental issues considered in the final three chapters.

This link was summed up very eloquently by Vandana Shiva, the Indian academic, activist and critic of globalization as:

> '*Diversity is the characteristic of nature and the basis of ecological stability. Diverse ecosystems give rise to diverse life forms and diverse cultures. The co-evolution of culture, life forms and habitats have conserved the biological diversity of the planet. Cultural diversity and biological diversity go hand in hand.*'[15]

*Chapter 17*

# Localizing International Development

This chapter contrasts the generally stated demands of development professionals for a 'fairer' liberalized trading system, with the reality of what the rules of trade liberalization have done to the poor in the developing world. It then looks critically at development NGOs' adherence to the concept that liberalized trade should be made kinder and gentler. This fixation occurs because of the flawed paradigm that exports from the South are the main route for their development. Finally, developing world criticisms of this approach are highlighted as is the alternative of a localist development policy.

## WHAT DEVELOPMENT NGOS WANT

Most development NGOs and movements want democratic control over the commons, national resources and productive assets in order to redistribute land, ownership and wealth such that basic needs can be met. This process should also evolve in a way that increases equality and protects the environment permanently. Crucial to the attainment of these goals is the relationship of the OECD countries, and the TNCs predominantly based there, to the developing world and Eastern Europe. Calls are made for more aid, for debts to be forgiven, for foreign investment to benefit the poor and for world trade to be fairer to meet such development aspirations.

Other requirements for development are adequate access to assets – that is the physical and financial resources needed for people to participate in the economy. Taxation policies and public spending must also be directed towards the poor and disadvantaged, by social group, gender and region. Health, education and skill provision are key since there are strong links between education, income and economic growth and equality. Universal primary education is of 'paramount importance' in this context.[1]

Those who consider that international trade can be made fairer claim for it a number of potential advantages, whilst making clear the disadvantages of what occurs at present. Thus, import liberalization, for example, improves access to productive technologies and new management skills; the resulting increased efficiencies are said to have the potential to promote employment and increase efficiency. It can also undermine livelihoods by exposing vulnerable producers, industries and service sectors to intensive and destructive competition.

Likewise, export growth is said to have the potential to play an important role in increasing household incomes of vulnerable communities, maintaining access to essential imports, and generating the public revenue required for public investment. The reality is far more frequently one of basic needs provision being undermined by resources flowing to export sectors that harm small farmers, in the case of cash crops, and involve bad working conditions in the case of mining and goods exports. In all sectors the environment is normally also the loser.

Official agencies like the World Bank, though admitting problems, still promote globalization and, in the Bank's case, have attempted to claim localization as part of this (see Box 17.1).

# WHAT TRADE LIBERALIZATION DOES TO DEVELOPMENT

'...the final shape of this GATT treaty reflected not an agreement between equal partners, but an agreement to tilt the playing field dramatically in favour of the most powerful nations and their most powerful interest groups – principally TNCs. Indeed during the GATT talks, representatives from TNCs chaired and staffed all the 15 advisory groups set up by the US administration to draw up the US negotiating position. The outcome, not surprisingly given the political and economic muscle of the US, was a treaty that favoured transnational interests over national interests; and US transnational and national interests over everybody else's.'[7]

'An analysis of the "winners" and "losers" from the Uruguay Round of trade negotiations showed the biggest winners to be the EU, USA, Canada and China. China is not (yet) even a member of the WTO! The losers were African countries.'[8]

There are inevitably unbalanced power relations within the WTO between industrialized and developing countries. The governments

## Box 17.1 World Bank Attempts to Hijack 'Localization'

*'Globalization is like a giant wave that can either capsize nations or carry them forward. Successful localization creates a situation where local entities and other groups in society – the crew of the boat if you will – are free to exercise individual autonomy but also have incentives to work together.'*
Joseph E Stiglitz, former World Bank Chief Economist[2]

Localization is defined by the World Bank as the increasing push by local communities to expand popular participation in politics and to increase local autonomy in decision making. This will be bolstered by the growing concentration of developing countries' populations in urban centres.[3]

The World Bank asserts that such urban centres have much to gain from the open world trading system and global capital flows and that FDI will play a significant role in providing the needed urban services.

The Bank feels that in meeting the urban challenges of the 21st century, the most effective institutions and policy initiatives will exploit the opportunities globalization and localization present. The former can provide the impetus for economic growth, while successful localization can empower communities to act as agents of change, promote transparency and accountability in public sector decision making. For developing countries willing to exploit them, these opportunities 'can have a lasting impact on the daily lives of millions of urban households'.[4]

It almost seems as these two forces are seen by the World Bank as a seamless web spun for global economic improvement. The Bank does concede that 'at first glance' globalization and localization may look like counterveiling forces, but in fact the Bank claims they often stem from the same source and 'reinforce each other'. The justification and example given of this is very limp. It sites advances in information and communication technology as key to globalization, as also often allowing local groups to bypass central authorities in the search for information, visibility and even financing.

On the contrary, the common technology has often been used by local people as a tool to fight globalization and its adverse effects on the majority. The example of the international campaign against the MAI was a case in point, as was the organization of the thousands of protestors who attended the 1999 WTO Seattle Ministerial meeting.

The Bank seeks to rewrite reality when it defines localization as a process that will be helped by, and will itself further, globalization. Indeed the claimed advantages of globalization, the potential for widespread prosperity through increased growth does not occur, and is admitted in other parts of the report. Thus it admits that recent studies suggest that rates of economic growth over the last 30 years reveal little about the rates of improvement in vital measures of development such as political stability, education, life expectancy, child mortality and gender equality.[5]

Indeed, the report concedes that given current projections, the number of people living in absolute poverty will continue to increase. In 2000 an estimated

2 billion will subsist on the equivalent of a dollar a day, up from 1.2 billion in 1987. By 2015 the number of people subsisting below this international poverty line could reach 1.9 billion. Inequality is also shown to be on the increase with the average per capita income in the world's poorest countries falling from 3.1 per cent of rich nations' incomes in 1970, to 1.9 per cent in 1995 – with no foreseeable prospect of improvement. Small wonder that at the launch of the *World Bank Development Report*, Joseph Stiglitz, their Chief Economist, admitted: 'We are not winning the fight against poverty.'[6]

At no point in the report is there any serious consideration of any path forward to tackle such problems, other than through globalization.

and NGOs of developing country members have bitterly complained that in past negotiations, including those that created the WTO, major decisions were made at informal group meetings between the US, the EU and Japan. Developing country participation is reduced to a proforma rubber-stamping of the agenda. In addition, disciplines on intellectual property rights and work programmes on investment, competition and government procurement have been advanced against their wishes. What follows is a number of examples of the way the WTO and its rulings act against development.

## WTO Sends EU Bananas but the Developing World is the Real Loser

The Lomé Treaty between the EU and its former colonies in Africa, the Caribbean and the Pacific (ACP countries) establishes preferential tariffs and sets aside some portion of the EU market for a set list of tropical products from these countries. In a world where all countries are attempting to compete with all others, the special treatment allowed to ACP poor countries by the Lomé Treaty is considered indispensable for their economic and political stability. Bananas account for up to 60 per cent of the exports of the countries concerned, yet only 3 per cent of the world trade. This still leaves Europe buying 90 per cent of its bananas from the big US companies.[9]

The EU negotiated a waiver for the Lomé Convention's tariff reduction requirements during the GATT Uruguay Round. However, the fact that the Lomé Treaty's quota preferences guarantees that the EU would import a certain amount of ACP products was thought to fall foul of WTO rules.

This was put to the test on 11 April, 1996, when the US, on behalf of the Chiquita Banana Corporation, requested a GATT panel to rule on the legality of the Lomé banana trade regime. The US itself does not export a single banana, but claimed on behalf of the US incorporated company that the EU's preferential quotas for bananas exported by ACP countries was unjustifiably discriminatory under WTO rules. Chiquita's Chief Executive Officer, Carl Lindner, had made major campaign contributions to both Democratic and Republic parties. Chiquita Brands paid US$500,000 to Democratic funds two days after the US Government asked the WTO to examine Chiquita's complaint.[10] This generosity earned Carl Lindner, the boss of the company, coffee with President Clinton and a night in the Lincoln Bedroom of the Whitehouse.[11] One month after the Republicans received a US$350,000 donation, their Senate leaders introduced the 'Uruguay Round Agreement Compliance Act of 1998', which imposed tariffs on the EU for not fully complying with the WTO.[12] Massive Latin American plantations are infamous for gross labour violations and pollution from intensive pesticide use.

In September 1997, a WTO panel confirmed the original panel's ruling that the Lomé waiver did not allow the EU to give privileged access to ACP bananas. According to the panel, the tariff and quotas enjoyed by ACP countries must be eliminated or provided to all, forcing ACP countries to compete against producers from Latin America and Asia.

The banana plantations of Latin America are almost exclusively controlled by large multinational corporations like Chiquita, which rely on cheap farm labour. Eastern Caribbean banana producers, on the other hand, tend to be small-scale farmers (average size, two to four acres) who own and work the land in a far less chemically intensive way, and whose production costs are therefore higher.

The EU issued a proposal to address the panel's ruling. It agreed to most of the panel's suggestions for changes, but stood firm on the quota issue, proposing to maintain the two-tier system for ACP and non-ACP banana producers. According to St Lucia's Secretary Trade Minister, Earle Hunteley, 'the simple tariff would leave us wide open to fruit from cheaper sources, thus making it even more difficult to compete.'[13]

The US challenge, and subsequent WTO ruling, could lead to the decimation of the ACP banana industry. This is made even worse by the fact that no material US interest is advanced by eliminating Lomé Treaty preferences. This opens the door for governments with no economic stake in a certain trade practice to be willing, if the price were right, to do the bidding of multinational corporations. Not surprisingly such behaviour has aroused suspicions that the WTO dispute resolution system operates on a 'rent-a-nation' basis.[14]

In fact, the US has many policy interests in the banana regime remaining intact: General John Sheehan, Commander of US forces in the Atlantic and Caribbean, noted that undermining the banana-based economy and the middle class it created would increase drug flow to the US.[15]

In the summer of 1999 the EU lost to the US in a WTO adjudication. It resulted in the US penalizing imports of a range of European goods, from Italian handbags to British bath salts resulting in US$191.4 million (£112 million) in trade sanctions.[16] In the face of this the EU backed down and announced that it would have no choice but to rescind the ACP preferences.[17]

## WTO Backs GM Foods

> '*Genetically modified foods will make bananas look like peanuts.*'
>
> WTO staffer[18]

> '*Genetic engineering is pushing out crop diversity and narrowing the genetic base of agriculture to only a few crops. The global trends of the growth of genetically engineered crops is as follows: 40% in the case of Soyabean, 25% Corn, 13% Tobacco, 11% Cotton, 1% Tomato, 1% Potato. This can hardly provide food security to rice-eating Asians or sorghum-eating Africans.*'
>
> Vandana Shiva[19]

The conflict between the EU and the US over GM foods will be covered in the environment section (see Chapter 19). However, for developing countries the ability of the US via the WTO to force them to either import GM products or to stop them excluding their use in poor countries poses very serious threats.

According to scientist and developing world activist, Vandana Shiva, genetic engineering in agriculture will increase food insecurity and environmental destruction in the following ways, which are particularly damaging for developing countries:

1   *Genetic engineering destroys biodiversity which is a major source of food and erodes the genetic basis of food production. This will make agriculture more vulnerable and increase food insecurity. Genetic engineering applications are spreading the cultivation of non-food crops such as cotton and tobacco. More cotton and tobacco will not increase food availability. It also concentrates on crops like the soya bean which has not been the staples for most cultures outside East Asia.*

2　*Genetic engineering maintains and deepens the monoculture paradigm of the Green Revolution and industrial agriculture which focuses on single functions of single species, and fails to take yields of diverse species and diverse function into account.*

3　*Genetic engineering is not aimed at crop improvement for food security. The most dominant genetic engineering application is herbicide resistant seeds which is designed specifically for the purpose of increasing the use of chemicals, not the production of more food. This will further increase the non-sustainability of agriculture and make it more vulnerable to crop failure caused by pests, diseases and weeds, thus increasing food insecurity.*

4　*The substitution of tropical crops such as pyrethrum, cocoa, vanilla and coconut through biotechnology will also have major impacts on Third World exports and the livelihood of Third World farmers, causing major dislocations and displacement, thus contributing to hunger among rural producers. An assessment has been made that in the medium term the estimated loss to the Third World could be more than $10 billion.*[20]

5　*Food security must take into account the healthiness and safety of food. The exclusion of concerns for food safety through the resistance to labelling of genetically engineered foods by the biotechnology industry and the denial to consumers of the right to know and the right to choose amounts to the denial of food safety will hence increase food insecurity.*

6　*The monopoly control on seeds through intellectual property rights and the growing concentration of ownership control over the entire agricultural system will increase food insecurity for the poor peasants who cannot afford to buy agrochemicals and patented seed and pay royalties each year and will hence be pushed off the land.*[21]

## NAFTA For Africa

In July 1999, the US African Growth and Opportunity Act (referred to by US opponents as 'NAFTA for Africa') was passed by Congress. Critics claim that it will open up Africa to increased foreign investment by transnational oil, mining and logging companies by threatening to raise tariffs on Africa's exports, unless Africa accepts the bill's investor-friendly rules. But without strong environmental laws, the increased investment will destroy more of the natural resources – the farmland, pure water, and forests – that the vast majority of Africans depend on for survival. Tropical deforestation in Central Africa, already worse than in Brazil, would only accelerate if the African Growth and Opportunity Act becomes law and opens the region to increased resource extraction. When the Act was first unveiled in 1998 the then South African President Nelson Mandela declared 'this is not acceptable'.[22]

Another provision of the Act could force African nations to comply with one of the worst features of the failed MAI. This provision could be used to force Africa to compensate foreign investors if new regulations – including environmental safeguards – hurt the profits of foreign investors. For instance, if an African nation adopted new laws to protect its forests or rivers from mining operations, a foreign mining company could sue for compensation, forcing rollback of the new safeguards.

### Sanctions Threaten Africa's Aids Sufferers

*'Important as our child survival, health, agriculture, educational and humanitarian programmes have been, they have not ... benefited the American economy. For that reason, it is time to re-evaluate our policy.'*

US Senator Richard Lugar[23]

Twenty-two per cent of South Africa's pregnant women are HIV positive and it is predicted that within 10 years the country's life expectancy will drop from 59 to 40. Although Aids is incurable there are drugs to delay its onset, treat its symptoms and prevent the transmission of the HIV virus from mother to baby. However, these drugs are exorbitantly expensive due in part to the huge profits taken by those drug companies owning the patents.

The South African government has therefore passed a law allowing the department of health either to compulsorily purchase the rights to manufacture the drugs, or buy them from the country which produces them, under licence, most cheaply.

Although the South African law would allow the huge pharmaceutical companies which own the patents to continue to make a profit, they launched a legal challenge and began lobbying the US Government. In July 1999, the US Congress voted overwhelmingly to allow the state department to continue putting economic pressure on South Africa to halt this aspect of its AIDS programme.

Despite pressurizing South Africa for the previous two years to withdraw this law, the WTO rules could not be used to halt it, because of a clause allowing waivers to protect serious threats to life. Instead the US, with support from other countries home to the drugs TNCs like France, Switzerland and Germany, have threatened to apply sanctions if South Africa persists.[24]

Thailand has already buckled under similar pressure. The US-based Pfizer company used to charge US$14 for a daily dose of fluconazole, an antibiotic that can fight off a fatal form of meningitis contracted by one in five AIDS sufferers in Thailand. Three Thai companies began making the drug at a cost of just over US$1 per daily dose. The US threatened Thailand with trade sanctions under the WTO. Since 25 per cent of its exports go to the US, the Thai government banned such cheap licencing even though it has a genuine health emergency and hence could use the WTO waiver.

The US pharmaceutical companies claim that the drugs are so expensive because of the enormous sums spent on R&D. Yet most of the important AIDS drugs were discovered using government money. These were then handed over to companies that produce the drugs at huge profit.

## Gerber Undermines Guatemala's Infant Health Law

In 1988, in accordance with recommended World Health Organization (WHO)/United Nations International Children's Emergency Fund (UNICEF) guidelines, Guatemala banned claims on packaging that equated infant formula with healthy, fat babies in order to encourage mothers to breast feed infants. According to UNICEF, 1.5 million infants die each year because their mothers are induced to replace breast feeding with artificial breast milk substitutes. The major cause of death being infant diarrhoea caused by mothers in poor countries mixing the infant formula with unclean water.[25]

Gerber Products Company (baby foods), whose trademark logo includes a podgy baby, refused to comply with Guatemala's law and in 1995 threatened a challenge to this regulation under the WTO, claiming that it was an infringement of trademark protection. Guatemala took these threats seriously and changed the law so that imported baby food products would be exempted from the country's stringent infant food labeling policy.[26]

## WTO Makes a Shrimp of Development

In April 1998, a WTO disputes panel ruled in favour of a complaint against the US law designed to protect endangered sea turtles. Thousands of highly migratory sea turtles are killed worldwide every year by shrimp nets fitted without 'turtle excluder devices' (TEDs). To protect endangered sea turtles, the US measures required that shrimp caught in the wild and then imported into the US be certified as having been caught in nets fitted with TEDs.[27]

Thailand, India, Malaysia and Pakistan have brought a case to the WTO challenging the legality of this US law. They have been supported by the trade group of the US importers, traders and marketers, the National Fisheries Institute. In April, 1998 the final report of the WTO panel found against the US.[28]

Activists and traditional fishing communities have attacked this 'profits above life' WTO decision. In the view of the fisherfolk, protection of the turtle needs to be linked to protection of traditional fishing communities and their culture of conservation. What is needed, they feel, is the strengthening of environmental laws, not their dismantling. At their heart must be the banning of trawlers. It is estimated that 150,000 turtles drown each year when they are caught in the nets of such large vessels involved in bottom trawling for shrimp in inshore waters. These vessels when in pursuit of shrimp use huge nets which also scoop up turtles and whole shoals of fish. In 1998, for the second year in a row, turtles did not come for mass nesting to Orissa along the Bay of Bengal.[29]

## Another WTO Hiding for India

In March 1998, the WTO dealt a further blow to the majority in India, when it announced the initiation of a dispute by the EU against India, which in effect forces India to kill animals. The EU sees India's restrictions on the export of raw hides and furs as a contravention of the WTO's free trade rules, since it limits EU industry's access to 'competitive sourcing of raw and semi-finished materials'.[30] Even with today's restrictions, India is exporting more meat than animals being replenished within the country. In the last decade there has been a significant decline of livestock in India, particularly the indigenous breeds known for their hardiness, milk production and draught power. The decline in livestock is primarily due to illegal slaughtering of cattle and buffalo for meat export. WTO-induced liberalization of India's exports of raw hides and fur skins is expected to lead to similar trends of serious decline in animal genetic diversity and threats to the economic survival of rural communities.[31]

## Watering Down National Control of Water

*'The wars of the next century will be about water'*
Ismail Serageldin, Vice President of the World Bank[32]

> '*As the water crisis intensifies, governments around the world
> – under pressure from multinational corporations – are
> advocating a radical solution: the commodification and mass
> transport of water ... experience shows that selling water on
> the open market does not address the needs of poor, thirsty
> people. On the contrary, privatized water is delivered to those
> who can pay for it, such as wealthy cities and individuals and
> water intensive industries, such as agriculture and high-tech.
> As one resident of the high desert in New Mexico observed
> after his community's water had been diverted for use by the
> high-tech industry: "Water flows uphill to money."*'[33]

Global consumption of water is doubling every year, at twice the rate
of world population growth. According to the UN more than one
billion people on earth already lack access to fresh drinking water.
Small wonder that water-related conflicts are on the increase. The
Middle East is a well-publicized example but in Asia, Malaysia threatened to cut off the half of Singapore's water it supplies after criticism
by Singapore of the Malaysian Government's policies. In Africa,
Namibia and Botswana have strained relations over the former's plans
to construct a pipeline diverting water from the shared Okavango
River to eastern Namibia.

Yet at the same time governments are signing away their control
over domestic water supplies by membership of the WTO and the
NAFTA. These agreements effectively give TNCs the unprecedented
right to the water of signatory countries.

An ominous instance is that of Sun Belt, a Californian company,
which is suing the government of Canada under NAFTA because
British Columbia banned water exports several years ago. The
company claims that BC's law violates several NAFTA-based investor
rights and therefore is claiming US$220 million in compensation for
lost profits.

The WTO, although not yet involved in any water dispute, could
be in the future. Its prohibition on the use of export controls for any
purpose and its elimination of quantitative restrictions on imports and
exports places water at risk. Quotas and bans on the export of water
imposed for environmental purposes could be challenged as a form of
protectionism. A GATT ruling forced Indonesia to lift its ban on the
export of raw logs and a NAFTA ruling against a similar practise in
Canada 'bode badly' for a nation's right to protect its natural
resources.[34]

Under the protection of these international trade agreements,
companies are planning mass transport of bulk water by diversion and

by super tanker. Several companies are developing technology whereby large quantities of fresh water would be loaded into huge sealed bags and towed across the ocean for sale.

A Canadian company, US Global Water Corporation, has signed an agreement with Sitka, Alaska, to export 18 billion gallons per year of glacier water to China. Here it will be bottled in one of the country's free trade zones to take advantage of cheap labour. The company's brochure urges investors: 'to harvest the accelerating opportunity as traditional sources of water around the world become progressively depleted and degraded.'[35]

## *Supporting Human Rights Breaks Trade Laws*

The serious human rights violations and the deliberate suppression of democracy perpetrated by the military junta ruling Myanmar (formerly known as Burma) since it came into power in 1988, are widely known throughout the world. Such blatant violations of human rights, and calls for pressure to be put upon the regime by Burma's pro-democracy movement, have lead a number of US municipal and county governments, and the state government of Massachusetts, to impose economic sanctions on Myanmar.

The sanctions have been enacted throughout the US as selective purchasing laws and were designed to allow local jurisdictions to avoid indirectly supporting a regime whose conduct their constituents strongly object to, and to encourage TNCs to divest from Burma. The selective purchasing laws are based on the effective divestiture and selective purchasing initiatives used by the anti-apartheid movement in this country in the 1980s, and are widely credited for hastening the successful transition to democracy in South Africa. To date, Siemens, Unilever and several Japanese companies are among those that have been penalized by the Massachusetts legislation, and the law was cited as one of the main reasons for Apple Computer's withdrawal from Myanmar.

The Massachusetts-Burma law has come under attack both on the US domestic front and internationally, particularly in the EU and Japan. The National Foreign Trade Council (NFTC), a coalition of some 600 US-based manufacturers and financial institutions, has taken the state of Massachusetts to court over the law. Oil companies such as Texaco and Mobil have expressed their concern about the impact of such laws on their activities in Burma and other dictatorial regimes.

In Europe, European Roundtable of Industrialists (ERT) companies, including Ericsson, Unilever and Siemens, also viewed the Massachusetts law as a dangerous precedent to be speedily eliminated. Industry mobilized its forces to pressure the European Commission to challenge the US Government to drop the Massachusetts law. Failing that strategy, corporations urged the initiation of action in the WTO. Japanese heavyweights such as Mitsubishi, Sony, and Nissan, some of the biggest losers in the Massachusetts law, applied the same pressure to the Japanese Government.

Thus the EU and Japan requested the creation of a WTO dispute panel in October of 1998, arguing that the Massachusetts law was discriminatory and in violation of the WTO's Agreement on Government Procurement (AGP).

Pending the outcome of a US constitutional challenge to the Massachusetts statute mounted by the corporate front group USA Engage, the EU and Japan have suspended their WTO challenge. Should Massachusetts win the domestic case, the WTO challenge will recommence. A WTO ruling would serve as an important test case on its potential to be used to counter democratic policy making, like the advancement of human rights around the world. It is very probable that if such an attack on sanctions had overridden state law during the 1970s and 1980s, the struggle against South African apartheid would have been seriously hindered.

The Administration's strategy in response to the EU's prospective threat of a WTO challenge against selective purchasing to support human rights has been to discourage such laws in other places. In the spring of 1998, the Administration actively lobbied the Maryland State legislature against adopting a selective purchasing law against Nigeria. The proposal subsequently lost by a single vote. This lobbying effort put the Administration in the same camp as the big business lobby and against pro-democratic activists. It thus questions the Administration's ability and willingness to defend vigorously the Massachusetts law against the EU–Japan challenge, although it is officially playing that role.[36]

# DEVELOPMENT NGOS MUST RECONSIDER

Though grass-roots activists are at the cutting edge of the fight for change, it tends to be the development NGOs that have the money and resources to develop policies in conjunction with them. Governments and the official development establishment virtually all accept trade liberalization. New approaches are not to be expected from this quarter, unless they are forced to respond to a more radical agenda that the development NGOs could help bring about. The way NGOs led the anti-MAI fight in many countries was a positive example of this. However, unless such demands are put within the context of an overarching change that prioritizes protecting and rebuilding local economies, then campaign gains will be very limited in their scope, and their potential for widespread replicability.

Development NGOs, championing export growth, albeit hedged with calls for a fairer system, are a roadblock to consideration of a radical alternative of concentrating on localization, rather than international trade. Their approach also provides enormous succour to big business and free market commentators.

> '...*movements which although deeply critical of the current global economy, do not oppose globalization itself, or see it as an unstoppable process. Rather their analysis – and resulting demands – are primarily addressed to ensure a more level playing field in world trade and national economic policy. In the words of Oxfam, "The challenge for Northern Governments – as it is for their Southern counterparts – is to harness the market to the cause of social justice through regulatory measures designed to generate and distribute wealth more equitably.'*[37]

Much of the development lobby needs to consider a fundamental rethink in its approach to aid and trade. Some are concerned about being seen to be anti-globalization because they appear to muddle it up with the concept of internationalism, where North–South solidarity is used to further development aims. Others consider the poor will gain export advantage in the reduced trade barriers of a more global economy.

Yet a brief perusal of the development lobbies' literature provides a litany of sobering case studies showing how this process is increasing poverty, inequality and environmental degradation, virtually everywhere. Official aid policies intertwined with structural adjustment policies, debt traps and the virtually unchallenged idea that all countries must gear their economies to producing cheaper exports, continuously add to the misery.

## The Infatuation with Exports

Ministries of development, UN agencies and development NGOs are virtually united in their belief that exports to the North are a route for funding improvements for living conditions of the poor in the South. The same approach has now been expanded to the former communist countries of Russia and Eastern Europe. Yet the NGO movement's own research and that of, for example, the World Bank (see Box 17.1) shows that with the exception of the newly industrialized countries (NICs), prior to the 1997 Asian crisis, the position of the majority in such export dependent countries did not improve and in many cases worsened. It is always possible to find those who might earn more than before, or of women who manage to escape the strictures of family life for a while in, for example, export zones, but most experience an oppressive and time-limited stay in such industrial establishments.

In cash crop exports, the position is even clearer due to decades of experience of the adverse effects. Cash crops worsen land tenure, deprive small farmers of a living, result in increased numbers of landless and neglect of the rest of a nation's rural infrastructure. (See also Vandana Shiva's criticisms of cash crop exports in Box 18.1 in the following chapter.) Should any group of export workers get organized to improve wages and conditions, then they are likely to be either personally intimidated or killed[38] or their governments threatened with, or experience, relocation of the employer to a more pliant country. This is even happening between export zones within China (see Chapter 14).

One of the most bizarre examples of the pitfalls of export dependence took place in Bangladesh in the late 1980s. The country was earning some US$10 million from exporting about 50 million frogs' legs per year. This resulted in the depletion of the frog population (to an estimated 400 million) and an increase in insect populations requiring the import of more and more pesticides. Bangladesh ended up spending some US$30 million on pesticide imports to counteract the loss of frogs, which earned just US$10 million. The winners were the companies, some of whom were both exporting frogs' legs and importing pesticides.

However, the response of the development lobby is generally to retreat to the theoretical possibilities of such worthwhile, but incredibly limited concepts, as 'fair trade', 'real aid', 'voluntary codes of conduct' somehow becoming the norm. In countless issue-specific campaigns, concerns about globalization are expressed. This never seems, even after years of reaching the same conclusion, to suggest to the development NGOs that they should start setting their campaigns within a radically different construct. It is crucial for them to reject export dependence as the route to poverty eradication. Trade liberalization will not radically change direction by having a few worst-case excesses exposed. Its very nature, and the TNCs and powerful sectors it serves, will ensure that the position of the majority, that the development lobby is supposed to support, will worsen.

The development lobby should reflect on whether it will be marginalized in terms of effectiveness, if not in terms of official consultation, unless it rejects globalization and returns to the concept of more self-reliance. It must challenge the need to be internationally competitive, and not just oppose the worst excesses of the WTO but also drop its counter-productive adherence to the idea of countries exporting their way to wealth.

## EXPORTS OVERALL DO NOT HELP THE SOUTH'S POOR

'*Free Trade Theorists claimed that the "rising tide will lift all boats", providing broad economic benefits to all levels of society. The evidence so far clearly shows that it lifts only yachts.*

'*...during the 1980s and 1990s, tremendous pressures were applied to all countries, particularly by the World Bank and the International Monetary Fund, to abandon the idea of self reliance... and instead to specialize in producing a much smaller number of commodities for export... In the end, self-reliant economies and communities, small businesses, and small farms were undermined by a system that sends mass-produced manufactured and agricultural goods steaming around the planet at staggering environmental costs in the form of ocean and air pollution, energy consumption, and devastating infrastructure developments (new roads, ports, pipelines, dams and airports).*'[39]

The demands of the development lobby have shadowed the changes in official development and political thinking. The traditional emphasis on the development of national industries with a strong state input in order to replace imports, was replaced by export-led growth and an ever bigger role for the private sector.

This shift from government to private control is often supported even by opponents of the worst excesses of globalization, because of the corruption and inefficiencies of some state-run organizations in the past. However, as recently as 25 years ago, less than a third of the world's countries were democracies, now it stands at nearly two-thirds.[40] Putting trade and domestic industrial policy in the hands of the private sector is far less likely to alleviate overall poverty.

In Côte d'Ivoire, for example, the cocoa market was turned over to the private sector in line with World Bank demands in 1995. This ended a state system of controlled credit and production designed to keep the market stable and small farmers' incomes secure. Liberalization has offered the farmers no protection, despite the fact that the reforms were supposed to benefit them.

Cisse Locine, National Secretary of the Cocoa Farmers Cooperative of Côte d'Ivoire complained that: 'What we have now is a lawless market where merchants are treating farmers any way they want. The merchants have become both referees and players in the market.'[41]

## The Poor Lose Out in Every Export Sector

It is not just the emphasis on agricultural exports that has damaged the poor, but also that on the other traditional large source of developing world export revenue – raw materials. The structural adjustment policies of the World Bank and the IMF encouraged increased exports as a way to repay debts and provide cash for development. The predictable result was a glut and a collapse in prices, made worse by the control in the international trade of such materials by TNCs seeking the biggest returns themselves via holding down the prices paid to producers. In India in 1996, for example, Cargill and Continental, two giant grain traders, bought wheat at US$60–$100 per ton from Indian farmers and sold it at US$230–$240 per ton in the international market. Indian farmers were deprived of millions in export earnings because of the concentrated power of the five major grain merchants.[42]

Mining has always had a history of bad working conditions and damaging environmental effects. Investment liberalization policies have led to an increase in mineral exploration and mining and creates a climate where countries eliminate or ignore environmental protections in order to attract new investment.[43]

The increasing model for developing countries' exports of manufactured goods is the Export Processing Zones (EPZs). At present there are 27 million people working in 850 EPZs worldwide. In these, global manufacturing firms and large local firms import most of their components from overseas subsidiaries and pay production workers very low wages in often appalling working conditions to assemble the products for exports in rich markets.[44] The International Labour Organization (ILO) expects the number of EPZs to grow, especially in the developing world.

The WTO's investment rules also favour such an expansion and it is usually at the expense of the development of a diverse domestic industrial and jobs base. The WTO's TRIMs Agreement forbids developing country governments from requiring that a certain portion of inputs be procured domestically. Also, countries' attempts to enforce labour rights such as workers' rights to organize unions and bargain for better wages and conditions are usually 'rewarded' by companies' relocation.[45]

## Women in Export Service-tude

> '...the widespread perception (is) that female employees are
> more tractable and subservient to managerial authority, less
> prone to organize into unions, more willing to accept lower
> wages, less likely to expect upward job mobility and easier to
> dismiss using life-cycle criteria such as marriage and childbirth.
> In short, behind women's labour force growth stands 'employ-
> ers' needs for cheaper and more 'flexible' sources of labour
> given the rigours of international trade competition.'[46]

The ILO has noted that many of the TNCs in EPZs employ young and
unskilled or semi-skilled women, provide minimal training and under-
take relatively frequent job shedding. Also found was that export
manufacturing and services do not seem to lead to job openings for
women in higher skilled, higher wage positions as the composition of
exports shifts towards more technology-intensive products.[47]

The service sector is a growing proportion of such exports. Entering
data on computer terminals for airline reservations, medical insurance
claims etc, is now carried out by women in countries such as India,
China, Singapore, Barbados, Jamaica, Haiti.

An example of the 'new factory' was described as:

> 'A hundred Barbadian women sit at rows of computer termi-
> nals. They enter 300,000 ticket reservations flowing from
> 2,000 daily flights of a single US airline. In the same building
> one floor above them other women enter data from American
> medical insurance claims. The average hourly wage is only
> $2.50 compared with the same company's $9.50 hourly wage
> for its US-based employees.'

Women have also been the first to lose their jobs. The UN's Economic
and Social Commission for Asia and the Pacific commented that 'This
was inevitable given that women were originally preferred as workers
largely because of the greater ease of dismissal.' Their report on
growing female unemployment in the wake of the East Asian crisis
warned of increasing numbers of women being driven into poverty
and prostitution across the region.[48]

## Export Models Only Success Story?

The one example that development-lobby supporters of the export
route to poverty eradication could point to was the manufacturing and
hi-tech sectors of the NICs. Such a head start was only made possible

by domestic protectionist policies in these countries coinciding with the opening up of markets in the North. Nowadays, under the WTO, such an approach by the South is impossible.

Even before the 1997 Asian crisis finally ended the NICs miracle, relocation was beginning to threaten the domestic advantages of these original countries. Workers there had begun to earn higher wages and the response was for Japanese, Korean, Thai, Taiwanese, and other owners of factories to go offshore in search of cheaper labour.

In mid-1996, a Bangkok-based subsidiary of the Austrian-owned Eden Group, which was manufacturing children's fashion products for the Walt Disney Corporation, sacked 700 workers who protested against the firm's strategy of cutting secure jobs and sub-contracting out work to cheaper workers in rural Thailand and abroad. When the state authorities tried to intervene, the company packed up and left the country surreptitiously, leaving behind millions of dollars in debts both to former employees and to local raw material suppliers.[49]

Once the 1997 crisis hit, the wages and levels of employment slumped in the original NICs. Competitive pressures also became more intense as they and China, Cambodia, Vietnam and the like undercut each other to enter the US market. Indonesia lost 8 million jobs during 1998, resulting in an unemployment rate of 20 per cent. In Thailand and South Korea unemployment more than doubled. The crisis also affected employment in East Asia, in Lao PDR and Vietnam, as well as in the South Asian countries of Sri Lanka, Nepal, Pakistan and Bangladesh. As many as 1.5 million migrant workers faced expulsion.

The Asian tiger economies had also become important providers of FDI for export sectors in other Asian countries and other continents. As the crisis became more acute, much of this investment was frozen or withdrawn, leading to job losses in countries thought to be unaffected by the crisis. Two-thirds of South Korean TNCs either cancelled, scaled down or postponed their investment plans, and intended to follow the same course of action in 1999.[50]

At the same time the NICs were forced to abandon the last vestiges of protection of their domestic economy as the IMF and World Bank investment packages demanded that foreign companies be able to enter domestically controlled sectors like banking. This is almost certain to lead to further relocations offshore as the search for higher investment profits is further disconnected from overall domestic priorities.[51]

## Ruthless Job Competition

Development lobby proponents demanding more access from the North to developing world exports tend to highlight the hypocrisy of the North in delaying opening up markets like agriculture and textiles, compared with the South having been bullied into opening up its markets far more quickly.

The unemployment implications for those in the North tend to be glossed over. A mixture of arguments are put forward, ranging from the South is owed this because of colonialism, to the assertion that the North can afford to shunt displaced workers into other work. The majority in the North have had their improving living standards underpinned to some extent by the fruits of colonial exploitation, but in the South the major gains have been made by a rich and powerful strata. The new colonialism of globalization is now increasing this wealth gap. As the North too is being forced to automate, relocate and curb labour-intensive public sectors, job losses to foreign competition becomes a much more damaging and intractable reality (see Chapter 14).

However, even if Northern opposition could be overcome and the last remaining barriers to the South's exports to the North were removed, the international competitive pressures would result in conditions worsening for the world's poor. Development priorities are and will be pushed aside in the race to the bottom in terms of price, and workers' and environmental conditions necessary to grab these export markets.

China, like Russia, has seen conditions for the majority worsen as both countries have opened up to the market (see Chapter 14 for the effects of relocation and the cheap labour force in China). Should China join the WTO things will worsen both internally and for their developing world competitors for export markets. Wages and conditions will remain very low and probably worsen. An estimated 100 million people have already left the land in search for work in towns and cities, thought to be the biggest migration in human history. WTO membership will result in cheap food imports, thus accelerating rural decline and the move to urban centres. In addition it is expected a further 150 million jobs will be lost as 'inefficient' state enterprises are made ready for international competition. Whatever the actual final numbers, this trend will ensure a permanent cheap labour force whose products will undercut workers in other developing countries as well as in the North.

When Canada removed cotton T-shirts from quota restrictions in 1997, China gained 95% of its market – at the expense of Bangladesh. Mohammed Uzair Afzal, chief executive of the Bangladesh garment manufacturers expressed worry having seen the Chinese Government's forecasts suggesting that its garment exports will double over the next few years, as the Multi-fibre Agreement is phased out by 2005 and their country joins the WTO.[52]

To point this out is not to be anti-Chinese, but anti the immiserating effects that Globalization is already having on them and its implications for their competitors, and for those who propose an export-led route to poverty alleviation for the South in general.

## DEVELOPING WORLD OPPOSITION

Developing world movements are already active in these areas. In addition to getting half a million farmers on the streets to protest against GATT in 1994, recent Indian grass-roots activity against their export economy have included prawn farming. This has taken place in India for 4000 years, but now with global trade and large-scale brackish water prawn aquaculture millions of farmers, farm labourers and fisherfolk, have been marginalized and displaced. It has also led to the destruction of mangrove forests, depletion of natural fishery resources and increased salinity of ground water.

Other areas where Indian farmers' coalitions are fighting large-scale export agriculture includes countering the 'illegal' rollback of land reform policies to enable TNCs and domestic industries to buy agricultural land for growing luxury crops for exports; fighting World Bank policies of privatization of water resources and demanding that water rights were common rights; and opposing new export policies encouraging the slaughtering of 'sacred' farm animals in slaughter houses for meat exports. Also, thousands of villages in Gopalpur in Orissa blocked the setting up of a new steel plant by Tata and Nippon. The steel plant is only for export production and will use iron ore from newly opened mines and energy from new dams. Millions will have to be uprooted for the dams, mines and plants.

Some developing world commentators give their reservations about export-led development in Box 17.2.

## A NEW DEVELOPMENT AGENDA – TRADE AND AID FOR SELF-RELIANCE

The WTO rules should be revised to become a General Agreement for Sustainable Trade (GAST, as detailed in Chapter 12). Aid, technological transfer and the residual international trade should be geared to the building up of sustainable local economies. The goal should be to foster maximum employment through sustainable regional self-reliance.

A handful of developing countries, mostly in Asia, dominate trade with, and until recently received most of the FDI from, the OECD.

## BOX 17.2 DEVELOPING WORLD COMMENTATORS REJECT THE EXPORT ROUTE TO DEVELOPMENT

'... the alternative to state centralisation is not corporate centralisation through global markets. The ecological and democratic model of food security is based as far as possible on ecological production and local consumption. Trade liberalization ignores this truth... Diverting food from rural households and communities to global markets or diverting land from food crops for local consumption to luxury crops for export to the rich north might show growth in dollars in international trade figures but it translates into increased hunger and deprivation in the rural areas of the Third World.'

Vandana Shiva[53]

'... the Southeast Asian governments' position in favor of more liberalization of agricultural markets in the North serves mainly the interests of organized lobbies of cash crop exporters and processors, like Malaysian palm oil plantations, Philippine coconut oil exporters, and Bangkok-based Thai rice middlemen. The vast majority of unorganized small farmers in these countries, who do not have political clout, are harmed by this position, for the quid pro quo of greater market openings for products like palm oil and coconut oil in the North is even greater liberalization of sectors like rice and corn in Asia, where small farmers are concentrated.

'... This is why it is important for ASEAN governments, small farmers, and consumer groups to study closely the arguments being advanced by the Japan and South Korean governments – under pressure from their small farmers – to oppose another round of liberalization: that small farm agriculture in Asia, though it may seem inefficient in terms of unit cost, actually produces net gains because agriculture is "multifunctional": that is, it protects biodiversity, guarantees food security against the volatility of world trade, promotes rural social development, is part of the national cultural heritage, and enhances the regional landscape.'

Walden Bello[54]

'The women call it "the Boundary". The barbed-wire fence which encloses them for up to 12 hours a day ... of the Noida Export Processing zone, 24 km from India's capital city... Inside, it is hot, dirty and dangerous. Security is tight – humiliating body-searches are routine – and trade union activity is forbidden... nearly 4000 women work in the zone... Dhiraj Singh, a manager at Garmex India, whose export-ready garments are stitched by 600 women and 100 men, is remarkably frank about hiring practices. "There are so many benefits with women employees" he says. "Administratively, it is easy to control women. We do not need to have too much security. We prefer the age group 18 to 30 years, preferably single"... For Sita and her daughters, the day (in a surgical glove factory) starts before dawn and ends at midnight.'

T K Rajlakshmi[55]

They could substitute this trade over a perhaps five- to ten-year transition period by increasing their inter-regional trade.

Increasingly, countries are in regional trading blocs; these can form the basis of the localized trading system by changing their end goals away from trade liberalization towards localization brought about by the *Protect the Local, Globally* policies in Part Two.

The key challenge is not to encourage further spirals of ruthless competition, but for new rules to facilitate the building up and diversification of local economies globally. These will be major engines for change that will help bring about conditions to meet the needs of the poor majority. Such a major transition requires the grass-roots movements and the development lobby to campaign actively for it.

# Chapter 18

# Localizing Food Security

*'Food security exists when all people, at all times, have physical and economic access to sufficient, safe, and nutritious food to meet their dietary need and food preferences for an active and healthy life.'*[1]

## GLOBALIZATION AND AGRICULTURE

The WTO Agreement on Agriculture (AOA) brought agriculture into GATT for the first time. It was negotiated initially between the US and the EU to provide a global framework for price support reduction and other measures. This was necessary because of the huge subsidies each bloc was giving to their respective agricultural sectors to cope with the effects of increased competition between the blocs. The AOA was opposed by many Southern governments as being biased to the advantage of Northern interests and they only agreed to it under pressure from the US and Europe.

The North claimed that the South benefited through the lifting of quotas and reducing tariffs on developing country exports such as palm and coconut oils. However, such concessions largely benefit huge corporate agribusiness in the South and Southern markets were opened up to cheap imports of rice and corn which mostly hurt small farmers.[2]

The free trade vision of the WTO AOA (see also Chapter 12) is a disaster for the food security of poor countries, as subsistence farms are increasingly replaced by export production. It also has adverse environmental and food safety effects as agricultural commodities are transported long distances and processed and packaged to survive the journey. Historically this has meant breeding programmes to improve durability, but more recently new varieties are literally being designed to withstand this transportation (eg the genetically altered tomato).

Global food production and trade is thought to consume more fossil fuel than any other industrial sector.[3] Vandana Shiva in India is a potent critic of trade liberalization and its effects on agriculture; an excerpt from her forthcoming report is given in Box 18.1.

# BOX 18.1 WHY CASH CROP EXPORTS HARM THE RURAL MAJORITY AND THE INDIAN ECONOMY

### By Vandana Shiva[5]

Trade liberalization policies were imposed on Indian agriculture in 1991 by the IMF through structural adjustment programmes linked to a $91b debt. One third of this debt was related to industrial agriculture – for dams, import of machinery, pesticides, fertilisers and fossil fuel.

When trade liberalization policies were introduced in 1991 in India, the Agriculture Secretary stated that 'food security is not food in the godowns [grain warehouses] but dollars in the pocket'. It is repeatedly argued that food security does not depend on food 'self-sufficiency' (growing and storing your own food as a country) but on food 'self-reliance' (buying your food from international markets).

Three areas of exports which have been heavily promoted under the new trade liberalization regime are aquaculture, floriculture and meat. According to the received ideology of free-trade the export earnings from exports of farmed shrimp, flowers and meat would finance imports of food, and hence any short fall created by the diversion of productive capacity from growing food for domestic consumption to growing luxury items for consumption by rich northern consumers would be more than made up.

However, it is neither efficient nor sustainable to grow shrimps, flowers and meat for export in India. In each case more food production capacity is destroyed domestically through diversion of resources and destruction of ecosystems than the food that can be purchased on global markets through exports. India can buy only one fourth of the food it could have grown with export earnings from floriculture. Our food security has therefore declined by seventy five per cent.

In the case of meat exports, for every dollar earned, India is destroying fifteen dollars worth of ecological functions performed by farm animals for sustainable agriculture. Cattle in India are the sources of organic fertilisers and renewable energy. When they are killed for exports, these essential services given freely by the cattle to the farmer are destroyed and we have to import chemical fertilisers and fossil fuels, thus increasing foreign exchange outflow and leading to increased climate instability.

In the case of shrimp exports, every Rupee of export earnings has generated more than five Rupees of ecological destruction of water, biodiversity, agriculture and fisheries. Industrial shrimp farming destroys 200 times more area than the actual size of ponds through salinisation of ground water, pollution of coastal waters, destruction of agriculture and mangroves. More food production is destroyed through destruction of domestic agriculture and fisheries than can be purchased by the export earnings from industrially farmed shrimp. Further, export earnings go to rich industrial houses, and the price of destruction is paid by poor peasants and artisanal fisherman.

Thus, as a society, we are paying more in terms of food insecurity and ecological destruction than we are earning through exports of luxury crops such as shrimps, flowers and meat.

The growth as projected in industrial agriculture is thus based on dissimulating the scarcity produced at 3 levels:

a) The ecological scarcity created by wasteful use of resources.
b) The food insecurity generated for producers by diverting more food to national or local markets or converting from food to non-food crops.
c) The economic insecurity generated for small farmers by rising costs and rising debts.

The ecological destruction of land, water and biodiversity undermines food security in the present and the future since those resources would have gone to produce more food.

## TNCs Take Over Global Food Supply

The winners in the North and South are the large industrial agricultural corporations, the losers are small family farms and subsistence farmers. In the US in 1998, for example, pork exports went up by 27 per cent, the large food processors had record profits, but the price paid to small pig farmers fell by over 200 per cent.

Current WTO rules limit the right of governments to support small family farms such as through tax breaks. One result has been their replacement with corporate-owned industrial-style livestock facilities, particularly in the US, and the increased takeover of agriculture by huge TNCs. Unlike small farmers these TNCs are subsidized by other means, such as export subsidies or foreign-investment insurance, as WTO rules have allowed the maintenance and even an increase in subsidies for export. As a result many countries now provide higher financial supports for companies involved in exports, or foreign investments.

Such subsidies have led to an increase in 'export dumping' as companies are able to sell products abroad at prices below their actual cost of production. The WTO has rules that ban dumping, but by permitting export subsidies, it hands corporations the loophole they need to circumvent the ban, to dump products at below cost, and to drive out smaller competitors, usually in smaller, poorer countries.[4]

## Changing the UK Food Systems

The current phase of globalization in agriculture is characterized by concentration at national, regional and international levels and the UK food industry is one of the most concentrated in Europe (see Box 9.1 in Chapter 9). Since the mid-1990s, there has been a wave of global mergers and acquisitions (M&As) in the food manufacturing sector. Between 1993 and 1995 there were almost 1500 M&As within the food and drink industry worldwide.[6]

*'In 50 years' time Britain's countryside could have become a factory, with big, mysterious sheds in a flawless prairie and irrevocably so, as the infrastructure needed to do otherwise will be gone. Or it could be an endless trail of golf courses and caravans, if farmers finally accept that in a globalised market they can no longer compete with other people's climates and their willingness to work for slave wages, both prospects are dire. We must do better...*

*We should acknowledge (for the first time in history) that farming is primarily for feeding people – which means providing sufficient amounts of food that meets the highest criteria of nutrition, gastronomy and safety. But farming should also be kind to livestock, be good for producers (plenty of people securely employed in interesting jobs) and provide a countryside that is both rich and aesthetically pleasing – though we should match our aesthetic standards with the needs of wildlife.'*

Colin Tudge[7]

Globalization always stresses the advantages for consumers of increased choice and keener prices from trade liberalization. Certainly, a hypermarket with 20,000 items is a cornucopia of choice and range, but questions about how important and superficial this advantage is has been a hallmark of the new food movement almost everywhere. Critics have argued that choice at the cost of environmental, cultural, safety and health considerations is a bad choice.[8]

## Who Benefits and Who is in Control?[9]

Most obviously, the poor are not the winners. In the UK, despite the fact that since the 1950s the percentage of household expenditure on food has dropped from about a quarter to a tenth of total household expenditure, the gaps between rich and poor are large. The poorest tenth spend a quarter to a third of their incomes on food, while the richest spend nearer 10 per cent. The poorest children eat less than half the fresh fruit and vegetables consumed by the richest children. Post-war, the gap in fruit consumption between rich and poor was narrowing, but is now widening again.

Even within commerce, the picture is mixed. Although dominated by highly profitable companies, the food trade gap of the UK food sector is in deficit with the rest of the world. According to government figures, the total food and drink trade imbalance has risen from £5.5 billion in 1989 to £7.7 billion in 1996, ie the country imported £7.7 billion more food than it exported. The fruit and vegetables trade gap in 1989 was £2.5 billion and by 1996 £3.84 billion.

Consumer food culture has been dramatically altered in the postwar period by the arrival of more processed foods and by changes in retailing, and the role of women in the waged labour force. In the EU as a whole, there has also been some convergence of food tastes and consumption patterns. Simple traditional dishes prepared from raw products in the household are being replaced with refined, industrially processed food; food consumption patterns no longer follow the seasonal cycle; and there is an increase in exotic foods among certain groups.

In the 1960s and 1970s, processed foods increased in both number and range in the UK, as in North America. By 1982 only a fifth of UK food was fresh with minimal packaging. Critics have predicted that a culture of dependency on pre-cooked food is in the making.

There is a dilemma for government here. On the one hand, health educators argue that people should take more control of their diets to meet health targets such as obesity and heart disease reduction. Yet on the other hand, one of the simple means for people controlling their diet, namely cooking their own, is made harder by a skills deficiency. There are 18 hours of food programmes on UK television, but cooking is in decline. The reality is that cooking now occurs mainly in the factory or commercial kitchen; TV makes it a voyeuristic experience and the introduction of a new compulsory National Curriculum for schools in the 1990s gave no room to practical food skills.

There is a growing backlash against some of these trends. There is an increasing demand from consumers for safer, more organically grown food. There is also a gradual increase in the number of farmers markets which only source from locally grown products. Recent health scares over food such as BSE and *E coli* have made people keener to know the source of their food where possible. Box 18.2 illustrates the tensions in the food system.

## CAN LOCALIZATION PROVIDE GLOBAL FOOD SECURITY?

The demands of the global food movement tend to concentrate on:

- Land reform and redistribution.
- The ability to put national food security before the concentration on exports and dependence on imports.
- Shifting subsidies from dumping Northern food surpluses to the detriment of the developing world and Eastern Europe, to paying for a transition to organic farming, marketed locally.

## BOX 18.2 TENSIONS IN THE FOOD SYSTEM

The future of food is one of tensions between different visions of the future, both being actively pursued and supported by different interests and 'constituencies'. In the table below, the left-hand column broadly represents those characteristics pursued within the food system driven by globalization, whilst the right-hand column represents counter trends associated with forces seeking the relocalization of food.

| Trends driven by globalization | Counter trends associated with relocalization |
| --- | --- |
| urban/rural divisions | urban-rural partnership |
| long trade routes (food miles) | short trade routes |
| import/export model of food security | food from own resources |
| intensification | extensification |
| fast speed, pace and scale of change | slow pace, speed, scale of change |
| non-renewable energy | re-usable energy |
| few market players (concentration) | multiple players per sector |
| costs externalized | costs internalized |
| rural de-population | vibrant rural population |
| monoculture | biodiversity |
| science replacing labour | science supporting nature |
| agrochemicals | organic/sustainable farming |
| biotechnology | indigenous knowledge |
| processed (stored) food | fresh (perishable) food |
| food from factories | food from the land |
| hypermarkets | markets |
| de-skilling | skilling |
| standardization | 'difference' and diversity |
| niche markets on shelves | real variety on field and plate |
| people to food | food to people |
| fragmented (diverse) culture | common food culture |
| created wants (advertising) | real wants (learning through culture) |
| burgerization | local food specialities |
| microwave re-heated food | cooked food |
| fast food | slow food |
| global decisions | local decisions |
| top-down controls | bottom-up controls |
| dependency culture | self-reliance |
| health inequalities widening | health inequalities narrowing |
| social polarization and exclusion | social inclusion |
| consumers | citizens |

- The rebuilding of rural economies and infrastructure to decrease wealth discrepancies within rural areas and between rural and urban areas.
- A move towards more ecologically sustainable organic agriculture which benefits small and medium-sized farmers.

- Production of safe food in a way that is environmentally sensitive and puts animal welfare at its core.
- A move away from hi-tech, intensive agriculture such as that depending on GM food and continued high uses of pesticides.
- Perhaps most fundamentally, a re-balancing of power and control away from TNCs (fostered by the trade rules of the WTO) and towards national control over the setting of food security priorities.

Prodigious numbers of books and reports illustrating the need for each of the above have been published. Issue-specific battles fought by NGOs and movements have had their degree of success; ranged from baby food campaigns, to land redistribution in Brazil, to fighting GMOs. Despite this, in most developing countries and much of Eastern Europe, the food security position is worsening for people.

The FAO have also said of this worsening situation:

*'We consider it intolerable that more than 800 million throughout the world and particularly in developing countries do not have enough food to meet their basic nutritional needs... the problems of hunger and food insecurity have global dimensions and are likely to persist, and even increase dramatically in some regions, unless urgent, determined and concerted action is taken.'*

## Food Security GATT Screwed

The results of the GATT Uruguay Round were bad for world food security. The WTO's disputes mechanism has ruled in ways that harm food security in its widest sense – see Chapter 19 for the ruling on beef hormones and the potential ruling on GM food and Chapter 17 about the banana dispute.

The WTO's AOA goes in the wrong direction. The world needs new food policy rules to protect local production for local need. The AOA enshrined the 1970s formulae – deregulation, economic efficiency, international competitiveness, and a dogmatic reliance on the market. Yet there is enough evidence that these policies do not increase food security. In the Northern model of industrialized efficiency, self-reliance is out, trade is in. Of course, with the vagaries of weather, terrain and season limiting the range of goods that can be grown in any one region, some trade in food is inevitable. The new goal, however, should be self-reliance where possible, deriving food from the locality first, then the geographical region and from world resources only as a last resort.

Already, Southern agricultural investment is too often export-led. In the Gambia, roads have been installed radiating from the airport to getting fresh foods to Northern Europe faster. This sets the Gambia in competition with Kenya – another developing country – a competition from which only the trader and the distant consumer benefit. This puts traders in the position to mediate between producer and consumer and creates a new dependency culture – developing world suppliers for the affluent. Some argue that this enables small farmers to make much-needed cash from a part of their acreage. Historically, as more competitors enter the market, this doesn't remain so.

Similarly, calls for a blanket reduction of tariff barriers both to developing countries' exports to the North and between developing world countries will be harmful. Zimbabwe's textile industry, for example, has been decimated by, amongst others, exports from South Africa, as the latter flexes its economic dominance as tariffs are lowered regionally.

The answer lies in less international trade overall, not more.

## Achieving Food Security

Mitigating trade liberalization's adverse effects by calling for the stabilizing of raw commodities' prices and trade in more value-added food products is inadequate. As are appeals to niche markets for ethically better 'fair trade' that supports small farmers and less environmentally damaging production. While both of these have their value, this policy still substitutes one form of dependency upon external trade for another. The real role of exports should be as a useful adjunct in the transition to an end-goal of maximum self-reliance.

In terms of the campaign goals of food activists listed earlier, the transition to maximum self-reliance using the policy tools of *Protect the Local, Globally* is a precondition for a number of reasons. Land reform cannot take place if the thrust of all government's policies is to compete internationally. This requires keeping costs low and encouraging inward investors seeking maximum returns to locate and not relocate. It also needs a pool of cheap labour and farming intensively to reap economies of scale. Finally, international competitiveness, means land reform can never happen on the scale required as investors must not be frightened off with too radical and egalitarian social and farm policies.

However, once a country's food goals and those of its regional neighbours are only to accept investment and to consider exports when they contribute towards greater self-reliance, then land reform also becomes a prerequisite. Similarly, surplus dumping, import dependence and export concentration will wither away as there is a much greater emphasis on national food needs and far less dependence on producing surpluses.

To have a more self-reliant food system will need the rebuilding of rural economies and infrastructure, and a decrease in wealth discrepancies. This is crucial, since for developing countries in particular, such spreading of opportunities and wealth in the rural sector will be necessary for building up the demand for the goods from a growing domestic manufacturing and services sector.

For both developed and developing nations, the increasing dependence on local food resources should act as a spur to improve the environmental sustainability of local resource use, since this is where the future food supply will predominantly come from. More labour-intensive, less intensive agriculture will not only improve the local economy, but also ensure that new techniques are developed that will not threaten the local agricultural resource base, since importing your way out of problems becomes less of an option. The emphasis on resource taxes, including energy and agricultural pollution taxes, to help fund the transition to localization, will also direct agricultural practices towards more sustainable patterns.

As economic security increases, and attention turns to more than just the quantity of food available, then issues such as food quality, animal welfare and their links to human health begin to go up the public agenda. The most significant improvement inherent in the *Protect the Local, Globally* form of localization is that it controls TNCs activities and investment patterns. These players will not be able to force down wages or conditions through the threat of relocation. Access to national markets depends on being in that market and staying there. The increased control of governments, plus the local competition laws, dramatically reduces the power of TNCs to control the world food system. The less trade internationally, the more local control under this system.

# Chapter 19

# The WTO and the Environment

## GREEN GLOBALIZATION – AN IMPOSSIBILITY

*'[Environmental standards in the WTO are] ... doomed to fail and could only damage the global trading system.'*
Renato Ruggiero, former WTO Secretary General[1]

At the heart of environmentalists' myriad demands is the necessity to use resources frugally, for industry, services and agriculture to cause minimal pollution, to preserve wildlife, wildernesses and biodiversity, and to maximize recycling. More recently, this agenda has been broadened to ensure that during the process of change that democratic control of the emerging society is increased, human, cultural and animal rights respected and strengthened, and inequality decreased. Globalization thwarts this with its trade rules. The transition from today's unequal and environmentally destructive world economy to a future where 'sustainable development' becomes the norm is made impossible.

What stops it occurring is that it is very expensive to extract resources with minimal pollution, use them frugally and ensure that the products of use are as recyclable as possible. It is far cheaper and hence the products are more competitive if the environment and the local community, particularly the poor, pay the real price in terms of ecological despoilation, pollution and ill-health.

The environmental movement has changed public attitudes, particularly in the business world, but the gap between attitude changes and adequate action is still large. Environmentalists have stopped some of the worst excesses, but the adverse processes are speeding up. The higher levels of environmental taxes necessary to shift our economies to a more sustainable path aren't being introduced because of international competitiveness.

Finally, the trade rules which outlaw measures deemed to be a 'barrier to trade' undermine effective protection of domestic activities which are employing good environmental practice. A nation transferring to more environmental production processes would have had to borrow and/or invest in improvements (eg clean production or the shift to organic agriculture). This would be reflected in the price of the goods or service they are providing, but they would not be able to prevent competition from cheaper imports from areas not having such stringent environmental regulations. Worse, such rules allied to the constant demands of international competitiveness can erode already existing laws and prevent the introduction of more stringent ones, for fear of losing potential foreign investors or companies

## BRIEF HISTORY OF THE TRADE AND ENVIRONMENT DEBATE

Many environmental activists are aware of these problems. Canadian environmentalists were among the first to raise concerns about the relationship between international trade and the environment during the Canada–US free trade negotiations nearly ten years ago. They also played an important role in bringing these important issues to the attention of environmentalists in the US, Europe and elsewhere.

As they predicted, trade dispute processes have now become a popular weapon for attacking environmental and conservation measures across the world. Indeed, a GATT challenge to US Marine Mammal Protection legislation played an important role in gaining the attention of US environmentalists and law-makers during the more recent NAFTA debates. Trade and environment issues actually became so troublesome in the US that NAFTA was amended to include (nominal) environmental concerns. The most significant of these amendments provided some protection from free trade rules for certain multilateral environmental agreements (MEAs), such as the 1992 Climate and Biodiversity conventions. The other accommodation to the environmental groups that were foolishly willing to support NAFTA[2] was the establishment of the North American Commission on Environmental Co-operation (NACEC).

### WTO Committee on Trade and the Environment

During the early 1990s, similar developments were also taking place in Europe and elsewhere, and the environmental implications of the Uruguay Round trade negotiations began to emerge as important issues. However, environmental concerns never achieved the prominence needed in this larger global economic context to force amendments to the agreement that created the WTO. Instead, a long-dormant GATT Committee on Trade and the Environment was reconstituted as the WTO Committee on Trade and the Environment (CTE). The CTE was given a very broad mandate and, in late 1996, reported to the first biennial meeting of the WTO in Singapore. While few environmentalists knew of its existence, a handful of environmental groups tracked its deliberations or became actively engaged in its discussions, which ultimately centred on three issues:

1   The relationship between the WTO and trade measures authorized by several MEAs, such as the Basel Convention on Toxic Wastes, the Montreal (ozone) Protocol and the Convention on International Trade in Endangered Species of Wild Flora and Fauna (CITES).
2   The use of eco-labelling, a way to convey information to the consumer about the product or about the production or harvesting processes associated with that product.
3   The effects of environmental measures on market access, within the context of 'considering the benefits of removing trade restrictions'.

In important ways, the CTE has actually become a forum for asserting the pre-eminence of trade over environmental goals. It has asserted the right of a WTO member to challenge measures adopted by another member, even when taken in accordance with the provisions of a MEA to which it is a signatory. The committee's work is likely to actually *undermine* the integrity of agreements such as the Climate Convention and the same criticism can be made of its discussions about eco-labelling.

The official rhetoric suggested otherwise with Vice President Gore at the signing of the Uruguay Round Agreement in Marakesh stating: 'As the world moves to resolve environmental problems and strengthen environmental protection, the corresponding trade implications will have to be discussed openly in the World Trade Organization, as well as other fora. The decision to create the Committee on Trade and Environment within the World Trade Organization provides the formal means to do so... This Committee ... has a mandate to develop recommendations for necessary change.'

But the CTE become a venue for identifying environmental measures that should be eliminated to avoid trade conflicts, and a flurry of proposals arose to place *greater* constraints on the MEAs to be enforced via trade measures.

## WTO Dispute Settlement Panels

*'[The WTO] ... is the place where governments collude in private against their domestic pressure groups. Allowing*

*NGOs in could open the doors to ... all kinds of lobbyists*
*opposed to free trade.'*

WTO official[3]

The WTO's greatest power lies in its Dispute Settlement Body and its cross-retaliation provisions. Any WTO member state can complain to the body about any other member's policies or laws that are perceived to restrict the free flow of trade. During its first four years, the dispute settlement mechanism has been invoked predominantly for disputes between the EU and the US and first decisions provide evidence of the WTO's anti-environmental stance and the central, although often behind the scenes, role played by TNCs. The beef hormone case is considered in detail, and others are then examined briefly to show the scale of the problem.

## WTO Versus European Consumers

In May 1997, a three-person WTO dispute settlement panel ruled that a nine-year ban imposed by the EU on hormone-treated beef was illegal under WTO rules. The ruling, which overturned an important consumer health law, caused outrage throughout Europe. On May 13th 1999 a deadline was set by the WTO for the EU to drop its ban and allow the imports of beef fed with growth promoting hormones. The EU refused and the WTO authorized the Clinton Administration to impose US$116.4 million of trade sanctions on European goods including Roquefort cheese, chewing gum, raspberry jam and motorcycles.[4]

The background to this dispute shows how TNCs use free trade rules to further their own interests. Over the past decade, Monsanto, a US-based TNC which formerly produced chemicals, has restyled itself into a life science corporation, leaning heavily on the manipulation of genetic material. One of its products is a recombinant bovine growth hormone (rBGH), used by large-scale dairy farmers in the US to increase milk production. Other 'natural' hormones such as oestradiol and testosterone are also commonly used by US cattle farmers. In 1995, 90 per cent of US cattle were treated with some type of growth hormone to make them grow faster and larger.

In January 1989, the EU, applying the 'precautionary principle', deemed safety claims by US industry unconvincing and imposed a ban on the import of hormone-treated beef and milk. The ban also applied to producers within the EU. In response to strong lobbying by Monsanto, the US National Cattlemen's Association, the US Dairy Export Council, the National Milk Producers Federation and other interest groups, then US Trade Representative, Mickey Kantor, initiated action in the WTO against the ban.[5]

On the EU side, industry groups such as FEDESA, the primary lobby organization for the European animal 'health' products industry, and the European Federation of Pharmaceutical Industry Associations (EFPIA), both members of EuropaBio (the primary biotech lobby group in the EU), pressured the Commission to lift the ban, which was affecting European companies as well. Echoing their US counterparts, they argued that there is always some risk with food involving genetic modification or hormone treatment.[6]

Pressure from consumer protection organizations and other NGOs made the Commission realize that the lifting of its ban on hormone-treated beef and milk could have a high political cost. Supported by a growing body of evidence suggesting that certain natural and synthetic hormones are linked to rising incidences of cancer, the Commission decided not to lift its ban, despite the WTO ruling.

The preliminary decision in the dispute over hormone beef is the first ruling thus far (see Chapter 12) based on a WTO agreement known as the Sanitary and Phytosanitary Agreement (SPS). This agreement requires that restrictions based on food health and safety be based on scientific evidence, and accepts internationally agreed standards, such as those decided within the UN system, as a justification for taking protective trade measures. Since the FAO deemed the hormones to be safe, the WTO panel ruled that the EU's ban was unjustified and should be lifted.

This ruling sets a dangerous precedent for national consumer health and safety protection laws. Many experts believe that various EU measures, such as those regulating other animal products, may now also be challenged by the US and other nations. The process of whittling away consumer protection laws and regulations in Europe and elsewhere will thus continue unabated unless steps are taken to reverse this trend.

The WTO justification was that the EU's ban was not backed up by the proper risk analysis and that the legal burden is on the EU to prove that such hormones are not safe in order to enact a ban. The EU public health ban on beef containing artificial hormones on the other hand was based on the 'precautionary principle' which would place the burden on the industry to show its product was safe. The US insisted that the EU complies fully with the WTO ruling. Failure by the EU to lift its ban on hormone-treated beef was to lead to the threat of punitive duties.

The EU has been importing only hormone-free beef from the US and other countries since 1989. Furthermore, the EU recently threatened to extend its ban to cover all US beef exports because of fears that US beef shipped as hormone free may actually contain hormone residue.

In addition, in an effort to satisfy the WTO's demand for scientific evidence, the EU's Scientific Committee on Veterinary Measures Relating to Public Health published a report on 3 May, 1999 on the threat to human health posed by growth hormones in US beef.[7] It stated that the growth hormone 17 beta-oestradiol: 'has to be considered as a complete carcinogen... It exerts both tumor initiating and tumor promoting effects. In plain language this means that even small additional doses of residues of this hormone in meat, arising from its use as a growth promoter in cattle, has an inherent risk of causing cancer.'

The committee said it also had inadequate data to make a definitive finding on other growth hormones used in US beef: progesterone, testosterone, zeranol, trenbolone and melengestrol acetate. Although the scientists said exposure to small levels of residues in meat and meat products 'carries risks.'

The report said the six hormones may cause a variety of health problems including cancer, developmental problems, harm to immune systems and brain disease, but it acknowledged 'the available data do not enable a quantitative estimate of the risk'. Its 'greatest concern' was for the most sensitive sub-group of the human population, prepubertal children, as they have the lowest physiological hormone levels.

It is not just the legal use of such hormones that caused the Committee concern, they also warned of the added dangers of illegal use. They assert that there is evidence that the abusive use of six growth hormones for growth promotion purposes creates a significant increase in risk. Human exposure and risk are in particular increased by the fact that regulatory controls over residues of hormones in meat placed on the market are 'deficient in the USA and are insufficient in Canada'.

Abusive uses can include misplacement of approved implants in places other than the ears, off-label uses of hormonal growth promoters, use of multiple implants simultaneously or within very short time intervals and the use of unapproved substances obtained on the black market.

The Commission asserted that 'there can be no question of lifting the ban' because of the health risks identified in the report. Emma Bonino, Brussels' consumer policy commissioner said the study vindicated the beef ban and provided the EU with a scientific defence of its position. The US response was that it was based on 'faulty science'.[8]

The Commission's reply was that it 'is deeply concerned about the US' attempt to belittle the risk which scientists have identified. (It) cannot understand why the US has not reacted in a more responsible way... It is all the more incomprehensible as pre-pubertal children are the population group most at risk.'[9]

The resulting WTO-authorized fine by the US of US$116.4 million of trade sanctions on European goods has led to fears that the TNCs will again use the US to force Europe to import GM foods and GM growth hormones to increase milk production.

## Other WTO Threats to Environmental Laws

The Tuna-Dolphin, Shrimp-Turtle and Venezuela Gas rulings described below reveal a systemic bias in the WTO rules and the dispute resolution process against the rights of sovereign states to enact and effectively enforce environmental laws. All three rulings have led (or will lead, if implemented) to weakening of US laws.

In 1992, a GATT panel ruled against the US Marine Mammal Protection Act (MMPA) law forbidding sale in the US of tuna caught by domestic or foreign fishers using techniques that had killed hundreds of thousands of dolphins. Four years later, the Clinton Administration lobbied Congress intensively to amend the MMPA to implement the GATT ruling after Mexican threats of a WTO enforcement case. In late 1999, the US will again import tuna caught using mile-long nets set around schools of dolphins. In fact, under the Clinton Administration-pushed MMPA amendments, this tuna can be certified as 'Dolphin-Safe.'[10]

In April 1998, the WTO also ruled in favour of a complaint against the US law restricting the import of shrimps from countries whose fishermen catch them with methods that drown thousands of turtles annually – see Chapter 17. The US turtle protection rules fall under the Endangered Species Act. But this ruling, if implemented, would debilitate the US law by requiring the elimination of its provisions requiring foreign countries to mandate use of Turtle Excluder Devices (TEDs) on their shrimp trawlers. The US will only be allowed to target individual shrimp boats, which is expected to encourage the practice of 'shrimp-laundering'. This involves shrimps that are harvested on boats without TEDs, being imported on boats with TEDs, and passed off to US consumers as 'turtle-friendly'.[11]

Anti-environmental bias is also prevalent in other recent WTO edicts. In January 1996, the WTO ruled in favour of complaints from Venezuela and Brazil opposed to the US Environmental Protection Agency's (EPA) Clean Air Act. The gasoline pollution regulation was deemed to have discriminated against the more polluting Venezuelan and Brazilian refineries. In May 1997, the EPA announced it was changing the Clean Air Act to comply with the WTO's decision. This involved adopting a policy towards limiting contaminants in foreign gasoline that the EPA had earlier rejected as effectively unenforceable.[12]

The US has also instigated WTO action in addition to the beef hormone case above and the Banana case described in Chapter 17. It is trying to get the EU to stop recycling components of electrical goods. Environmentalists fear that the WTO might eventually strike down provisions in MEAs to protect the ozone layer (Montreal Protocol), control the dumping of toxic waste overseas (Basle Convention) and to ban trade in endangered species (CITES).[13] All of these treaties involve constraints in trade.

Finally, some governments are using uncertainty over WTO rules to prevent the incorporation of trade measures of any description into new and existing environmental agreements. Thus, trade officials at environmental negotiating fora have been arguing that eco-labelling should not be encouraged by the Intergovernmental Panel on Forests; trade measures should not be incorporated into the Prior Informed Consent Convention on trade in toxic products, or the proposed Biosafety Protocol to the Convention on Biodiversity.[14]

Countries can initiate challenges to other countries' trading practices when limits are imposed due to their environmental or consumer laws. Business has taken advantage of this and a process of mutual undermining of such regulations is underway. US corporations lobby the US government to target EU regulations; their subsidiaries and partners in Europe lobby the EU to target US regulations.

As has been seen above, North American interests have sought to overturn European bans on the use of bovine somatotrofin (BST), a genetically engineered growth hormone for cattle, as well as on the sale of furs caught with steel leg-hold traps. Meanwhile, the EU has challenged US fuel consumption standards in cars, food safety laws including the Delaney Amendment which bans carcinogenic chemicals from food, limitation on lead in consumer products, state recycling laws, and restrictions on driftnet fishing and whaling.[15]

## Deregulating the Environment

Deregulation is also a useful route for TNCs to undermine environmental laws. In Europe, the German and UK governments set up a business group who published *Deregulation Now*. It concentrated on deregulating the food, chemicals and transport sectors and stated 'any overlay of European standards, over and above existing international and national standards, should be resisted otherwise the competitiveness of European industry will be damaged.'[16]

In the UK, for example, since 1994, 605 regulations have been identified for deregulation, 129 of these concerned the Department of the Environment and included measures covering health and safety, biotechnology, advertising in sensitive areas, hedgerow preservation, food standards and energy efficiency.[17]

## And Then There is GM Food

> 'Absolute definitions of food safety are impossible. Any
> decision about acceptable levels of risk cannot be purely scien-
> tific – it must be political. Governments should decide what
> level of risk they are prepared to accept for their citizens... But
> just because the US chooses to accept the risks – whatever they
> might be – of unregulated use of GM foods, there is no justifi-
> cation for them to impose their choice, and this risk, on every
> other country through the mechanism of the WTO.'
>
> Duncan Brack, Royal Institute of International Affairs[18]

In the summer of 1999, the EU lost twice to the US in WTO disputes,
and paid heavily for the privilege. The banana trade row resulted in
sanctions of around US\$190m (£121.8m) and the dispute over
hormone-treated beef cost a further US\$116m. Yet all this will pale
into insignificance when compared with the massive collision between
the blocs over GM food.

The WTO's rules can effectively be used to impose the US' choice
on GM food on the whole world because the rules demand that
countries prove such products are unsafe before they can refuse to
import them. In a logical world, the exporters would have to prove
that their exports are safe.

In the case of GM food, European concern about their impact on
human health and biodiversity has led to widespread public protest, a
huge public debate and the major retailers withdrawing GM foods
from their shelves as fast as possible. Austria and Luxembourg
maintain bans on biotech products that have been approved by the
EU Commission.[19] The European Green Party is implacably opposed
to the technology. The Greens are against the use and sale of animal
products produced with hormone growth promoters and all GM
foods, feedstuffs and growth promoters for livestock. They have
demanded these products be banned and their import halted and
instead there be a shift to organic food production.[20]

In the US, there is less public debate but concern is growing, particularly among some farmers. They are worried that yields have not been
as high as predicted, foreign markets have been lost and the fact that
Monsanto is taking farmers to court to prevent them from obtaining
patented seeds illegally to protect the company's billions of dollars of
investments.[21] Yet in a few years, almost all US food exports are
expected to contain some element of GM products.[22] This will lead to
increased pressure from Europeans for the EU to impose restrictions.

Given the way one US banana company, Chiquita, was able to 'rent' the US government to get the WTO to protect its commercial interests,[23] the billion dollar GM industry could do the same over GM products. On past record the US would take the EU to the WTO should the EU try to impose any restrictions. Richard Rominger, US deputy agricultural secretary, has already accused the EU of costing America about £100 million in sales of US maize because of its delays in setting labelling standards for GM-free food. Kenneth Hobbie, president of the US Grains Council, asserted that GM food was the 'hottest issue in agriculture today'.[24]

## Less Public Expenditure, Less Environmental Protection

A lot of public expenditure is likely to be required for measures to adequately protect the environment. Free trade requires continuous curbing of the public purse. Some countries have a history of higher taxes and welfare than others and yet are competitors. However, in Europe, the examples of the pressure on Sweden and Germany, traditionally high-tax countries, to curb public expenditure to improve competitiveness are likely to reduce the gap between high-tax and low tax countries.

The trend towards limiting tax and public expenditure will make it more difficult to tackle perhaps the major environmental threat: climate change. This will require a total reorientation of our use and abuse of energy and of our transportation systems. Moving away from fossil fuels towards renewables, energy efficiency and conservation is potentially self-financing over the longer term, on paper. However it will require enormous amounts of up-front resources in terms of grants, loans, tax breaks and so on to pay for the initial transition to different fuels and reduced energy use.

Although money can be saved by measures such as the cancelling of nuclear programmes and mega road schemes, huge financial inducements and cash outlays will be required for the rebuilding of public transport to levels where car use is dramatically curtailed. To lubricate the transition will be very costly, regardless of whether the service is eventually provided publicly or privately.

Similarly, if countries are to shift their food and agricultural system towards organic farming, local food production and marketing, and more healthy, fresh and less highly processed food, this too will require enormous funds to pay for it. Money will also be required to enable the poorer sections of society to be able to afford the more expensive farming and food products.

In terms of the day-to-day workings of industry and services, moving from today's polluting activities to cleaner production methods and less materials use will also require financial inducements.

Free traders and some techno-optimists respond that if the market signals are clear enough, (eg tighter regulation or rising energy, resource and pollution taxes) then industry and services will adapt and respond. Many environmentalists repeat the arguments of the last 20 years that if only green taxes were introduced then the true costs to the environment of the energy, transport, food and production processes would be felt. Thus behaviour would change with or without massive public expenditure.

This ignores the fact that most dramatic technological innovations which could help such a transformation (fax machines and the internet are recent examples) were in fact born of, and funded by, public expenditure via the defence budget. It also overlooks the economic reality that business understandably seeks to get as much as possible from the public purse via grants, or loans, tax breaks whenever faced with dramatic government-induced changes caused by regulation or the taxation regime.

The reining-in of public expenditure therefore severely limits the potential for dramatic improvements in the environment, across a whole range of concerns.

## LOCALIZATION IS THE GREEN SOLUTION

Ecological taxes on energy, other resource use and pollution would help pay for the radical economic transition, would be environmentally advantageous and could allow for the removal of taxes on labour. Competition from regions without such taxes could be held at bay by reintroduced tariffs and controls. Relocalization would mean less long-distance transportation and energy use and resulting pollution. Also, any adverse environmental effects would be experienced locally, thus increasing the pressure, impetus and potential for control and improved standards.

The transition to more environmentally sustainable local economies would of course have huge job-creating potential as detailed in Chapter 5.

The environment will be better protected under this system than under any attempt to put minor environmental constraints on liberalization. The paramount necessity to be internationally competitive in today's system inevitably sacrifices adequate local environmental protection measures. Thus, for activists concerned about protecting the environment, it would be more effective to put their issue-specific demands within the overarching context of campaigning for policies resulting in localization (see Chapter 15).

# TRADE LIBERALIZATION CAN'T BE GREENER AND KINDER

## Green about NAFTA

As the massive effort to gain US Congressional approval of NAFTA came to a head in November of 1993, the Clinton Administration released a comprehensive report on NAFTA and environmental issues which recognized that 'there are serious environmental problems in North America, particularly along the US–Mexican border, that must be addressed in the context of expanded trade.' The report identified the issue at the core of the controversy on NAFTA and the environment: 'The question that Congress now faces, and this Report attempts to answer, is whether passage of the NAFTA will exacerbate our environmental problems or give us effective mechanisms to ameliorate them.'

In 1993, US political and corporate proponents made numerous impressive promises in an attempt to pass the trade agreement through the US Congress. If Congress would pass NAFTA, there would be an increase in jobs, wages would rise, the environment – particularly the area along the US–Mexico border – would improve, relations between the peoples of North America would be enhanced, illegal drug trafficking between NAFTA nations would be reduced, enforcement of each nation's labour and environmental laws would be strengthened, illegal immigration would decrease and so on.

The promises on the environment were particularly compelling. The health and living conditions along the US–Mexico border became a highly emotional and visible aspect of the debate. The border area already had small free trade zones there housing US-owned manufacturing plants, known as 'maquiladoras'. As a result of large-scale poverty, concentrated industrial development, pollution and overpopulation, the border area had turned into 'a virtual cesspool and breeding ground for infectious disease', according to the American Medical Association.

There was a division in the US environmental movement over NAFTA and its side agreements with five major US environmental organizations endorsing it: the National Wildlife Federation, the World Wildlife Fund, the Environmental Defense Fund, the Natural Resources Defense Council and the National Audubon Society. Most local and national environmental organizations, including the Sierra Club, FoE, Greenpeace, the Humane Society of the United States, the American Society for the Prevention of Cruelty to Animals, Clean Water Action, Rainforest Action, Environmental Action and hundreds of others opposed NAFTA, seeing it as a as a threat to the North American environment.

NAFTA proponents argued that NAFTA would solve the health and environmental problems in the border free-trade zone. If NAFTA were implemented, they argued, the concentration of industries in the border, and thus industrial pollution and human population would lessen, reducing the strain on the environment and the massively overburdened border infrastructure. NAFTA would also increase the prosperity of Mexico, raise its standard of living and result in an increase in spending on environmental clean up. Finally, proponents argued that the new environmental institutions that were to be created parallel to NAFTA (see later) would provide the funding and oversight to organize large-scale environmental clean up and improvements to the infrastructure, as well as ensuring strong environmental law enforcement.

'There's going to be a near-term resolution of some incredibly difficult environmental degradation problems,' said Jay Hair, President of the National Wildlife Federation. 'And there's going to be a long-term benefit of NAFTA, by ripening the very investment process, that environmental impacts will be increasingly be considered.'

### The NAFTA realists

For NAFTA opponents, the environmentally devastated, impoverished border zone was an example of what free trade arrangements like NAFTA would mean for public health, the environment, and the living conditions of workers. They argued that the border area's problems would not be improved by NAFTA, but would intensify and spread to the rest of Mexico. By promoting and making secure investment in Mexico, without enforceable environmental and labour standards, NAFTA would exert a downward pull on environmental and health standards throughout North America, opponents argued. Also increased trade under NAFTA would not necessarily lead to increased prosperity and would be more likely to lead to a 'race for the bottom' in wages and living standards.

### NAFTA's Green Toll

Such predictions have been born out by later analysis. In late 1995, Washington DC-based Public Citizen, in coordination with the Mexico

City-based Red Mexicana de Acci-n frente al Libre Comercio (RMALC), examined this very question. They found that NAFTA had resulted in job losses and a worsening of the environmental conditions in Mexico and the border area. Around 200,000 American jobs were predicted to be created in the first two years of NAFTA, as well as increased earnings.[25] The reality was an increase in American unemployment and a decline in US wages by 4.1 per cent between 1993 and 1996 and for those displaced US workers who managed to find re-employment, it was largely in the low-wage service sector.[26] In Mexico an estimated 2 million jobs were lost during NAFTA's first two years and by 1996 wages were half that of the 1980 level.[27]

In environmental terms, urban pollution is amongst the highest in the world in Mexico and there are serious environmental problems along both sides of the border. Three and a half years later, the Public Citizen/RMALC study showed that the Maquila workforce had risen by 60 per cent and there had been no significant changes in pollution control facilities. There was also an increase in toxic-waste production and disposal, diminished water quality and a greater incidence of environmentally-related disease. Tuberculosis and hepatitis had soared on both sides of the border, whilst the number of babies born with fatally exposed or missing brains (anencephaly) had continued to rise.

The Clinton Administration also promised that the environmental side agreement, the NAAEC would strengthen environmental law-enforcement, as well as laws affecting other aspects of public health and safety.[28] The Agreement set up three institutions: the Commission for Environmental Co-operation (CEC); the Border Environmental Co-operation Commission (BECC); and the North American Development Bank (NADbank).

They have been found to be inadequate. The CEC has no punitive authority, as only in certain, limited circumstances can it recommend sanctions. The process is so cumbersome and there are so many exclusions, however, that Jaime Serra Puche, the Mexican commerce secretary who negotiated the NAFTA deal, was quoted as reassuring a group of Mexican business people that it was 'highly improbable that the sanction stage would ever be reached'. The BECC although empowered to evaluate funding for border environmental infrastructure projects, which in theory are eligible to receive low-interest loans from the NADBank. However, because the bank is self-financed, it may only loan for commercially viable projects. Border clean-up projects do not fulfil this criteria.

After three and a half years of existence the bank had failed to provide a single direct loan. In any case the funds at their disposal at around US$2 billion are considered too little. The US Sierra Club estimated in 1993 that at least US$20 billion would be required to have some impact on the environmentally devastated region.[29]

### NAFTA's Lesson – 'Won't get Fooled Again?'

This case has been looked at in detail because it is vital that one key lesson be drawn from it. That is that free trade agreements like NAFTA, even with environmental side agreements, will by their nature and purpose inevitably fail to protect the environment. (The same holds true for labour rights, as the failure of NAFTA's parallel side-agreement, the North American Agreement on Labour Cooperation shows, see Chapter 10).

NAFTA was designed as a mechanism to lock-in the neo-liberal reforms of structural adjustment, thereby guaranteeing security for foreign, and predominantly American, TNC investment. Constraining profit levels by regulations requiring expenditure to improve environmental conditions is both the opposite of what NAFTA intended and what has, in fact, occurred.

# WTO – SOME ENVIRONMENTALISTS STILL HAVE TO LEARN

'*Currently, WTO members* fail to give priority to trade liberalizing measures that would deliver direct and immediate benefits to the environment... *WTO members should begin the process now of forging* rules that respect the environment without closing markets *or strengthening the hand of the already strong against the weak.*' [Emphasis added][30]

'*It is the underlying principles on which the free trade system is based that are fundamentally flawed. The current economic model places growth and profits above all other considerations: and is based on unsustainable rates of resource use.* These defects cannot be addressed by tinkering with the structure and/or regulations of the WTO.' [Emphasis added][31]

At its third Ministerial Meeting in Seattle in November 1999 the WTO had planned to expand the world trading system by initiating a new Millennium Round of trade negotiations. The public protests against this, and the internal problems inside the WTO, stalled this move towards further trade liberalization. Thus those social, environmental and developing world movements and groups who demanded a halt to all further liberalization, and to review and revise global trade rules, did potentially more to prevent further WTO-induced setbacks for the environment, than those attempting to put environmental add-ons to free trade rules.

Before and during Seattle, such environmentalists pointed to its potential to reduce tariff escalation, or increases, particularly on imports of products where natural resources could be processed domestically to add value. The argument goes that this allows countries – usually poor, raw material-exporting dependent countries – to increase their profit per unit of raw material used and potentially result in less resource use. However, under free trade rules, the higher the unit profit the greater the likely pressure to increase resource use and product output. Also the companies involved will demand the minimal imposition of profit-limiting environmental constraints, both on the raw material use and its further processing. In short, environmentally, conditions would worsen.

'Environmentally perverse subsidies' are also seen as something that could be dealt with by 'trade liberalizing measures. The usual example cited is agricultural subsidies that cause environmental problems in the polluting forms of the intensive agriculture they encourage. Also correctly highlighted is the way such subsidies can produce surpluses which are then dumped on the world market to the detriment of those farmers in the importing countries, especially in the South.

But the answer to this is to only use subsidies that encourage environmentally sound farming practices and which only produce small surpluses that can be exported in times of specific food shortages. If maximum feasible self-reliance were the end goal then such subsidies would make sense. With all countries geared to international competitiveness, those with the geographical potential to export food will go in the very opposite direction – and still seek domestic subsidies and/or environmentally damaging agricultural practices to ensure the cheapest prices and the maximum volume of production and exports. Again, the environment and the poorer sections of importing countries will be the losers.

Finally, those arguing for an environmentally kinder trade liberalization look to the social part of the sustainable development package to be delivered by giving increased market access to developing countries. The flaws in this approach were dealt with in more depth in Chapter 17. However, in summary, trade liberalization invariably means reducing expenditure on domestic social and environmental improvements in favour of allocating resources to produce the cheapest and the greatest volume of exports. This maximizes the profits for the wealthy companies and individuals which control such trade as well as taking market from competitors. In most cases it is the poor of the exporting countries and their environment who suffer.

## TINKERING WITH FREE TRADE – A TRAP FOR ANIMAL WELFARE

*'If any solution is to benefit both animal welfare and trade liberalization,* a complimentary relationship needs to be established in which policies to promote animal welfare, social justice and environmental protection are facilitated rather than obstructed by free and fair trade.' [Emphasis added][32]

Since the WTO's establishment, a wide range of laws and policy measures to protect animals have been deemed to be in conflict with its rules. New measures to improve the protection of animals are also being impeded by their perceived incompatibility with the WTO.

For example, leghold traps, a cruel and indiscriminate trapping method outlawed in 60 countries, were banned throughout the EU in 1995. It also established restrictions on imports of furs and fur products from 13 commonly trapped and traded species, unless the exporting countries had banned the use of leghold traps or used internationally agreed humane trapping methods. The two exporting countries most affected, Canada and the US were prepared to use WTO rules to overturn the EU provisions and Europe backed down as it didn't believe it could defend a WTO challenge. Instead, it negotiated bilateral agreements with Canada and the US and the resulting standards are substantially weaker with leghold traps continuing to be used.[33]

Cosmetics tested on animals were opposed by millions of EU citizens, who signed petitions in support of a total ban on such products. In 1993, the EU agreed to prevent the use of animals in cosmetic testing from 1998, so long as there were scientifically validated alternative tests available. Import restrictions were only applied to individual products, were dependent upon the availability of alternative tests, and still allowed scope for some derogations in exceptional circumstances. However the measure was thought to be incompatible with WTO rules and the EU did not implement it.[34]

Following growing public concern about intensive egg production, the European Commission (EC) in 1998 proposed to modify substantially the conditions in which laying hens are kept in the EU, in particular by increasing the minimum size of living space for each hen. However to do so would increase costs to domestic producers to the extent that they could become uncompetitive with non-EU country egg producers, operating lower welfare standards. Low transport costs add to the vulnerability of EU eggs to such imports. The Commission has been reluctant to introduce a comprehensive mandatory egg labeling scheme to help consumers decide between different production schemes, because it fears that this too might be considered as contrary to WTO rules.[35]

The fundamental problem in all these cases is that, in WTO jargon, animal welfare is a 'non-product related process and production' (PPM). WTO rules do not generally permit distinctions between 'like products' on the basis of PPMs, ie all eggs are treated the same regardless of whether they derive from a cramped battery cage or a free range production system. The Commission seems to have concluded that trade measures relating to animal welfare PPMs will not be supported by the WTO. It is not even prepared to propose mandatory labeling schemes based on animal welfare criteria, because it believes that this would also be contrary to WTO rules.[36]

PPMs are not some minor sticking point, but are utterly central to free trade and international competitiveness. Once any country is allowed to ban a product on the basis of how it was made, a floodgate of trade restrictions could result. Products made where labour costs were hugely less, workers oppressed, environmental standards too low or not enforced, or animals harmed in the process could all be banned as unfair to 'fair' trade. These would be hugely beneficial to workers, the environment and animals, but not to the powerful interests that benefit from liberalized trade.

In their efforts to overcome this hurdle, some animal welfare groups have suggested border measures to enable continued improvements in domestic standards, whilst allowing the promotion of 'trade liberalization in goods produced to equivalent welfare standards'.[37] The raising of domestic standards of animal welfare is likely to require transitional support (for farmers) and will still be undermined unless something can be done to ensure that domestic producers do not find themselves commercially disadvantaged as a result of adopting higher standards. Tariffs, quotas and financial aid have all been suggested by animal lobbyists. This is claimed to have a positive effect for domestic producers, but need not necessarily worsen the position of foreign producers. This is because improved market access or tariff reductions can be linked or weighted towards those exporters who can meet domestic (animal welfare) requirements.

Such suggested tamperings with the free market are understandable for a lobby that recognizes that concern for animals differs from society to society and hence such trade rule alterations seem the best hope for progress. What it fails to take into account is that this is still a method of putting barriers to free trade on the basis of how a product is produced and are against the interests of TNCs. It is possible to argue that extra profits could be made in the short term by demanding a higher price for the 'niche marketing' of products produced in a way that furthered animal welfare, as at present happens to a limited degree. However, big business is well aware that the end goal of such campaigners is the improvement in conditions for all animals. This will require higher costs and, if having to be marketed to all sectors, higher prices and potentially lower demand and profits, so will be fought against vigorously. But the biggest reason such an approach would fail, however, is that it would open the door to putting up barriers to trade because of factors such as labour costs or conditions, and a myriad of environmental concerns.

Within the context of the *Protect the Local, Globally* set of localization policies, the animal rights aims become much more attainable. Countries or groups of countries choosing to improve animal welfare would produce most of their meat and fish requirements from within their own borders, and in the desired animal-friendly manner. Food that had to be imported could be taken from countries that have comparable standards, via the tariff and quota system. Finally, animal welfare could be encouraged to increase globally by funding through the trade and aid for localization policies outlined in Chapter 12.

## TINKERING WITH FREE TRADE – A TIMEWASTING DIVERSION

The key thing to be considered by those lobbying for improvements in labour conditions, the environment and animal welfare, but who still put resources into trying to reform free trade to do so, is they in fact wasting their time and efforts. To really achieve their aims it is time such groups reconsidered whether the growing international calls for no further trade liberalization and a revision of trade rules should be where they should put their weight.

This would of course be at a cost of having less credibility with governments, who always prefer to engage in consultation over minor modifications, rather than fundamental changes. Yet perhaps the crucial debate to be had in these circles is what really constitutes credibility and effectiveness. Might their credibility in terms of achieving their aims in the end be best earned by considering the path of championing localization? Shouldn't they put their issue specific demands within the context of calls for policy changes to bring about the protection and diversification of local economies? This would be far more effective than chasing the mirage of a kinder, gentler, greener, more labour friendly globalization.

# A Controversial Conclusion – Localization will Bale Out the Market

'...*The industrial system must be reinvented to save the earth. The social values that are precious to most people must be freed from the confinements of economic imperatives and allowed to find fuller expression. These ideas are not utopian platitudes but the hard practical work of the future.*

*... human nature does not change over the millennia, but human behaviour has changed – when people applied their natural inventions to constructing a new context for their lives, freeing themselves of narrow debilitating habits that the old system required of them. This means thinking outside the framework of what is – imagining new economic and social understandings that deliver real value to the human experience, instead of destructive repetitions. Capitalism is in need of such examination.*'[1]

'*They surged in thousands down to Whitehall, passionate for their cause, and exulting in the power of the crowd. For most it was a peaceful protest. But the activists saw it differently. For years they had been building up their international connections. They had the courage to defy the law, to use violence and, if necessary, to go to prison.*

*That protest was against slavery. The year was 1832... Edmund Burke, the political theorist, complained that the abolitionists were guilty of confusion and oversimplification. Just like the anti free traders are today, right?*'[2]

The bad ship *Globalization* is drifting like a supertanker with the control room under siege from pirates. Its momentum was slowed significantly by the 'Battle of Seattle' in December 1999. Delegates from the developing world and street protestors successfully opposed the WTO's proposed further acceleration of trade liberalization – the so called Millennium Round. Despite this, 'serious' commentators still sagely nod their heads in unison as to the wonder or at least the inevitability of its direction. The supertanker's safe passage is now being threatened by two very deep icebergs coming towards it in a pincer movement. Of course noone can predict exactly their effect on the ship, but both have already caused it to slow down somewhat. The twin pincers are the instability of the world trading system and the growing international resistance to the effects of being caught in this huge vessel's damaging wake.

The Asian economic crisis that began in July 1997, sent shockwaves throughout the region, then moved onto Russia, Brazil and beyond. As a response the unthinkable became the acceptable. The unfettered movement of capital, once an untouchable bulwark of globalization, was to be regulated to some degree. Malaysia, Thailand, Russia and China introduced constraints and even the IMF went on record saying that in some circumstances there was a case for capital controls. The World Bank's former Chief Economist and Senior Vice President, Joseph Stiglitz, called for 'where necessary some form of restrictions on short-term private capital flows'.[3]

Although there has been some rallying in stockmarkets since, particularly in the US, things remain very volatile. The serious decline for the majority in the Asian economies affected by the crisis remain. The vulnerability of the US stockmarket, and hence the potential for US consumers to continue to go into debt, is being highlighted. Warnings range from the investment banking division of the UK bank HSBC, which predicted how the US Bubble will burst,[4] to Massachusetts Institute of Technology's economics professor, Paul Krugman's, comment: '... a Dow Jones index at 11,000. There is no rational way to justify stock prices at these levels'.

The present global economic crisis and the lack of solid success in dealing with it will require a comprehensive political response. Uncertainty over the US stockmarket and the pressures on the OECD economies at a time of burgeoning exports from Asia is likely to see a rise in protectionism from long-distance trade. This could follow the 1998 rise in protectionism from long-distance capital flight that occurred in the wake of the Asian crisis.

Indeed, the WTO's 1998 Annual Report expected that protectionist pressures will increase as the crisis-hit economies of Asia step up exports to kick-start recovery. US, Brazil, Mexico, and Australia are toughening anti-dumping or anti-subsidy rules and the WTO notes pressures on the US and EU, among others, to block 'unfair' imports in sectors such as steel and textiles.

On the ground, resistance from citizen's groups and movements has been growing dramatically over the past few years. It has been fuelled by high profile disputes from tuna–dolphin to bananas, from steel imports to the threat of GM pollution. More and more activists are resisting trade liberalization, as its adverse affects on the majority become ever clearer. In 1998, an unprecedented coalition, making full use of the Internet, brought enough pressure to bear to finally kill the OECD's MAI.

*The Financial Times* compared the fear and bewilderment that seized the OECD to a scene from the film 'Butch Cassidy and the Sundance Kid'. The article asked the reader to picture a group of politicians and diplomats looking over their shoulders at an encroaching 'horde of vigilantes whose motives and methods are only dimly understood in most national capitals' and asking despairingly, 'Who are these guys?' Veteran trade diplomats called it a first in global politics.[5]

Of course, the activists were under no illusions about the temporary nature of their win. They expected the MAI to return in some form at the Seattle WTO Ministerial meeting at the end of November 1999, and so turned up in their tens of thousands. But this time the protest had moved up a gear. Whilst still protesting against specific adverse incidences of trade liberalization and WTO rulings, over 1600 organizations from 90 countries in every continent of the world called for opposition to any further liberalization negotiations and for a review of the system.

It is not just activists who are calling for a pause. Developing world governments, reeling under the adverse effects of the Uruguay Round, called for no new topics to be added to the WTO's jurisdiction, such as those proposed covering investment, competition policy and government procurement at the Seattle Ministerial meeting.

The NGO's document went far further calling for: 'a review of the system that will provide an opportunity for society to change course and develop an alternative, humane and sustainable international system of trade and investment relations'. Their shorthand for this at Seattle was 'No New Round – Turn Around'.

These pressures resulted in unprecedented revolts against the WTO agenda, both by the developing world delegates inside the conference and protestors from around the world out in the streets. The collapse of the talks means that there is now the opportunity to put flesh on the demands of opponents at Seattle, ie to 'review and revise' world trade rules.

The details of such an alternative has been the theme of this book. It is becoming increasingly clear that to tackle unemployment and rebuild healthy, stable and sustainable societies can only be done when citizens and nations take back control of their economies. Localization is the route to achieve this. It will require the protection, encouragement and revitalizing of local economies, geared to the sustainable provision of basic needs. In the process, not just capital, but also the siting of production would be controlled, constraints on long-distance trade would be introduced, as would adequate resource taxes to fund a sustainable transition. The end goals of aid and trade rules would be redirected so that they, at last, serve domestic needs. In short, a rejection of globalization in favour of the concept of *Protect the Local, Globally*.

The real engine for this transition will come from the realization that in the end it is only localization that will provide the secure demand levels needed to bail out the market. The question is what kind of market will emerge. David Korten in his innovative and insightful book *The Post-Corporate World*[6] draws a novel and telling distinction between the potentially positive role of what Adam Smith described as the market economy, and capitalism. The former, Korten asserts, consisted of place-based economies. These comprized small, locally owned enterprises that functioned within a community-supported ethical culture to engage people in producing for the needs of the community and its members. Capitalism, on the other hand, was defined by European philosophers of the mid-1800s as an economic regime in which the benefits of productive assets are monopolized by the few to the exclusion of the many. Yet, it is through this majority's labour that these assets are made productive.

Korten's novel insight is to realize that the:

> '*relationship of capitalism to a market economy is that of a cancer to a healthy body. Much as the cancer kills its host – and itself – by expropriating and consuming the host's energy, the institutions of capitalism are expropriating and consuming the living energies of people, communities and the planet. And like a cancer, the institutions of capitalism lack the foresight to anticipate and avoid the inevitable deathly outcome.*'[7]

What he terms 'mindful markets' on the other hand combines an ethical approach to self-organizing economic relationships, which parallel the design and structures and processes of healthy living systems.

The inability of the present system to deal with the deflation caused by globalization will provide an enormous opportunity for a new alliance around such a new agenda. This will eventually embrace those working at the local level, those politically active at other levels and the small and medium-sized businesspeople threatened by what is happening. They will need to come together to work out how to achieve a localist future to provide the jobs and livelihoods required, the rebuilding of communities needed and the adequate protection of the environment that is crucial. In short, they will need to activate the process of localization. Just as the last century saw the battle between the left and the right, so this century will see an alliance of localists, reds, greens and small 'c' conservatives pushing a localist agenda, whilst challenging the doomed globalists of the political centre.

So, with apologies to Karl Marx and Margaret Thatcher, this book ends with the rallying cry: 'Localists of the World Unite – There is an Alternative!'

*Appendix I*

# Answers to Some Criticisms of the *Protect the Local, Globally* Form of Localization

A number of arguments are often put forward against this approach.

## THE WORLD LIVES BY INTERNATIONAL TRADE AND COUNTRIES WILL SUFFER WITHOUT IT

This argument fudges the greater question: what sort of trade? Today, international trade pressures are causing a loss of jobs, driving the deregulation of wages and social and environmental conditions, reducing elected governments' control over their economys, and thus undermining the value of democracy. Of course, the transition from the present economic emphasis on competitive exports to one where trade takes place as locally as possible to rebuild sustainable local economies will take place over a number of years. This will allow those involved with long-distance trade to reorientate to markets closer to home. There will continue to be some sectors involved in long-distance trade, because their output is not available in many parts of the world. Examples are likely to include some cash crops and minerals and certain location-specific luxury items like Scotch whisky.

## LACK OF COMPETITION IS INEFFICIENT

This argues that consumers lose if countries and domestic companies are protected. Who wants expensive and shoddy goods and services? The scourge of inefficiency is competition. The assumption is that giant corporations compete for purchasers' favours, but their power frequently results in them having virtual monopoly positions. By delineating markets more locally, *Protect the Local, Globally* policies promote the positive aspects of competition – the impetus to be cost competitive, utilize better design, make more efficient use of resources and so on – will be maintained. Lack of competition from those countries where wages, conditions and environmental laws are laxer will allow standards to be increased. Although there would be constraints on long-distance trade of goods and services, it is crucial that there be no impediments to the international flow of new information and relevant technology where it contributes to the localization end goals.

## NO ONE COUNTRY CAN GO IT ALONE

Since the retreat from the Exchange Rate Mechanism, all European governments know the power of the global financial markets only too well. The turmoil in the Asian Tiger economies has made this realization global. *Protect the Local, Globally* policies cannot be achieved through autarky (or go-it-alone) policies. They will only emerge if the countries of the most powerful blocs in the world, such as the EU or North America, promote them. They alone are big and powerful enough markets to be able to dictate conditions to international capital and TNCs. Other regions would follow suit very quickly. In any case, established trade blocs as well as newer regional trading blocks (ASEAN, Mercosur, SADEC etc) are increasing intraregional trade, which could make such a transition easier.

## WHY REDUCE LONG-DISTANCE TRADE, WHEN MOST TRADE ALREADY OCCURS WITHIN REGIONS ANYWAY, AND RELOCATION FROM NORTH TO SOUTH IS NOT THAT SIGNIFICANT?

It is true that trade between nations in regional blocs is already on the increase, which could make this basic localization approach easier. It requires an acceleration of this trend, but with one crucial difference – the end goal of protecting, rebuilding and rediversifying the local economy. At present, such intra-regional trade is highly competitive, involves relocation, or the threat of it, and so reduces the potential for maximum employment and environmental protection. Enough companies are moving from North to South, ranging from low-tech to hi-tech, from sandals to software, to make the disciplining threat to workers and governments effective should they threaten the competitiveness and profit levels of business and capital by 'excessive' improvements in wages, conditions, tax rises and environmental protection.

## A FORTRESS ECONOMY IN EUROPE OR NORTH AMERICA WOULD BE UNFAIR TO THE POOR OF THE DEVELOPING WORLD WHO DEPEND ON TRADE TO ESCAPE POVERTY

A handful of developing countries, mostly in Asia, dominate trade with, and receive most of the FDI from the OECD. They could substitute this trade over the perhaps five- to ten-year transition period to the *Protect the Local, Globally* by increasing their inter-regional trade. For the rest of the developing countries, and indeed for most of Eastern Europe, the present system forces such countries to distort their economies to produce the cheapest exports, usually in competition with other poor countries. Competition is not just setting poor against richer workers, but poor against poor. This drains resources from meeting the basic needs of the poor majority in these countries. The key challenge is not to encourage further spirals of ruthless competition, but for aid and trade rules to be drastically rewritten such that they facilitate the building up and diversification of local economies globally. Only then will the needs of the poor majority be met. Transfer of information, skills and appropriate technology would be actively encouraged to further the end goal of rebuilding local economies.

## PROTECT THE LOCAL, GLOBALLY WILL PANDER TO RIGHT-WING NATIONALISM

At present, the adverse effects of the present globalization process on the majority's sense of security is leading to the spread of what could be termed 'free market fascism'. In Europe, for example, the increased insecurity heightened by the public sector job losses and expenditure cut-backs needed to meet the convergence criteria of the single currency, have resulted in mass demonstrations greater than anything seen since the thirties. Ominously, the conditions created by EMU and other effects of globalization have led to the rise of the extreme right in France, Germany, Austria and Italy. The Asian crisis has led to increased racial tensions towards migrant labour and ethic minorities and the Russian upheavals have seen an increase in anti-Jewish and anti-foreigner sentiment.

The hope and security offered by the localization of *Protect the Local, Globally* can help reverse the very conditions of insecurity which are fostering the rise of this ugly nationalist right.

# PROTECTIONISM FAILED IN THE 1930S AND FAILED IN COMMUNIST COUNTRIES EVERYWHERE

In the 1930s, protectionism was nationalist and designed to protect the powerful. The goal was for each protected industry or country to increase its economic strength and then compete at the expense of others. Not surprisingly the more countries did this the less trade there was between them.

The closed economies attempted by communist regimes are different from the *Protect the Local, Globally* in that internal competition, the international flow of ideas and technology and resource taxes will ensure that the stagnation and environmental degradation so often found in these regimes will not be repeated. Localization leads to global protection for workers, communities and the environment because different goals are set: the minimization of the need to trade so much with other countries, if the traded goods and services can be met domestically. This involves a transition from the beggar-your-neighbour competition of globalization and the old protectionism to the better-your-neighbour supportive internationalism of localization.

# 'Making' Money to Fund Employment, a Citizen's Income, and the Shift to Localization

The array of *Protect the Local, Globally* policies is based on reintroducing many of the controls on trade, capital and competition that existed earlier this century. The policies also have the more contemporary addition of increased resource taxes.

What follows is a consideration of two *potentially* significant additional ways to generate jobs and livelihoods and increase the potential for localization – the introducing of a Citizen's Income and Monetary Reform. They are much more theoretical and are therefore in this appendix but they still merit serious debate. The former provides an income by right. The latter could potentially provide governments with a way of generating the money required to match the tasks society needs carrying out with the people to do such work. This discussion is included to fuel further debate.

## A Citizen's Income

*'The plan we are advocating amounts essentially to this: that certain small income, sufficient for necessaries, should be secured to all, whether they work or not.'*

Bertrand Russell[1]

*'Another radical change that should be evidenced as an offset to the distributional difficulties of a full-employment policy is the payment to every citizen of a tax-free social benefit to be referred to as a citizen's income.'*

James Meade, Nobel Laureate[2]

A Citizen's Income (sometimes referred to as Basic Income) is a modest payment payable to each individual as a right of citizenship, without means test or work requirement – see Chapter 11 for an initial description of its purpose.

There is a considerable body of literature published in recent years from both the left and the right justifying both the economic as well as the philosophical case for a Citizen's Income.[3] However, the idea is generally regarded as too expensive and utopian. One of the most recent attempts to counter these objections has come from the London School of Economic's Lord (Megnad) Desai. Using the University of Cambridge's POLIMOD computer program (using data from the Office of National Statistics Family Expenditure Survey) he has calculated that a Citizen's Income of £50 per week (with a £12.50 supplement for those over 65), paid unconditionally to all adults over 18 (eligible to vote) would be paid for by raising the basic tax rate to 35 per cent.

Lord Desai estimates that under this system Income Support, Jobseekers Allowance, pensions and Family Credit would be replaced by the Citizen's Income. All other benefits would be left unaltered. It would be paid whether a person was seeking work or not, economically active of not. Thus there is no need for a means test and other intrusion into people's private lives.[4]

The entire cost of financing Lord Desai's approach is paid for by changes in the income tax rates. Everyone receives £2,600 per annum (plus £650 for pensioners) and beyond that level, all income is taxable. The basic tax rate is raised to 35 per cent and the higher tax rate is left unaffected. Although today's base rate is 23 per cent, it was 33 per cent 'within living memory'. This increases income tax revenue by more than £79 billion, more than doubling it.

The largest gain in absolute terms, as well as in percentage terms, is for the households in the lowest 10 per cent. They gain £34.40 on average or 47 per cent. The next 10 per cent also gain and those in the next 70 per cent have practically no significant gain or loss. The tenth and highest 10 per cent loses, but the loss is £42.64 around 6.26 per cent of its income.[5]

A more gradualist approach is what has been termed a small Transitional Basic Income (TBI) of £20 a week for every man, woman and child, plus a minimum wage of £4 per hour. This could then be gradually increased in the light of experience. The TBI would replace virtually all income tax allowances and is deducted from most existing social security benefits. Using the same POLIMOD programme as Lord Desai, Parker and Sutherland calculated that the £20 per week TBI plus the £4 per hour minimum wage would be revenue neutral if existing social security benefits were reduced by the £20, and there were some increases in the income tax rates. The current 20 per cent rate of income tax is abolished and the standard rate is raised from 23 per cent to 26 per cent (with the latter increase partly off-set by reducing Class 1 National Insurance contributions from 10 per cent to 9 per cent.) The threshold for higher rate income tax remains virtually unchanged, but a 45 per cent income tax is introduced on taxable incomes (excluding the BIs) above £46,000. Income tax revenues will in any case be higher due to the pay rises inherent in the minimum wage.[6]

The outright gainers would be people on low benefit, those who at present have no entitlement to benefit, or do not claim the benefit to which they are entitled. Single-wage couples with children (married and unmarried), lone parents and people with disabilities would also gain.

On the question of political feasibility of such suggestions, the insecurity that is being felt by ever more people in a wide range of what was previously regarded as safe jobs or careers could make the idea of a guaranteed Citizen's Income more appealing. Another potential positive result would lie in its universality rather than being contingent on being unemployed, low paid or poor. It can thus be seen as an entitlement of citizenship, not a welfare handout to the needy. Desai asserts that other advantages include the fact that the Citizen's Income is an improvement on the existing structure of welfare payments:

> '*which distorts and destroys incentives, encourages – indeed rewards – staying off work, taxes couples who stay together rather than live separately, incites cheating and lying. The state in turn treats claimants with condescension, suspicion and contempt. It sees fraud in every corner and asks neighbours to report on one another.*'[7]

In terms of political support, the Citizen's Income pension should be seen as positive for the vast majority of the increasing number of pensioners. Another large reservoir of support could be found in the 7 million carers, of whom only about one quarter receive Carers Allowance.[8] They would no longer need to draw on their savings or do part-time work to make ends meet if they didn't want to. Finally, this money would be the beginnings of an acknowledgement of the vital role played by unpaid work in nurturing family, community and political life. It would not, like most benefits, allocate resources preferentially on the basis of paid work over unpaid work. The only difference is that the paid work would be subject to tax.

The fact that the Citizen's Income is beginning to enter mainstream political debate can be seen by the fact that the Irish Government is seriously considering adopting such an approach. A Green Paper has been promised and a Committee chaired by a member of the Prime Minister's office, is looking at the viability of such a strategy and its implication for the wider economy. A special study has been commissioned to evaluate the economic, social, budgetary and administrative impact of the introduction of a Basic Income scheme.[9]

The concept of a Citizen's Income is not just to be found in developed countries. Brazil has the concept on the political agenda and the government intends to introduce a national scheme. On a local level, 40 Brazilian cities have already introduced a variant of Basic Income, largely for women and children. The condition generally attached is that a certificate showing that children have attended school must be provided. It is expected that now this has been introduced it will be difficult to get rid of, since it can take children off the streets and give women more employment opportunities.[10]

## MONETARY REFORM

*'The bank hath benefit on the interest on all monies which it creates out of nothing'*
The Bank of England's Royal Charter, 1698[11]

*'The process by which banks create money is so simple that the mind is repelled. Where something so important is involved, a deeper mystery seems only decent...'*
John Kenneth Galbraith[12]

*'The modern banking system manufactures money out of nothing. The process is perhaps the most astounding piece of sleight of hand that was ever invented. Banking was conceived in iniquity and born in sin. Bankers own the earth; take it away from them, but leave them with the power to create credit, and with the stroke of a pen they will create enough money to buy it back again... If you want to be slaves of the bankers, and pay the costs of your own slavery, then let the banks create money.'*
Lord Josiah Stamp, former Director of the Bank of England, public address in Central Hall, Westminster, 1937[13]

### How Banks Create Money and Governments Borrow

The government should create the money required to meet the needs of society, rather than the present situation whereby it is the prerogative of the banks and financial institutions such as building societies. In the UK as in most developed countries, over 96 per cent of the entire money stock currently consists of bank and building society credit, created in the process of these bodies lending to private borrowers.

Most people mistakenly imagine that these institutions lend other people's money. However, if individual A loans individual B £1000, then A can't use that money until repaid by B. However if A deposits the money in a bank and B borrows the same sum from the bank, then they both now have access to £2000 rather than £1000. Thus, the bank didn't loan A's money to B, it created the second £1000 and credited it to B's account. Neither is the bank lending B the undrawn out money deposited by individuals C, D–Z. The scale of this creation of money out of nothing is simply too great to be explained by new deposits from C–Z. The growth in total money stock since 1963 also shows the parallel growth in the total of outstanding debt carried by industry and individuals. The money that is provided by the government free of debt (coins and notes) is a dramatically declining percentage of the total money stock.

Thus when a bank or building society advances a loan, this sum is added to the money stock. It is thus not just a loan, but a creation of additional money. This increase in the money stock then provides the banking system with additional money against which to advance further loans. This then in turn also contributes directly to the ever growing money stock. Money is thus 'borrowed into existence' and into circulation from banks and building societies.

This method of money creation and supply ensures that any increase in the money stock is directly paralleled by a pro-rata increase in the total of outstanding debt. It is this supplying of the money stock by lending institutions on condition of future repayment, which has given rise to the descriptive term, the 'debt-based money system'.

For example, of the £780 billion of private/commercial debt currently associated with the supply of UK money stock, some £490 billion is owed by individuals, mostly as house mortgages, whilst the remainder is the backlog of debt carried by various industries. Thus, housing debt principally provides the money supply to an economy. In Britain, £411 billion, 60 per cent of the money stock, relies on housing debt and in the US the outstanding mortgages are at US$4.2 trillion, over 80 per cent of the money supply. Both are examples of property-owing rather than property-owning democracies

Extensive debt is also carried by industry, agriculture and other forms of commerce. In the UK commercial debt has increased from 11 per cent of GDP to 20 per cent of GDP between 1963 and 1996, debt from other financial institutions, eg insurance companies, pensions and trust funds, stock market brokers and discount houses, grew from 4 per cent to 18 per cent.

These figures illustrate the severe monetary pressure under which businesses and citizens in developed countries operate.[14]

## National Debts

National debt also acts as a vital part of the money supply to an economy. It involves the assumption of debt by a national government in order to obtain the additional revenue needed to cover any annual shortfall of taxation. The government calls on two principle sources of revenue: the banking sector (all lending institutions) – commercial banks and building societies, and what is termed the non-banking sector – savings, insurance, pension and trust funds.

Governments draw up official treasury or federal bonds to fund the Public Sector Borrowing Requirement (PSBR), and these bonds are auctioned on the money markets. Lending institutions create money by the act of bank lending to the government, or money is recycled from savings and in the process, creates parallel debt (as described above). Thus, when government bonds are bought by the banking sector, additional money is created provided it doesn't exceed the amount allowed to be created by the bank's 'fractional reserve' (ie the minimal percentage of a bank's deposit reserves that have to be held in cash, the rest can be used to multiply into existence new money.) Additional bank credit is thus created and new deposits of bank credit result.

When government bonds are bought by the non-banking sector (eg funds held in pensions, private purchase of gilts), then money previously locked in savings is brought back into everyday circulation via the government spending it on public services and other spending. Parallel debt is undertaken by the government and registered against the nation's assets.

## Matching Money to Work

To match the work that needs to be done in society with those who want to work requires an increase in the supply of money – this is rarely realized. Yet, when governments want to increase their supply of money they increase their borrowing. This in turn increases their debt and the need to direct money to repay this debt, rather than add that money to fund more of the nation's employment, social and environmental priorities.

The usually perceived constraint on this process is the idea that creating more money will be inflationary. Were the money supplied to be debt free and carefully linked to accurately costed spending priorities, this should not cause a harmful level of inflation. What causes inflation is the process whereby government has to raise finance to repay the borrowed money needed to create the resources it requires. In order to service its own debt it has to raise taxes higher than would be the case merely to provide for the nation's needs. Such a debt-based money system results in both extra government taxation as well as commercial and personal debt. Producers and working people all have to demand higher prices for their goods and services to cover these costs leading to inflation.

The alternative is for the government to create debt-free money and this credit source would restrain the creation of credit by banks and building societies. The increase in money supply from a government's debt-free credit creation would be compensated for by a decrease in debt-inducing lending by the banks and building societies. A likely division of funding sources would be the use of government debt-free money to pay for public works, for subsidies to, for example, help pay the upfront cost of making the nation's buildings energy efficient, moving towards renewable energy supplies, transforming agriculture to being predominantly organic and providing adequate and affordable public transport. Government money could also be used to fund the Citizen's Income.

Banks and building societies would continue to provide loans for property and businesses. To prevent them contributing to the creation of too much money chasing too few goods their lending could be capped, for example, by gradually reducing the number of times a person's income can be multiplied to work out their mortgage loan. This would have a tremendous impact since 60 per cent of the annual money stock increase comes from mortgage growth. Bank lending for hedge funds and asset stripping should also be stopped.

## Government Should Create Money

'Government, *possessing the power to create and issue currency and credit as money and enjoying the right to withdraw both currency and credit from circulation by taxation and otherwise need not and* should not borrow capital at interest as a means of financing governmental work and public enterprise. The Government should create, issue, and circulate all the currency and credit needed to satisfy the spending power of the Government and the buying power of consumers. *The privilege of creating and issuing money is not only the supreme prerogative of government, but is the Government's greatest creative opportunity.*

*By the adoption of these principles, the long-felt want for a uniform medium will be satisfied. The taxpayers will be saved immense sums of interest, discounts and exchanges. The financing of all public enterprises, the maintenance of stable government and order progress, and the conduct of the Treasury will become matters of practical administration. Money will cease to be master and become the servant of humanity. Democracy will rise superior to the money power.'* [emphasis added]

Abraham Lincoln[15]

From 1882 to 1885, Abraham Lincoln had to pay for the US Civil War. The banks only offered to loan his government funds at cripplingly high interest rates. Abraham Lincoln therefore had US$432 million of new bills printed instead, with Congressional authorization. In order to distinguish them from private bank notes in circulation, he had them printed with green ink on the back side. Hence the term 'Greenbacks'. With this new money, Lincoln paid the troops, and bought their supplies. During the course of the Civil War, nearly all of the US$450 million of Greenbacks authorized by Congress were printed at no interest to the federal government.

Within four days of the passage of the law which allowed Greenbacks to be issued, bankers met in Washington and agreed that Greenbacks would be their ruin. They therefore devised a scheme to undermine their value. The scheme was so effective that the next year, 1863, with Federal and Confederate troops beginning to mass for the decisive battle of the Civil War, and the Treasury in need of further Congressional authority at that time to issue more Greenbacks, Lincoln gave in to the banker's pressure. He allowed the bankers to push through the National Banking Act of 1863 in exchange for additional money. This gave them virtually tax-free status and the new banks also got the exclusive power to create the new forms of money – National Bank Notes. Though Greenbacks continued to circulate, their quantity was limited and no more were authorized after the War.

Not since Lincoln has the US issued debt-free US notes. It was almost 50 years before there was another short-lived government creation of debt-free money by Lloyd George in the UK in 1914. When war broke out people started to exchange their bank notes and withdrew their deposits in gold. At the start of the war the Bank of England held just £9 million in gold, yet there were total recorded bank deposits amounting to some £240 million. Lloyd George and the commercial banks feared a run on the Bank of England they could not contain.

In May 1914, Lloyd George as Chancellor of the Exchequer, declared the suspension of gold payments. He then extended the bank holiday by three days, during which the stock market was also to be closed. The Bank and Lloyd George held discussions as to how the crisis could be overcome and decided that the government should create its own money. When the commercial banks opened again a few days later, those who asked for gold were given, in exchange for their old bank notes, new Treasury notes, a new legal tender. The total issue was £3.2 million and the creation of this money helped the government to fund the initial stages of the war effort.

However, this was not the intention of the notes. Had they not been issued, the private banking houses would have been forced to default to their creditors in a week's time. The banks fully supported this initiative and had pleaded and interceded for it. However, once the government had successfully alleviated the initial crisis by the issue of these Treasury notes, the Bank of England according to Christopher Hollis, a respected journalist of the time: 'insisted forcibly that the state must upon no account issue any more money on this interest free basis: if the war was to be run, it must be run with borrowed money, money upon which interest must be paid ... and to that last proposition the Treasury acceded.'[16]

## FINANCING LOCALIZATION AND EMPLOYMENT BY GOVERNMENT – CREATED CREDIT AND A CITIZEN'S INCOME

The government, by printing money to pay for a carefully costed set of programmes, would be able to create jobs by paying for a labour-intensive social infrastructure of health, education, transport etc as well as a more environmentally sustainable energy and agricultural sector. The government could also print the money needed to fund a Citizen's Income – see Chapter 11 and Appendix II. These policies combined would mean that instead of running an underfunded public sector, a national debt, a dependency culture and a wasteful economy, there could be a decent public sector backed up by a financial system that supports a productive economy and allows a modest basic income to be paid. Workers and contractors benefiting from the increased public expenditure plus that portion of the Basic Income that is not saved would both result in money being spent into the economy and contribute to a stable, circulating money stock.

Monetary reform, plus the provision of a Citizen's Income will, like the *Protect the Local, Globally* alternative to the present neo-liberal model, depend on two things for its success. Firstly, there will need to be serious enough financial crisis to prompt a basic rethink. Secondly, citizens and the politically active in the OECD, Eastern Europe and the developing world will need to consider whether organizing around these end goals will provide the overarching context which will allow the specific improvements in their societies, that they seek.

The provision of adequate government debt-free money would fund the work that needs to be done to improve societies internally. The *Protect the Local, Globally* policies plus monetary reform and Citizen's Income would be of value not just to developed countries, but also the rest of the world because it would also allow the debt problem that is such a scourge to Eastern Europe and the developing world to be eradicated. Existing debt would gradually be forgiven and government provision of the money for adequately costed programmes should limit new debt.

With the security of a gradual reduction in debt, this will enable debtors and so called lender countries to concentrate on providing livelihoods for their people, tackling the needs of each country rather than dancing to the tune of international bankers and driving their economy to meet the debts owed to the banks.

# A Global Manifesto

## LOCALIZATION – AN IDEA WHOSE TIME HAS COME

(Introduction)
Globalization and free trade are under unprecedented attack as its adverse effects becomes ever clearer. Now is the time for a comprehensive and radical alternative which must be based on a new direction for the global economic system. It must reduce inequality, improve the basic provision of needs, and adequately protect the environment. Its end goal must be to ensure, aid and increase the democratic control and involvement of citizens in the rebuilding of sustainable local economies. A *Protect the Local, Globally* approach.

(Chapter 1)
This process is **Localization** – a set of interrelated and self-reinforcing policies that actively discriminate in favour of the local. It provides a political and economic framework for people, community groups and businesses to rediversify their own local economies. It has the potential to increase community cohesion, reduce poverty and inequality, improve livelihoods, social provision and environmental protection and provide the all-important sense of security.

It is the very antithesis of globalization, which emphasizes a beggar-your-neighbour reduction of controls on trade and contorts all economies to make international competitiveness their major goal. Localization involves a better-your-neighbour supportive internationalism where the flow of ideas, technologies, information, culture, money and goods has, as its end goal, the protection and rebuilding of local economies worldwide. Its emphasis is not on competition for the cheapest, but on cooperation for the best.

## GLOBALIZATION – A WORLDWIDE REALITY BASED ON UNREALISTIC THEORIES

(Chapter 2)
Trade liberalization is built on the flawed theory of comparative advan-

tage, the unchallenged diktat of being internationally competitive, and the illusionary promise of growth generating future wealth for all. Comparative advantage – do what you do best, and trade for the rest – was an ivory-tower theory that ignored the reality of the differences in power between traders and producers as well as those between nations. It was also originally assumed that money would remain local. Despite these fundamental flaws and the theory's irrelevance to today, the World Trade Organization (WTO) is the global cheerleader and enforcer of comparative advantage.

(Chapter 3)
Capital advantage holds that the free flow of money internationally ensures its efficient and rational use, allows financial investors to diversify risks globally and, in the process, ensure that governments run their economy to the benefit of such investors. The reality is the opposite, with investors exhibiting a herd instinct. To woo footloose capital, countries try to provide the low inflation, low tax and low government expenditure policies investors deem prudent. This means giving up power over major domestic control mechanisms like interest rates and government borrowing and risking reduced demand levels through lower domestic expansion. Recent economic crises have highlighted the adverse effects of global money flows and the Multilateral Agreement on Investment (MAI) designed to speed up this process was defeated by international opposition.

## THE ADVANTAGES OF SHIFTING FROM GLOBALIZATION TO LOCALIZATION

(Chapter 4)
The international resistance to the adverse effects of globalization is on the rise, providing an opening to pursue localization. The parameters of the 'local', although predominantly the nation state, depend to some extent on the goods and services being considered. These range from the sub-national for food stuffs, to the geographic region for aeroplanes. Localization requires widespread involvement; it will therefore be something done by people, not something done to them. The huge potential of localization includes devolved power, control of the economy, increased environmental and social protection and benign technological developments. Global financial instability makes such a radical departure ever more timely.

(Chapter 5)
Localization can foster and build sustainable local communities to help rebuild local economies. It allows the achievement of social cohesion and economic renewal particularly through investment in labour-intensive, infrastructural renewal and face-to-face caring. Local businesses have a central role and much to gain. Globalization, on the other hand, poses a triple threat to sustainable local communities. Its fetishism of international competitiveness leads to public expenditure curbs which constrain community renewal; to the opening up of government purchasing to foreign interests, thus cutting local jobs; and the shifting of agriculture away from smaller scale farming for local markets to agribusiness methods to feed the wealthy, globally.

# ACHIEVING LOCALIZATION

(Chapter 6)
The first step to localization is a 'mindwrench' away from the passive acceptance that globalization is as inevitable as gravity and towards support for a set of self-reinforcing measures that will bring about a *Protect the Local, Globally* end goal internationally. Protective safeguards, such as import and export controls, quotas, subsidies etc, will need to be introduced over a clearly agreed transition period to all continents. This will not be old-style protectionism which seeks to protect a home market whilst expecting others to remain open. The emphasis will be on local trade. Any residual long-distance trade will be geared to funding the diversification of local economies. Such a dramatic, radical change will need to overcome TNC opposition and so will need to take place at the level of regional groupings of countries, especially the most powerful – in Europe and North America.

## Localizing Production and Controlling TNCs

(Chapter 7)
Industry will be localized by site-here-to-sell-here policies to ensure localized production. Threats by TNCs to relocate, thus become less plausible, as the market is lost to existing, or government encouraged, new local competitors. Once TNCs are thus grounded, then their domestic activities and the levels of taxation paid are back under democratic control. Campaigners' demands for social, labour and environmental standards also become feasible. Adequate company taxation can help compensate the poor for any increases in prices.

## Localizing Money

(Chapter 8)
The disastrous effects of the unfettered international flow of money has led to global calls for some controls to be reintroduced. What is required is a regrounding of money to remain predominantly in the locality or country of origin to fund the rebuilding of diverse, sustainable local economies. Measures include controls on capital flows, Tobin-type taxes, control of tax evasion, including offshore banking centres, the floating of civic bonds and the rejuvination of locally orientated banks, credit unions, LETS schemes etc. Public and private flows of money to other countries must also be directed to strengthen the local economies of the countries concerned.

## A Localist Competition Policy

(Chapter 9)
Local competition policies will ensure that high-quality goods and services are provided by ensuring a more level, but more local, playing field. Free of the 'race to the bottom' competitive pressures from foreign competition, business can be carried out within the framework of ever improving labour, social and environmental regulations, enhanced by the best ideas and technologies from around the world. Government competition policy will cover the structure and market share of businesses, plus regulate the behaviour of firms.

## Taxes For Localization

(Chapter 10)
To pay for the transition to localization and to improve the environment the majority of taxation will come from gradually increasing resource taxes, such as on non-renewable energy use and pollution. To promote a more equitable society, the removal of the option of relocation or the availability of foreign tax havens will make it possible to tax companies and individuals according to their wealth, their income, their spending through value added tax and their land. Part of this taxation will be used to compensate the poorer sections of society for any price rises and by shifting taxes away from employment to encourage more jobs.

## Democratic Localism

(Chapter 11)
A diverse local economy requires the active democracy of everyday involvement in producing the maximum range of goods and services

close to the point of consumption. To ensure the broadest distribution of the ensuing benefits will simultaneously require wider, political, democratic and economic control at a local level. A Citizen's Income will allow involvement in the economy as a matter of right. Political funding will be strictly constrained and power will pass from the corporations to the citizens. This will involve the encouragement of maximum participation in defining priorities and planning local economic, social and environmental initiatives. This will require a balance of involvement of the state, community networks and organizations and citizen's movements.

### Trade and Aid for Localization

(Chapter 12)
The GATT rules at present administered by the WTO should be revised fundamentally to become a General Agreement for Sustainable Trade (GAST), administered by a democratic World Localization Organization (WLO). Their remit would be to ensure that regional trade and international aid policies and flows, information and technological transfer, as well as the residual international investment and trade, should incorporate rules geared to the building up of sustainable local economies. The goal should be to foster maximum employment through a substantial increase in sustainable, regional self-reliance.

# How Localization Might Come About

### Growing Opposition

(Chapter 13)
The widespread resistance to globalization can be built upon to help fashion a viable localist alternative. There are already countless people and groups strengthening their local economies from the grass roots up. The greatest spur to consideration of such radical local alternatives at the governmental level will be the need to respond to global economic upheavals and the deflation, the job losses and inadequate consumer demand that will come in its wake. Equally crucial in shaping a different localist imperative amongst politicians will be the pressure that the politically active can bring to bear. This must shift from just fighting separate issue-specific aspects of globalization to realizing that their individual successes can only be secured as part of an overarching change to localization, but in an internationally supportive manner. In short, to *Protect the Local, Globally.*

## Destroying Jobs, Increasing Deflation

(Chapter 14)
Global deflation is being driven by relocation to cheaper labour countries, automation and public spending cuts, all accelerated by trade liberalization's diktat to be internationally competitive. This has resulted in the worst level of global under- and unemployment in most countries since the thirties. Increasing employment would be the end result of successful campaigns for large-scale improvements in domestic social provision and working conditions, as well as those concerned about more global issues like food security, environmental protection and development. However, unless these are placed firmly within a localization framework they will never experience the level of success they seek.

## A Localist Wake-Up Call to Political Activists

(Chapter 15)
The primary goal of the WTO is to limit government law-making and regulatory authority that are deemed an impediment to trade. Thus, national control is shifted from domestic priorities to facilitating the goals of trade liberalization. Activists must consider whether, in order to achieve their issue-specific goals, they should have an equally all-challenging, overarching demand to overcome the process of globalization, that is the major *roadblock* to their aims. They should evaluate whether it is only through the *roadway* of something like the *Protect the Local, Globally* form of localization, that their priorities and those of their supporters can be met. In this way, they will constantly contribute to the rejection of this dominant paradigm and its replacement by the localist one, which could enable these activists to experience success in their chosen areas.

## Failure to Champion Localization – A Campaign Loser for Social Services, Unions and Culture

(Chapter 16)
Campaigns for improved social provision too frequently fail to realize the constraints posed by globalization and its regional offshoots, such as European Monetary Union (EMU) on government's ability to raise and allocate financial resources. Unions and other campaigners for workers' rights muddle globalization and internationalism. They want a kinder, gentler trade liberalization, whereas the combination of lower trade barriers and growing unemployment in the poorer countries means that job security, wage levels and working conditions are mostly

driven ever downwards. Cultural diversity requires the media and those interested in sustaining national culture to replace globalization, the cultural homogenizer, with the variety implicit in localization.

## Localizing International Development

(Chapter 17)
Development professionals' calls for a 'fairer' liberalized trading system ignore the reality of what the rules of trade liberalization have done to the poor in the South. Development NGO's also adhere to the flawed paradigm that exports from the South to the North are a major route for the poor's development. Southern critics of this approach point to the inevitability of adverse competition between poor export-ing countries, its hijacking of national priorities to the provision of the cheapest exports, the adverse working conditions and country-hopping demanded by the companies involved and instead propose the alterna-tive of a localist development policy.

## Localizing Food Security

(Chapter 18)
Globalization is increasing control of the world's food system by transnational companies (TNCs) and big farmers. There is a backlash from both consumers and farmers to this process that provides less safe food, environmental threats and rural impoverishment. Localization can reverse this trend. Food security both for rich and poor countries requires an increase in the level of self-sufficiency. Also needed is a dramatic reduction in international trade in foodstuffs until the commerce left becomes a useful adjunct to increased self-reliance. This should be governed by fair trade rules benefiting small farmers and food producers, animal welfare and the environment. Land reform and the rebuilding of rural economies is an integral part of such food localization.

## Green Globalization – An Impossibility

(Chapter 19)
At the heart of environmentalists myriad demands are the necessity to use resources frugally, for industry and agriculture to cause minimal pollu-tion, to preserve wildlife, wildernesses and biodiversity, and to maximize recycling. More recently, this agenda has been broadened to ensure that during the process of change democratic control of the emerging society is increased, human, cultural and animal rights respected and strength-ened, and inequality decreased. Globalization thwarts this by its mix of

trade rules that maximize international competitiveness, its emphasis on the cheapest product and the encouragement of inward investment and foreign companies and reduced public expenditure. The transition from today's unequal and environmentally destructive world economy to a future where the 'sustainable development' of the paragraph above becomes the norm is made impossible.

## Green Localization

Ecological taxes on energy, other resource use and pollution would help pay for the radical economic transition to localization, would be environmentally advantageous and could allow for the removal of taxes on labour, thus helping unemployment. Competition from regions without such taxes could be held at bay by reintroduced tariffs and controls. For the environment in general, relocalization would mean less long-distance transportation and energy use and resulting pollution. Also any adverse environmental effects would be experienced locally, increasing the pressure, impetus and potential for control and improved standards. Thus, for activists concerned about protecting the environment in the broadest sense, it would be more effective to put their issue-specific demands within the overarching context of localization.

# A CONTROVERSIAL CONCLUSION – LOCALIZATION WILL BALE OUT THE MARKET

A major engine for the transition from globalization to localization will come not just from NGO reaction or specific adverse global economic events, but the realization that in the end it is only the potential for secure local demand and conditions offered by localization that will bail out the market. The question is what kind of market will emerge as a result. The inability of the present system to deal with deflation caused by globalization will provide an enormous opportunity for a new alliance and a new agenda. This will eventually embrace those working at the local level, those politically active at other levels, the small- and medium-sized businesspeople threatened by what is happening. They will need to come together to work out how to achieve a localist future to provide the jobs and livelihoods required, the rebuilding of communities needed and the adequate protection of the environment, which is crucial. In short, they will need to activate the process of localization.

Just as the last century saw the battle between the left and the right, so this next century will see an alliance of localists, red-greens and small 'c' conservatives pushing a localist agenda, whilst challenging the doomed globalists of the political centre. So, with apologies to Karl Marx and Margaret Thatcher, the rallying cry should be:

*'Localists of the World Unite – There is an Alternative'.*

# Notes and References

## An Intemperate Introduction

1 Speech to the World Trade Organization, 18 May, 1998
2 Speech to the World Trade Organization, 19 May, 1998

## Chapter 1 Globalization – What it is and the Damage it Does

1 Caborn, R (1999) Letters to the Editor, *The Guardian,* 11 October
2 Wilson, B (1999) Letter to Alan Simpson MP, 19 February
3 International Society for Ecology and Culture (1999) From Global to Local: Resisting monoculture, rebuilding community, ISEC, Devon
4 International Labour Organisation (1995, 1996, 1998) World Employment Reports, 1995, 1996–97 & 1998–99, International Labour Organisation, Geneva
5 UN figures quoted in Elliot, L (1998) 'Why the poor are picking up the tab', *The Guardian,* 11 May
6 Quoted in Coyle, D (1997) The Weightless World, Capstone, Oxford, p11
7 United Nations Development Programme (1999) *Human Development Report,* UNDP/Oxford University Press, Oxford
8 Ahuja, V et al (1997) *Everyone's Miracle? Revisiting Poverty and Inequality in East Asia,* World Bank, Washington, DC, p9, quoted in Hildyard, N (1998) *The World Bank and the State: A Recipe for Change?* Bretton Woods Project, London, p15
9 Gray, J (1998) *False Dawn: the Delusions of Global Capitalism,* Granta Books, London, p57
10 Ruigrok, W and van Tulder, R (1995) *The Logic of International Restructuring,* Routledge, London p188, quoted in Hildyard, N, Hines, C and Lang, T (1996) 'Who Competes? Changing Landscapes of Corporate Control' *The Ecologist* 26(4), July/August, p130
11 UNCTAD (1996) *Conclusions and Recommendations of the Interagency Seminar, Globalization and Liberalization: Effects of International Economic Relations on Poverty,* UNCTAD, New York and Geneva, Chapter 1

# CHAPTER 2  HISTORY AND WTO ENFORCING OF COMPARATIVE ADVANTAGE

1   Dunkley, G (1997) *The Free Trade Adventure, The Uruquay Round and Globalism: a Critique,* Melbourne University Press, Australia, Chapter 6
2   Gray, J (1998) *False Dawn: the Delusions of Global Capitalism,* Granta Books, London, p6
3   Morris, D (1996) *Free Trade: The Great Destroyer,* in Mander, J and Goldsmith, E (1996) *The Case against the Global Economy and for a Turn Towards the Local,* Sierra Club Books, San Francisco, p226
4   Dunkley (1997) op cit, Note 1, pp108, 109
5   Smith, A (1776) *Wealth of Nations,* quoted in Daly, H and Cobb, J (1989) *For the Common Good,* Beacon Press, Boston, Mass, p215
6   Gray (1998) op cit, Note 2, p82
7   Lazonick, W (1993) *Business Organization and the Myth of the Market Economy,* Cambridge University Press, Cambridge, p3
8   Clarke, T (1996) *Mechanisms of Corporate Rule,* in Mander, J and Goldsmith, E (1996) *The Case Against the Global Economy* Sierra Club Books, San Francisco, p298; Barnet, R and Cavanagh, J (1994) *Global Dreams: Imperial Corporations and the New World Order,* Simon and Schuster, NewYork, p423
9   Balanya, B et al (2000) *Europe Inc, Regional and Global Restructuring and the Rise of Corporate Power,* Pluto Press, London, p95; *New Internationalist* (2000), January–February, p24
10  Korten, D (1995) *When Corporations Rule the World,* Earthscan, London, Chapters 9 and 10; Balanya et al (2000) op cit, Note 9, p21
11  *New Internationalist* (2000) op cit, Note 9, p24

# CHAPTER 3  THEORY AND ATTEMPTED ENFORCEMENT OF CAPITAL ADVANTAGE

1   This section draws heavily on Blecker, R (1999) *Taming Global Finance: a Better Architecture for Growth and Equity,* Economic Policy Institute, Washington, DC, Chapter 1
2   Keynes, J M (1936) *The General Theory of Employment, Interest, and Money,* Harcourt Brace, London, p383, cited in Blecker (1999) op cit, Note 1, p4
3   *Foreign Policy in Focus* (1999) Interhemispheric Resource Center and the Institute for Policy Studies, New Mexico, September, pp5–8
4   Brittan, S (2000) 'Market euphoria cannot last', *The Financial Times,* 20 January; King S (1999) *Bubble Trouble: the US bubble and how it will burst,* HSBC Economics & Investment Strategy: Economics, July; 'Trapped by the bubble' *The Economist,* 25 September, 1999, p17
5   Balanya, B et al (2000) *Europe Inc, Regional and Global Restructuring and the Rise of Corporate Power,* Pluto Press, London, Chapter 12

6    Ibid, Chapter 11
7    Ibid, Chapter 11
8    *Le Monde Diplomatique*, May 1999

## Chapter 4 From Globalization to Localization – A Potential Rallying Call

1    The Council of Canadians (1998) *The MAI Inquiry: A Citizen's Search for Alternatives*, Council of Canadians, Ottawa, Autumn
2    International Society for Ecology and Culture (1999) *From Global to Local: Resisting monoculture, rebuilding community*, ISEC, Devon; 'Beyond the Monoculture, Shifting from Global to Local', *The Ecologist* 29(3), May/June, 1999; Shuman, M (1998) *Going Local Creating Self-Reliant Communities in a Global Age*, Free Press, New York; Mander, J and Goldsmith, E (1996) *The Case against the Global Economy and for a Turn Towards the Local*, Sierra Club Books, San Francisco; Douthwaite, R (1996) *Short Circuit, Strengthening Local Economies for Security in an Unstable World*, Green Books, Devon
3    Shuman (1998) op cit, Note 2, p6
4    Douthwaite (1996) op cit, Note 2, p52
5    Kretzman, J and McKnight, J (1996) *A Guide to Mapping and Mobilizing the Economic Capacities of Local Residents*, The Asset-Based Community Development Institute, Illinois, p2
6    Kretzman, J and McKnight, J (1995) *Building Communities from the Inside Out*, The Asset-Based Community Development Institute, Illinois
7    Ibid, p6
8    Ibid, pp367–75
9    Shuman (1998) op cit, Note 2

## Chapter 5 Localization – Increasing Community Renewal

1    Chanan, G et al (1999) *'Regeneration and Sustainable Communities'* Community Development Foundation, London, p16
2    Shuman, M (1998) *Going Local: Creating Self-Reliant Communities in a Global Age*, Free Press, New York, p180
3    Chanan et al (1999) op cit, Note 1, p19
4    Harker, D et al (1996) *Community Works! A guide to community economic action*, New Economics Foundation, London
5    Mayo, E (1999) 'Local loans bake Hackney's cakes', *New Statesman* Special Supplement, 19 March, pxviii
6    Chanan et al (1999) op cit, Note 1, p28
7    Personal communication, 13 October 1999

8    Lovering, J (1999) 'Celebrating Globalization and Misreading the Welsh
     Economy: The "New Regionalism" in Wales', *Contemporary Wales* 11,
     University of Wales Press, p11
9    Jenkins, T and McLaren, D (1999) *Regions and Sustainability,* Friends of
     the Earth, London, 18 May, p5
10   *The Scotsman,* 3 March 1999
11   Department of the Environment, Transport and the Regions (1999)
     *Towards an Urban Renaissance: Report of the Urban Task Force.*
     *Chaired by Lord Rogers of Riverside,* DETR, London
12   Kennedy, M (1999) 'Regeneration. The heritage dividend pays out', *The
     Guardian,* 1 July
13   Young, J (1999) 'Give our town centres a chance to recover' *The
     Financial Times Letters,* 30 June; personal communication 30 June
14   Shuman (1998) op cit, Note 2, pp180–198
15   Leadbeater, C and Christie, I (1999) *To Our Mutual Advantage*, Demos,
     London, June, p7 and pp98–105
16   Mayo, E et al (1996) *Taking power, an agenda for community economic
     renewal*, New Economic Foundation, London, p4
17   Shuman (1998) op cit, Note 2, p189
18   Ibid, p84
19   Ibid, p116
20   Ibid, p45
21   Pandya N (1999) 'Sheffield's sons lend cash to cut local dole queues' *The
     Guardian,* 12 June; Clark, M (1999) *A £5,000 Sheffield Employment
     Bond: what it achieves and what it costs,* CityLife, Sheffield, May
22   Jones, S (1999) 'Investment bond launched to boost job hopes' *The
     Financial Times,* 23 April
23   Martinson J (1999) 'They succeeded in New York', *The Guardian,* 24
     November
24   Kramer S (1999) 'Bonds: they'll work here', *The Guardian,* 24
     November
25   Martinson J (1999) op cit, Note 23
26   Renewing the Regions, 1996, p207
27   Anon (1997) 'Regional Economic Development Bonds: Labour Party
     Consultation Paper', London, p3
28   Simpson, A and Hines, C (forthcoming) 'Civic Bonds: the Secure
     Returns', Peoples Europe, London
29   Harker et al (1996) op cit, Note 4, p1
30   Mayo et al (1996) op cit, Note 15, p1
31   Khor M (undated) 'The WTO and The South: Implications and Recent
     Developments', *Third World Network*, Penang, Malaysia, pp20, 21
32   Ibid, p20
33   Shiva, V (1998) *Globalisation, Gandhi, and Swadeshi*, Research
     Foundation for Science, Technology and Ecology, New Dehli, May
34   'United Colours of Swadeshi', *Outlook,* India, 13 April 1998

# CHAPTER 6 'PROTECT THE LOCAL, GLOBALLY' – A ROUTE TO LOCALIZATION

1 Black, J (1997) *Oxford Dictionary of Economics,* Oxford University Press, Oxford, p458
2 Ibid, p220
3 Ibid, p385
4 Dunkley, G (1997) *The Free Trade Adventure, The Uruquay Round and Globalism: a Critique,* Melbourne University Press, Australia, p35
5 Black (1997) op cit, Note 1, p167
6 Ibid, p325
7 Ibid, p497

# CHAPTER 7 LOCALIZING PRODUCTION AND DISMANTLING TRANSNATIONAL COMPANIES

1 Leadbeater, C (1999) *Living on Thin Air,* Viking Press, London, p193
2 Kaplinski, R (1998) 'Globalisation, Industrialisation and Sustainable Growth: the Pursuit of the Nth Rent', Institute of Development Studies, Discussion Paper 365, June
3 Personal communication from Department for Trade and Industry, November 1998
4 Karliner, J (1997) *The Corporate Planet: Ecology and Politics and World Development,* Sierra Club Books, San Francisco, pp5, 226
5 Ibid p5
6 Clarke, T (1997) *Silent Coup: Confronting Big Business Takeover of Canada* CCPA & Lorimer, Ottawa, p5
7 Anderson, A and Cavanagh, J (1998) 'The rise of global corporate power', *Third World Resurgence,* no 97
8 Balanya, B et al (2000) *Europe Inc, Regional and Global Restructuring and the Rise of Corporate Power,* Pluto Press, London, p96
9 Hirst, P and Thompson, G (1996) *Globalisation in Question,* Polity Press, Cambridge, p98
10 See for example: World Development Movement (1998) *Law unto Themselves: Holding Multinationals to Account,* WDM, London, September
11 Greer, J and Bruno, K (1996) *Greenwash, the Reality Behind Corporate Environmentalism,* Third World Network & The Apex Press
12 Personal communication with Maggie Burns of Ethical Trading, 11 March 1998
13 *The Thor, Connelly and Cape Cases,* Leigh, Day and Co, London, November, 1997; Meeran, R (1995) '"Process" Liability of Multinationals: Overcoming the Forum Hurdle' in *Journal of Personal Injury Litigation*

14   World Development Movement (1998) op cit, Note 10 p9
15   Roddick, A (1999) 'Transnationals must face responsibilities', *The Financial Times Letters*, 16–17 January
16   Wheeler, D (1998) *Trade, Investment and the Environment: Building markets for sustainable trade*, Chatham House, London, 29 October, p205
17   Wright, M (1999) 'Do the Right Thing', *Green Futures*, March/April, p24
18   Cowe, R (1999) 'The cannibals adopt cutlery', *The Guardian*, 18 March
19   Ethical Trading Initiative (1998) *Purpose, Principles, Programme, Membership Information*, ETI, London, undated
20   Wright (1999) op cit, Note 17, p27
21   Cowe, R (1999) 'End of an era as Body Shop jobs go', *The Guardian*, 27 January
22   Wheeler (1998) op cit, Note 17, p205
23   Greer, J and Bruno, K (1996) *Greenwash: the reality behind corporate environmentalism*, Third World Network & the Apex Press, Malaysia

## Chapter 8   Localizing Capital

1    Blecker, R (1999) *Taming Global Finance: a Better Architecture for Growth and Equity*, Economic Policy Institute, Washington, DC
2    Crotty, J and Epstein, G (1996) 'In Defence of Capital Controls', in Panitch, L (ed) *Are There Alternatives?* Socialist Register, Monthly Review Publishing Company, New York
3    Ibid
4    UNCTAD (1997) *World Investment Report*, United Nations Conference on Trade and Development, Geneva
5    Keynes, J M (1936) *The General Theory of Employment, Interest, and Money*, Harcourt, Brace, London
6    Blecker (1999) op cit, Note 1, p2
7    UN figures quoted in Elliot, L (1998) 'Why the poor are picking up the tab', *The Guardian*, 11 May
8    Felix, D (1999) 'Repairing the Global Financial Architecture', *Foreign Policy in Focus*, Special Report, Interhemispheric Resource Center and Institute for Policy Studies, New Mexico, no 5, September
9    Bello, W (1999) 'Architectural blueprints, development models, and political strategie', paper prepared for Conference on Economic Sovereignty in a Globalised World, Bangkok, 23–26 March
10   Statement by International Forum on Globalization, San Francisco, 1998
11   Bello (1999) op cit, Note 9
12   IMF (1998) *World Economic Outlook*, International Monetary Fund, Washington, DC, October
13   Bello (1999) op cit, Note 9
14   Shrybman, S (1999) *A Citizen's Guide to the World Trade Organization*, Canadian Centre for Policy Alternatives, Ottawa, p122

15  Clarke, T and Barlow, M (1998) *MAI and the Threat to Canadian Sovereignty*
16  Hines, C (1997) 'Europe Must Control Capital to Create Jobs', *The Guardian*, 17 November
17  Originally jointly drafted by Morehouse, W and Hines, C, 1998

# CHAPTER 9  A LOCALIST COMPETITION POLICY

1  Korten, D (1999) *The Post-Corporate World, Life After Capitalism*, Kumarian Press, Connecticut, p40
2  Scherer, F (1994) *Competition Policies for an Integrated World Economy*, The Brookings Institution, Washington, DC, p2
3  Ibid, pp44–46
4  Korten (1999) op cit, Note 1, p43
5  Black, J (1997) *Oxford Dictionary of Economics*, Oxford University Press, Oxford, p329
6  DTI (1998) *Our Competitive Future, Building the Knowledge Driven Economy*, Department of Trade and Industry, London, December, p5
7  Lang, T (1999) *The Complexities of Globalization: the UK as a case study of tensions within the food system and the challenge to food policy*, Centre for Food Policy, Thames Valley University, London, Summer
8  DTI (1998) op cit, Note 6, p8
9  Ibid, p51
10  Hildyard, N (1998) *The World Bank and the State: a Recipe for Change?* Bretton Woods Project, London, p8
11  Monbiot, G (1999) 'The Wal-Mart monster hits town', *The Guardian*, 17 June
12  Breverton, T (1994) 'Rules Under Different Visions of Economy and Society: The Economic Vision', a paper presented at The Evolution of Rules for a Single European Market, Exeter University, 8–11 September
13  Karliner, J (1997) *The Corporate Planet: Ecology and Politics in the Age of Globalization*, Sierra Club Books, San Francisco

# CHAPTER 10  TAXES FOR LOCALIZATION

1  Black, J (1997) *Oxford Dictionary of Economics*, Oxford University Press, Oxford, p179
2  Roodman D (1998) *The Natural Wealth of Nations, Harnessing the Market for the Environment*, WW Norton/Worldwatch Books, New York, p246
3  Tindale, S and Hotham, G (1996) *Green Tax Reform: Pollution Payments and Labour Tax Cuts*, Institute for Public Policy Research, p112
4  Ibid, p113

5    Roodman (1998) op cit, Note 2, p243
6    Balanya, B et al (2000) *Europe Inc: Regional and Global Restructuring and the Rise of Corporate Power*, Pluto Press, London, Chapter 17
7    von Weizsäcker, E and Jesinghaus, J (1992) *Ecological Tax Reform*, Zed Books, London, p9
8    'Climate Crisis' *The Ecologist* 29, March/April 1999
9    Stockholm Environment Institute (1993) *Towards a Fossil Free Energy Future: The New Energy Transition*, Boston
10   von Weizsäcker, E , Lovins A B and Lovins, L H (1997) *Factor Four: Doubling Wealth, Halving Resource Use,* Earthscan, London, p288
11   Roodman (1998) op cit, Note 2, p151
12   Ibid, p180
13   Round, R (2000) 'Time for Tobin!', *New Internationalist,* January/February, p20
14   Boyle, S (1999) 'Making Progress Towards a Fossil Free Energy Future', *The Ecologist* 29, March/April, pp129–132
15   Goldsmith, E (1999) 'The Crash Programme: A Solution-multiplier', *The Ecologist* 29, March/April, p143
16   Ibid, p144
17   Ibid
18   Ibid
19   von Weizsäcker et al (1997) op cit, Note 10
20   Ibid, p24
21   Tindale and Hotham (1996) op cit, Note 3, p114
22   Boardman, B (1999) et al *'Equity and the Environment: Guidelines for Green and Socially Just Government',* Catalyst/ Friends of the Earth, London, September, p5

# CHAPTER 11  DEMOCRATIC LOCALISM

1    Barber, B (1996) *Jihad vs McWorld: How Globalism and Tribalism are Reshaping the World,* Ballantine, New York, p285
2    Ibid, p300
3    World Bank (2000) *Entering the 21st Century,* World Development Report 1999/2000, World Bank, Washington, DC, p8
4    Ibid, p28
5    Gindin, S and Robertson, D (1991) *Democracy and Productive Capacity: Notes Towards and Alternative to Competitiveness,* Canadian Centre for Policy Alternatives, Ottawa, September
6    Greider, W (1997) *One World Ready Or Not: The manic logic of global capitalism,* Simon and Schuster, New York, p38
7    Chossudovsky, M (1997) *The Globalisation of Poverty: Impacts of IMF and World Bank reforms,* Zed Books/Third World Network, London, 1997
8    Altieri, M and Rojas, A (1999) 'Ecological impacts of Chile's Neoliberal Policies, with Special Emphasis on Agroecosystems', *Environment,*

*Development and Sustainability,* Kluwer Academic Publishers, Netherlands

9  World Bank (2000) op cit, Note 3, p43
10  'Putting the Case for a Citizen's Income: a New Dimension of Welfare Reform', *Citizen's Income Trust,* London, 1998.
11  Castells, M (1996) 'An introduction to the information age', *City* 7, p11
12  Hencke, D (1999) 'Straw caps election spending', *The Guardian,* 27 July
13  'The next president, it's time for voters to pay attention', *The Guardian Editorial,* 27 July 1999
14  Brown, P (1994) *Restoring the Public Trust,* Beacon Press, Boston, p71
15  Ibid, p131
16  Clarke, T (1997) *Silent Coup: Confronting the Big Business Takeover of Canada,* Canadian Centre for Policy Alternatives & James Lorimer and Company, Ottawa, p2
17  Gindin and Robertson (1991) in Clarke, T, ibid, p3
18  Ibid
19  *Global Challenges,* p92
20  Ibid, p82
21  *Global Challenges,* p86
22  Personal communication with Tony Clarke, 2 December, 1999

# CHAPTER 12 TRADE AND AID FOR LOCALIZATION

1  Dunkley, G (1997) *The Free Trade Adventure, The Uruguay Round and Globalism: A Critique,* Melbourne University Press, Australia
2  Ibid, p250
3  Ibid, p251
4  Ibid, p255
5  This section is based on Shrybman, S (1999) *A Citizen's Guide to the World Trade Organization,* Canadian Centre for Policy Alternatives, Ottawa and Shrybman, S (1999) 'The World Trade Organization The New World Constitution Laid Bare', *The Ecologist* 29(4), July, and the author is indebted for being allowed to quote extensively from them.
6  Shrybman, S (1999) 'The World Trade Organization: The New World Constitution Laid Bare', *The Ecologist* 29(4), July, p270; Wallach, L and Sforza, M (1999) *Whose Trade Organization? Corporate Globalization and the Erosion of Democracy,* Public Citizen, Washington, DC, pp19–21
7  Shrybman (1999) op cit, Note 6, p271
8  Dunkley (1997) op cit, Note 1, p261
9  Ibid, pp26–27
10  EUROSTEP and ICVA (1998) *The Reality of Aid 1998/1999: An Independent Review of Poverty Reduction and Development Assistance,* Earthscan, London, p5

11　Ibid, p4

12　*The Guardian*, 10 November, 1998

13　*Global Challenges*, p86

14　Watkins, K (1995) The Oxfam Poverty Report, Oxfam, Oxford, p200

15　Whiteside, M (1999) *Empowering the Landless*, Christian Aid, London, April, p17

16　Ibid, p18

17　Ibid, p5

18　Girardet, H (1992) *The Gaia Atlas of Cities: New directions for sustainable urban living*, Gaia Books, London, pp177–180

19　Watkins (1995) op cit, Note 14, p174

20　Padgett, B (1999) 'Technology transfer services and financing, factors that assist and inhibit development', *Tech Monitor*, March–April

## CHAPTER 13　GROWING OPPOSITION

1　Shuman, M (1998) '*Going Local Creating Self-Reliant Communities in a Global Age*', Free Press, New York; Gabriel Chanan et al (1999) '*Regeneration and Sustainable Communities*' Community Development Foundation, London; International Society for Ecology and Culture (1999) *From Global to Local: Resisting monoculture, rebuilding community*, ISEC, Devon; 'Beyond the Monoculture, Shifting from Global to Local', *The Ecologist* 29(3), May/June, 1999; Shuman, M (1998) *Going Local: Creating Self-Reliant Communities in a Global Age*, Free Press, New York; Shiva, V(1998) *Globalisation, Gandhi, and Swadeshi*, Research Foundation for Science, Technology and Ecology, New Dehli, May; Mander, J and Goldsmith, E (1996) *The Case against the Global Economy and for a Turn Towards the Local*, Sierra Club Books, San Francisco; Douthwaite, R (1996) *Short Circuit: Strengthening Local Economies for Security in an Unstable World*, Green Books, Devon; Harker, D et al (1996) *Community Works! A guide to community economic action*, New Economic Foundation, London; Mayo, E et al (1996) *Taking Power: An agenda for community economic renewal*, New Economic Foundation, London; Kretzman, J and McKnight, J (1996) *A Guide to Mapping and Mobilizing the Economic Capacities of Local Residents*, The Asset-Based Community Development Institute, Illinois; Kretzman, J and McKnight, J (1995) *Building Communities from the Inside Out*, The Asset-Based Community Development Institute, Illinois

2　de Jonquieres, G (1998) 'Network guerrillas', *The Financial Times*, 30 April; Arden-Clarke, C (1998) *The Financial Times, Letters*, 7 May; Dunne, N (1998) 'Democrat obstacle to IMF funding', *The Financial Times*, 4 May

3　Hines, C (1999) 'What next after the battle of Seattle?', *Tribune*, 10 December

4　Shiva (1998) op cit, Note 1

5   Steltzer, I (1998) 'US hit out as free trade slips on banana skin', *The Sunday Times, Business,* 15 November
6   'Closing Down', *Panorama,* BBC TV, 30 November, 1998
7   Williams, F (1998) 'Rate of global trade growth likely to halve', *The Financial Times,* 4 December
8   Brown, K and de Jonquieres, G (1998) 'Close to melting point', *The Financial Times,* 23 October
9   'Soros on Soros', John Wiley, New York, 1995, quoted in Gray, J (1998) *False Dawn: The delusions of global capital,* Granta Books, London, p1
10  Quoted in Rothstein, R, *'As the Good Jobs Go Rolling Away...Who Will Buy?',* CEO/International Strategies, December 1993/ January 1994, p25
11  Quoted in Barnet, R and Cavanagh, J (1994) *Global Dreams: Imperial Corporations and the New World Order,* Simon and Schuster, New York, p261
12  Reich, R (1998) 'Deflation: the real enemy', *The Financial Times,* 15 January
13  See for example Brittan, S (2000) 'Market euphoria cannot last', *The Financial Times,* 20 January; 'The Threat of Deflation', *Business Week,* 10 November, 1997; Shultz, G, Simon, W and Wriston, W (1998) 'Who Needs the IMF?', *Wall Street Journal,* 30 January
14  Elliot, L (2000) 'History points the way to another crash landing', *The Guardian,* 28 February
15  Denny, C (2000) 'IMF stakes its name on a Thai miracle', *The Guardian,* 21 February
16  Madeley, J (1998) 'Africa Squeezed by Asia's Crisis', *Independent on Sunday, Business,* 10 May
17  'Trapped by the bubble', *The Economist,* 25 September, 1999, p17
18  King, S (1999) *Bubble Trouble: The US bubble and how it will burst,* HSBC Economics & Investment Strategy: Economics, July
19  Elliot, L (1998) 'The buck pops here', *The Guardian,* 7 December

# CHAPTER 14   DESTROYING JOBS, INCREASING DEFLATION

1   WTO (1998) *WTO Annual Report 1998,* WTO, Geneva, p47
2   Collins, P (1994) *Dictionary of Banking and Finance,* Peter Collins Publishing, London
3   Panos (1999) 'Globalisation and Employment, new opportunities, real threats', *Panos Briefing* No 33, May, p5
4   Ranney D and Naiman, R (1997) *Does 'Free Trade' Create Good Jobs?,* Institute for Policy Studies and Great Cities Institute, Washington DC and Illinois, January, p11
5   *Today Programme,* BBC Radio, 7 December 1998
6   Wainwright, M (1999) 'Threat to put tin lid on Yorkshire's flat caps', *The Guardian,* 8 December

7  'Men's Economic Inactivity and Unemployment in the UK', Economic
   and Social Research Council, UK, February 2000
8  *The Guardian*, 13 September 1999
9  ILO (1997) *ILO Yearbook of Labour Statistics*, ILO, Geneva; exchange
   rates in *The Financial Times*, 12 June, 1998
10 Palley, T (1998) *Plenty of Nothing: The Downsizing of the American
   Dream and the Case for Structural Keynesianism*, Princeton University
   Press, New Jersey, p81
11 Wood, A (1994) *North–South Trade, Employment and Inequality:
   Changing Fortunes in a Skill-Driven World*, Oxford University Press,
   Oxford
12 Wallach, L and Naiman, R (1998) 'NAFTA: Four and a Half Years
   Later', *The Ecologist* 28(3), May/June
13 'Rapport Arthius sur les délocalisations', Assemblé Nationale, Paris, 1993
14 Genillard, A (1994) 'German plans to shift production abroad', *The
   Financial Times*, 31 May
15 Quoted in Abrahams, P (1994) 'The dye is cast by growth and costs', *The
   Financial Times*, 31 May
16 Personal communication with Kelvin Hopkins, MP for Luton North,
   based on press releases from himself and Electrolux
17 'The Globalisation of the Civil Aviation Industry, and its Impact on
   Aviation Workers', a report prepared for the International Transport
   Workers' Federation Civil Aviation Section Conference, London 11–13,
   1992; personal communication with Stuart Howard, International
   Transport Worker's Federation
18 Wallach, L and Sforza, M (1999) *Whose Trade Organization? Corporate
   Globalization and the Erosion of Democracy*, Public Citizen,
   Washington, DC, p155
19 Greenfield, G (1998) 'Flexible Dimensions of a Permanent Crisis: TNCs,
   Flexibility, and Workers in Asia', Asia Monitor Resource Centre, paper
   to ASEM II NGO Conference, 'ASEM and the Crisis: People's Realities,
   People's Responses', London, 31 March–1 April, p3
20 Gray, J (1998) *False Dawn: The delusions of global capital*, Granta
   Books, London, p3
21 Greider, W (1997) 'One World Ready Or Not: The manic logic of global
   capitalism', Simon and Schuster, p148; Lloyd, J (2000) 'Will this be the
   Chinese century?', *New Statesman*, 10 January
22 Buxton, J (1998) 'Work on Hyundai plant hit by crisis in Asia', *The
   Financial Times*, 10 February
23 Gates, J (1999) 'The Ownership Solution: Towards a Stakeholder Society
   for the 21st Century', Addison Wesley, Massachusetts, p84
24 Egan, T (1997) 'Old-Fashioned Town Sours on Candymaker's New
   Pitch', *New York Times*, 6 October, cited in Gates (1999) op cit, Note
   23, p84
25 Panos (1999) 'Globalisation and Employment, new opportunities, real
   threats', *Panos Briefing* No 33, May, p6

26 On 17 January 2000, a proposed merger was announced between GlaxoWellcome and SmithKline Beecham, and approved by the European Commission on 8 May 2000 (http://www.glaxowellcome.co.uk)
27 Panos (1999) op cit, Note 25
28 Wallach and Sforza (1999) op cit, Note 18, p156
29 Gates (1999) op cit, Note 23, p86
30 Rifkin, J (1995) *The End of Work: The Decline of the Global Labor Force and the Dawn of the Post-Market Era*, Tarcher/Putman, New York
31 *Wall Street Journal*, 16 March 1993, p1, quoted in Rifkin, J (1994) 'Laid Off! Computer Technologies and the Re-Engineered Workplace', *The Ecologist* 24(5), p183
32 Martin, H and Schumann (1997) *The Global Trap: Globalization and the Assault on Democracy and Prosperity*, Zed Books, London
33 Speech to the American Society of Newspaper Editors, 1997
34 Secrett, C (1998) Letters, *The Guardian*, 14 November
35 See for example: Wolf, M (1998) 'Why liberalisation won', in 'The World Trade System at 50', *The Financial Times Survey*, 18 May

# CHAPTER 15 A LOCALIST WAKE-UP CALL TO POLITICAL ACTIVISTS

1 Wallach, L and Sforza, M (1999) *Whose Trade Organization? Corporate Globalization and the Erosion of Democracy*, Public Citizen, Washington, DC, pp36–38
2 Ibid, p89
3 Ibid, p131
4 Shrybman, S (1999) 'The World Trade Organization: The New World Constitution Laid Bare', *The Ecologist* 29(4), July, p271

# CHAPTER 16 FAILURE TO ADEQUATELY CHALLENGE GLOBALIZATION – SOCIAL SERVICES, UNIONS AND CULTURE

1 Walker, D (1999) 'Malignant growth', *The Guardian,* 5 July
2 Martin, G and Lister, J (1998) *EMU and the NHS*, People's Europe Campaign and London Health Emergency, London, p14
3 Harvey, P (1998) *Developing Effective Mechanisms for Implementing Labor Rights in the Global Economy*, International Labor Rights Fund, Washington, DC, August, pp34–35
4 Jones, R (1999) 'What About Labour Rights?', a paper for From the MAI to the Millenium Round, a Green Party Conference in the European Parliament, Brussels, 27–28 April 1999, pp5–6

5   Clinton, W (1992) 'Expanding Trade and Creating American Jobs', speech, North Carolina State University, 4 October
6   Coote, B (1995) *NAFTA, Poverty and Free Trade in Mexico*, Oxfam, Oxford, p8
7   Public Citizen (1997) *The Failed Experiment: NAFTA at Three Years*, Public Citizen, Washington, DC, p12
8   Ibid, p 12
9   See, for example, Coote (1995) op cit Note 6, p27; and Teamsters (1998a) 'Workers' groups in three NAFTA countries bring new charges against US firm for beatings at Mexican plant', 25 February in Borcik, E 'Themes and issues in Latin American Politics', December, unpublished
10  Coote (1995) op cit, Note 6 p27
11  Barlow, M (1999) 'The battle over culture at the WTO', *Third World Resurgence*, Malaysia, No 108/109 August/September, p51
12  Ibid, p52
13  Ibid
14  Ibid
15  Quoted in Shrybman, S (1999) *A Citizen's Guide to the World Trade Organization*, Canadian Centre for Policy Alternatives, Ottawa, p30

## CHAPTER 17  LOCALIZING INTERNATIONAL DEVELOPMENT

1   Watkins, K (1995) *The Oxfam Poverty Report*, Oxfam, Oxford, p81
2   Joseph E Stiglitz, former World Bank Chief Economist and Senior Vice President, Development Economics, at the launch of the *World Bank's World Development Report 1999/2000*, 15 September 1999
3   World Bank (1999) *Entering the 21st Century: World Bank's World Development Report 1999/2000*, September, World Bank/Oxford University Press, Washington DC, pp43, 173
4   Ibid, p140
5   Ibid, p19
6   Stiglitz (1999) op cit, Note 2
7   Watkins, K (1996) 'Global Market Myths', *Red Pepper*, UK, p14
8   Friends of the Earth (1999) *'The Emperor Has No Clothes': Opposing Trade Liberalisation by stopping the Proposed 'Millennium Round' Negotiations of the World Trade Organisation (WTO)*, FoE, London, p4
9   *The Independent on Sunday*, 17 July 1999
10  Bates, S (1999) 'Billion dollar banana split', *The Guardian*, 6 March
11  Hines, C (1997) 'Big-stick politics', *The Guardian*, 8 October
12  Wallach, L and Sforza, M (1999) *Whose Trade Organization? Corporate Globalization and the Erosion of Democracy*, Public Citizen, Washington, DC, p140
13  Speech to 'From the MAI to the Millenium Round', a Green Party Conference in the European Parliament, Brussels, 27–28 April 1999

14 Wallach and Sforza (1999) op cit, Note 12, p140
15 Ibid, p145
16 *The Independent on Sunday* (1999) op cit, Note 9
17 Wallach and Sforza (1999) op cit Note 12, p143
18 quoted in Lucas, C (1999) *Watchful in Seattle: World Trade Organisation Threats to Public Services, Food and the Environment*, The Greens/European Free Alliance, European Parliament, Brussels, November, p9; Kilman, S and Cooper, H (1999) 'Monsanto Fails Trying to Sell Europe on Bioengineered Food', *Wall Street Journal*, 11 May
19 Shiva, V (2000) 'Why Industrial Agriculture Cannot Feed the World', *The Ecologist Special Issue*, forthcoming
20 RIS (1985) *Biotechnology Revolution and the Third World*, RIS, New Delhi, p218
21 Shiva (forthcoming) op cit, Note 19
22 Sierra Club briefing, San Francisco, 8 September 1999
23 One of the sponsors of a US 'African Growth and Opportunity Act'
24 Monbiot, G (1999) 'Hanging on to the profits of Aids', *The Guardian*, 5 August
25 Wallach and Sforza (1999) op cit, Note 12, p115
26 Ibid, p117
27 Ibid, p26-29; Arden-Clarke, C (1998) *The Final Report of the WTO Shrimp-Turtle Panel: WWF's Response*, WWF International, Switzerland, May
28 Arden-Clarke (1998) op cit, Note 27
29 Shiva, V (1998) 'The WTO is Pushing Turtles and Traditional Fishworkers to Extinction, Research Foundation for Science, Technology and Ecology, New Delhi, April
30 World Trade Organization (1998) WT/DS120/1, WTO, Geneva, 23 March, quoted in Shiva, V 'WTO Rules Force India to Kill Animals' Research Foundation for Science, Technology and Ecology, New Delhi, April
31 Ibid
32 Barlow, M (2000) *Blue Gold: The Global Water Crisis and the Commodification of the World's Water Supply*, International Forum on Globalization, San Francisco, June, p2
33 Ibid, p2
34 Ibid, p35
35 Ibid, p3
36 Wallach and Sforza (1999) op cit, Note 12, pp186,188; Balanya, B et al (2000) *Europe Inc: Regional and Global Restructuring and the Rise of Corporate Power*, Pluto Press, London, pp127–127
37 Watkins, K (1997) *Globalisation and Liberalisation: The Implications for Poverty, Distribution and Inequality*, paper prepared for UNDP Human Development Report Advisory panel, Oxfam, Oxford, 22 January, quoted in Hildyard, N (1998) *The World Bank and the State: A Recipe for Change?*, Bretton Woods Project, London, p37

38   Jones, R (1999) 'What About Labour Rights?', paper prepared for 'From the MAI to the Millenium Round', a Green Party Conference in the European Parliament, Brussels, 27–28 April 1999, p5

39   Barker, D and Mander, M (2000) *Invisible Government: The World Trade Organization: Global Government for the New Millennium*, International Forum on Globalization, San Francisco, pp4,3

40   World Bank (1999) op cit, Note 3 p8

41   Panos (1998) 'Trading in Futures: EU-ACP Relations: Putting Commerce before Cooperation?, *Panos Briefing*, No 31, p5

42   Barker and Mander (2000) op cit, Note 39, p25

43   Ibid, p13

44   Wallach and Sforza (1999) op cit, Note 12, p176; Barnet, R and Cavanagh, J (1994) *Global Dreams: Imperial Corporations and the New World Order*, Simon and Schuster, NewYork

45   Wallach and Sforza (1999) op cit, Note 12, p178

46   Panos (1999) 'Globalisation and Employment, New Opportunities, real threats', *Panos Briefing*, No 33, May, p14

47   ILO (1998) *World Employment Report 1998-99*, International Labour Organisation, Geneva, p142

48   United Nations (1998) 'Gains by women reversed in economic downturn', United Nations Information Services, Bangkok, 23 November

49   Panos (1999) op cit Note 50, p10

50   Ibid, p8

51   Ibid, p10

52   Denny, C (1999) 'From Maesteg to Dhaka, the same fears', *The Guardian*, 29 November

53   Shiva (forthcoming) op cit, Note 19

54   Bello, W (1999) 'Asia, Asian Farmers, and the WTO', *Far Eastern Economic Review*, 24 June, p54

55   Rajlakshmi, T K (1999) 'The terrible price that workers in developing country pay when it embraces a policy of export-led growth', *Third World Resurgence*, Malaysia, No 107, July, p42

# CHAPTER 18   LOCALIZING FOOD SECURITY

1   FAO (1996) *World Food Summit Plan of Action, Report of the World Food Summit, Part 1*, FAO, Rome, 13–17 November

2   Barker, D and Mander, M (2000) *Invisible Government: The World Trade Organization-Global Government for the New Millennium*, International Forum on Globalization, San Francisco

3   Shrybman, S (1999) *A Citizen's Guide to the World Trade Organization*, Canadian Centre for Policy Alternatives, Ottawa, p12

4   Barker and Mander (2000) op cit, Note 2, p24

5   Shiva, V (2000) 'Why Industrial Agriculture Cannot Feed the World', *The Ecologist Special Issue*, forthcoming

6   Lang, T (1999) *The Complexities of Globalization: The UK as a case study of tensions within the food system and the challenge to food policy*, Centre for Food Policy, Thames Valley University, London, Summer

7   Tudge, C (1999) 'Fields of Dreams', *New Statesman*, 12 July, p35

8   Lang T (1998) *The Complexities of Globalization: The UK as a case study of tensions within the food system and the challenge to food policy*, in Dahlberg, K and Koc, M (eds) 'The Restructuring of Food Systems: Research and Policy Issues', *Agriculture and Human Values*, Kluwer Academic Publishers, Netherlands, Summer

9   This section is based on Tim Lang's paper (ibid) and the author is indebted for being allowed to quote extensively from it

# CHAPTER 19 THE WTO AND THE ENVIRONMENT

1   Evans, R (1998) 'Green Push Could Damage Trade Body: WTO Chief', *Reuters*, 15 May, 1998

2   Wallach, L and Sforza, M (1999) *Whose Trade Organization? Corporate Globalization and the Erosion of Democracy*, Public Citizen, Washington, DC, p13

3   de Jonquieres, G (1998) 'Network guerillas', *The Financial Times*, 30 April

4   Wallach and Sforza (1999) op cit, Note 2, pp59–61; *Independent on Sunday*, 17 July, 1999

5   de Jonquieres (1998) op cit, Note 3

6   Balanya, B et al (2000) *Europe Inc: Regional and Global Restructuring and the Rise of Corporate Power*, Pluto Press, London, pp125–126

7   Report from the European Union's Scientific Committee on Veterinary Measures Relating to Public Health, Brussels, 3 May, 1999

8   *The Financial Times*, 5 May, 1999

9   *The Guardian*, 5 May 1999

10  Wallach and Sforza (1999) op cit, Note 2, p26

11  Ibid, pp26–29

12  Ibid, pp21–22

13  *The Independent*, 17 July 1999

14  Arden-Clarke, C (1996) *The WTO Committee on Trade and the Environment: Is It Serious?*, WWF, Switzerland, December

15  Nader, R and Wallach, L (1996) 'GATT, NAFTA and the Subversion of the Democratic Process' and Goldsmith, E (1996) 'Global Trade and the Environment', both in Mander, J and Goldsmith E (1996) *The Case Against the Global Economy*, Sierra Club Books, San Francisco, pp89, 97–98; Hines, C (1996) 'The "New Protectionism"', *Economic Affairs, Journal of Institute of Economic Affairs* 16(5) Winter, pp29–32; Lang, T and Hines, C (1993) *The New Protectionism: Protecting the Future Against Free Trade*, Earthscan, London, pp65–67

16  'Deregulation Now', report by the Anglo-German Deregulation Group, March 1995, p32
17  Ibid
18  Brack, D (1999) *The Guardian*, 19 July
19  *The Daily Telegraph,* 11 June
20  Lucas, C (1999) 'The Greens "Beef" with the World Trade Organisation', A Green Party Report, UK, 10 May
21  *The Financial Times*, 13 July 1999
22  *The Guardian*, 19 July 1999
23  Wallach and Sforza (1999) op cit, Note 2, p140
24  *The Daily Telegraph*, 11 June 1999
25  Wallach, L and Naiman, R (1998) 'NAFTA: Four and a Half Years Later', *The Ecologist* 28(3), May/June, p172
26  Ibid, p173
27  Heredia, C (1996) 'Downward Mobility: Mexican Workers After NAFTA', *NACLA Report on the Americas* XXX(3), November/December, p34
28  Public Citizen (1997) *The Failed Experiment: NAFTA at Three Years,* Public Citizen, Washington, DC, p14
29  Wallach and Naiman(1998) op cit, Note 25, p175
30  WWF (1999) *Initiating an Environmental Assessment of Trade Liberalisation in the WTO,* WWF International, Switzerland, March
31  Friends of the Earth (1999) *'The Emperor Has No Clothes': Opposing Trade Liberalisation by stopping the Proposed 'Millennium Round' Negotiations of the World Trade Organisation (WTO)*, FoE London, p2
32  RSPA/Eurogroup for Animal Welfare (1998), *Conflict or Concord?,* RSPCA/Eurogroup, UK, p5
33  Ibid, p7
34  Ibid, p12
35  Ibid, p6
36  Ibid, p12
37  'Farm Animal Welfare and the World Trade Organisation (WTO)', Eurogroup for Animal Welfare, European Parliament Briefing, Brussels, undated

# A Controversial Conclusion

1  Greider, W (1997) *'One World Ready Or Not: The manic logic of global capitalism'*, Simon and Schuster, New York, p470
2  Wilkinson, M (1999) 'The changing face of protest', *The Financial Times*, 31 July/1 August
3  Stiglitz, J (1998) 'Lessons of the Asia crisis', *The Financial Times*, 3 December
4  King S (1999) *Bubble Trouble: The US bubble and how it will burst,* HSBC Economics & Investment Strategy: Economics, July

5   de Jonquieres, G (1998) 'Network guerillas', *The Financial Times*, 30 April

6   Korten, D (1999) *The Post-Corporate World, Life After Capitalism*, Kumarian Press, Connecticut

7   Korten, D (1999) 'The Post-Corporate World', *YES! A Journal of Positive Futures*, Spring, pp17–18

# APPENDIX II

1   Bertrand Russell (1918) *Roads to Freedom*, Unwin Paperbacks, London, 1985, quoted in Basic Income European Network, Belgium, 1997

2   Meade, J, Nobel Laureate quoted in Basic Income European Network, Belgium, 1997

3   Desai, M (1998) 'A Basic Income Proposal', *The State of the Future*, Social Market Foundation, London, p112

4   Ibid, pp113, 114

5   Ibid, pp117, 121

6   Parker, H and Sutherland, H (1998) *How to get rid of the poverty trap: Basic Income plus national wage*, Citizen's Income Bulletin 25, London, February, pp11–14

7   Desai (1998) op cit, Note 3, p123

8   Ibid, p122

9   Standing, G (1998) speech at 'Increasing Labour Market Participation' Citizen's Income Trust, plus personal communication, 11 February

10  Ibid

11  Rowbotham, M (1998) *The Grip of Death: A Study of Modern Money, Debt-Slavery and Destructive Economics*, Jon Carpenter Publishing, Charlbury, p189

12  Galbraith, J (1998) *Money: Whence it Came, Where it Went* Harmondsworth, Penguin, p29, quoted in Hutchinson, F, *What Everybody Really Wants to Know about Money*, Jon Carpenter Publishing, Charlbury, p110

13  Rowbotham (1998) op cit, Note 11, p35

14  Ibid, Chapter 2

15  Ibid, pp205,221

16  Ibid, p222

# Suggested Reading

Balanya, B et al (2000) *Europe Inc, Regional and Global Restructuring and the Rise of Corporate Power*, Pluto Press, London

Barker, D and Mander, M (2000) *Invisible Government: The World Trade Organization: Global Government for the New Millennium*, International Forum on Globalization, San Francisco

Barnet, R and Cavanagh, J (1994) *Global Dreams: Imperial Corporations and the New World Order*, Simon and Schuster, New York

Blecker, R (1999) *Taming Global Finance: a Better Architecture for Growth and Equity*, Economic Policy Institute, Washington, DC

Clarke, T and Barlow, M (1998) *MAI Round 2: New Global and Internal Threats to Canadian Sovereignty*, Stoddart Books, Toronto

Dunkley, G (1997) *The Free Trade Adventure, The Uruquay Round and Globalism: A Critique*, Melbourne University Press, Australia

Gray, J (1998) *False Dawn: The Delusions of Global Capitalism*, Granta Books, London

Greider, W (1997) *One World, Ready Or Not: The manic logic of global capitalism*, Simon and Schuster, New York

Korten, D (1995) *When Corporations Rule the World*, Earthscan, London

Korten, D (1999) *The Post-Corporate World, Life After Capitalism*, Kumarian Press, Connecticut

Lang, T and Hines, C (1993) *The New Protectionism: Protecting the Future Against Free Trade*, Earthscan, London

Mander, J and Goldsmith, E (1996) *The Case against the Global Economy and for a Turn Towards the Local*, Sierra Club Books, San Francisco

Rifkin, J (1995) *The End of Work: The Decline of the Global Labor Force and the Dawn of the Post-Market Era*, Tarcher/Putman, New York

Shrybman, S (1999) *A Citizen's Guide to the World Trade Organization* Canadian Centre for Policy Alternatives, Ottawa

Shuman, M (1998) *Going Local Creating Self-Reliant Communities in a Global Age*, Free Press, New York

Wallach, L and Sforza, M (1999) *Whose Trade Organization? Corporate Globalization and the Erosion of Democracy*, Public Citizen, Washington, DC

# Index